OUT OF PLACE

Cross Cultural Theologies

Series Editors: Jione Havea and Clive Pearson, both at United Theological College, Sydney, and Charles Sturt University, Australia, and Anthony G. Reddie, Queen's Foundation for Ecumenical Theological Education, Birmingham

This series focuses on how the "cultural turn" in interdisciplinary studies has informed theology and biblical studies. It takes its leave from the experience of the flow of people from one part of the world to another.

It moves beyond the crossing of cultures in a narrow diasporic sense. It entertains perspectives that arise out of generational criticism, gender, sexual orientation, and the relationship of film to theology. It explores the sometimes competing rhetoric of multiculturalism and cross-culturalism and demonstrates a concern for the intersection of globalization and how those global flows of peoples and ideas are received and interpreted in localized settings. The series seeks to make use of a range of disciplines including the study of cross-cultural liturgy, travel, the practice of ministry and worship in multi-ethnic locations and how theologies that have arisen in one part of the world have migrated to a new location. It looks at the public nature of faith in complex, multicultural, multireligious societies and compares how diverse faiths and their theologies have responded to the same issues.

The series welcomes contributions by scholars from around the world. It includes both single-authored and multi-authored volumes.

Published:

Global Civilization
Leonardo Boff

Dramatizing Theologies: A Participative Approach to Black God-Talk
Anthony G. Reddie

Art as Theology: The Religious Transformation of Art from the Postmodern to the Medieval
Andreas Andreopoulos

Black Theology in Britain: A Reader
Edited by Michael N. Jagessar and Anthony G. Reddie

Bibles and Baedekers: Tourism, Travel, Exile and God
Michael Grimshaw

Home Away from Home: The Caribbean Diasporan Church in the Black Atlantic Tradition
Delroy A. Reid-Salmon

Working against the Grain: Black Theology in the 21ˢᵗ Century
Anthony G. Reddie

The Non-Western Jesus: Jesus as Bodhisattva, Avatara, Guru, Prophet, Ancestor or Healer?
Martien E. Brinkman
Translated by Henry and Lucy Jansen

Another World is Possible: Spiritualities and Religions of Global Darker Peoples
Edited by Dwight N. Hopkins and Marjorie Lewis

Alternatives Unincorporated: Earth Ethics from the Grassroots
George Zachariah

Forthcoming:

Towards a Systematic Spirituality of Black British Women
Marjorie Lewis

Christian Worship: Postcolonial Perspectives
Stephen Burns and Michael N. Jagessar

OUT OF PLACE

DOING THEOLOGY ON THE
CROSSCULTURAL BRINK

Edited by

Jione Havea and Clive Pearson

LONDON   OAKVILLE

Published by Equinox Publishing Ltd.

UK: 1 Chelsea Manor Studios, Flood Street, London SW3 5SR
USA: DBBC, 28 Main Street, Oakville, CT 06779

www.equinoxpub.com

First published 2011

British Library Cataloguing-in-Publication Data

A catalogue record for this book is available from the British Library.

ISBN-13   978 1 84553 389 2   (hardback)
          978 1 84553 390 8   (paperback)

Library of Congress Cataloging-in-Publication Data

Out of place : doing theology on the cross cultural brink / edited by
Jione Havea and Clive Pearson.
    p. cm. – (Cross cultural theologies)
    Includes bibliographical references and indexes.
    ISBN 978-1-84553-389-2 (hbk) – ISBN 978-1-84553-390-8 (pbk) 1.
Theology. I. Havea, Jione, 1965- II. Pearson, Clive.
    BT80.O98 2010
    230—dc22
                            2009033849

Typeset by S.J.I. Services, New Delhi
Printed and bound in Great Britain by Lightning Source, Milton Keynes, UK

Contents

Contributors

Anastasia Boniface-Malle
United Bible Societies
Nairobi, Kenya
(abnatse@yahoo.com)

Mercedes L. García Bachmann
Instituto Universitario ISEDET, Argentina
(garciabachmann@gmail.com)

Jacqueline Grey
Alphacrucis College
Chester Hill, NSW, Australia
(jacqui.grey@alphacrucis.edu.au)

Jione Havea
School of Theology, Charles Sturt University
United Theological College
North Parramatta, NSW, Australia
(jhavea@csu.edu.au)

Albert W. Jebanesan
Methodist Headquarters
252 Galle Road, Colombo-3, Sri Lanka
(jebi@sltnet.lk)

Namsoon Kang
Brite Divinity School
Texas Christian University
TCU Box 298130
Fort Worth, TX 76116, USA
(n.kang@tcu.edu)

Hisako Kinukawa
Center for Feminist Theology and Ministry in Japan
Tokyo, Japan
(hkinukawa@nifty.com)

Peter Matheson
Dept. of Theology and Religious Studies
University of Otago
Dunedin, Aotearoa/New Zealand
(peter.m@compassnet.co.nz)

Joseph Mathew
Church of South India
Chennai, Tamil Nadu, India
(josemath30@yahoo.com)

Fumitaka Matsuoka
Pacific School of Religion
Graduate Theological Union
Berkeley, California, USA
(fmatsuoka@psr.edu)

Clive Pearson
School of Theology, Charles Sturt University
United Theological College
North Parramatta, NSW, Australia
(cpearson@nsw.uca.org.au)

Joerg Rieger
Wendland-Cook Professor of Constructive Theology
Perkins School of Theology
Southern Methodist University
Dallas, Texas, USA
(jrieger@smu.edu)

Gerald O. West
Ujamaa Centre
School of Religion and Theology
University of KwaZulu-Natal
Pietermaritzburg, South Africa
(west@ukzn.ac.za)

Vítor Westhelle
Lutheran School of Theology at Chicago
Chicago, Illinois, USA
(vwesthel@lstc.edu)

Foreword

Anthony Reddie

I am the eldest child of Caribbean migrants. My parents were born in the Caribbean island of Jamaica and came to Britain in 1957 as part of the post-Second World War mass migration of Black people from the British Commonwealth, in what is often called the "Windrush Generation."[1] One of the most formative, indeed, transformative experiences in my life occurred in the summer of my seventeenth year. That year, my parents paid for me and the older of my two younger brothers to travel to Jamaica, for the first time, to see our grandmother.

Neither of us had ever left the shores of Britain before and, while we had heard a great deal about Jamaica from our parents, nothing in our previous experience had prepared us for the cultural shock we would face when we arrived on the island. It was at this point that I was reminded of my sense of "in-between-ness." I use this inelegant phrase to describe the profound sense of unease and displacement I felt struggling to reconcile the romantic images of "homecoming" and "belonging" I expected to feel, alongside the acute feelings of embarrassment and culture at being the "little Black English boy lost at sea" in rural Jamaica.

Like many from the second generation of post-War Black, Caribbean people living in Britain, I was already an instinctive "postcolonialist." I did not identify with the incipient Whiteness that signified the sense of being "English" for the majority community, and I did not support England in any sporting endeavour. (Incidentally, I still continue to support any foreign nation against the English, especially in the classic colonial game of cricket.)[2] I had always felt alienated from the country of my birth and had travelled to Jamaica expecting to feel "at home" and a sense of place in terms of a need to belong. It was only after prolonged reflections on this formative experience that I realized that I was a hybrid person. I was located somewhere across the Atlantic, between the Caribbean of my immediate forbears and the British postcolonial landscape of my birth and upbringing. I was "out of place."

In more recent times, scholars such as R. S. Sugirtharajah and Edward Said, to whom mention has been made in this text, have explored in exemplary, eloquent fashion the notion of hybridity that lies at the heart of the postcolonial subject. It has become much more de rigueur to speak of postcolonial subjects who embrace their "in-between-ness" and the sense that one's subjectivity often transcends the binary of "either/or" but, rather, is characterized by a "both/and" mode of engagement.

As the twenty-first century witnesses the greater flow of human traffic and the accompanying cultures and perspectives on the divine inherent within that movement, we are witnessing the ever-burgeoning phenomenon of the sense of being "out of place." Perhaps it is now becoming more normative to talk of "out of place" as being the new "belonging"?

It is at this creative moment in human history – perhaps a Kiros moment – that we witness the unveiling of this landmark text. I commend my colleagues, Jione Havea and Clive Pearson, co-editors of this book series, for the creative leadership they have provided for this seminal piece of work. *Out of Place* provides a kaleidoscopic range of perspectives, narratives, subjectivities and thematic and methodological bursts of colour to ignite the imagination of all but the dullest of readers. This text provides insight into the myriad notions of what it means to be human in a world of marked change and where the sense of "solid ground" and being rooted in a specific and solidified space is becoming increasingly a rarity if not a misnomer.

Reading this text from my esteemed colleagues reminded me yet again of my own sense of being out of place in my daily interactions as a theologian and a person of faith. *Out of Place* speaks to me in a way that so many theological texts have failed to do in more recent times. It reminds me that we are all living through a time of relentless change where the indices for sameness and normativity are increasingly receding.

Indeed, this book emerges at a time when the leader of so-called free world is the archetypal hybrid subject. Barack Obama may well become the essentialized out of place spokesperson for the intercultural, hybridized, inter-subjective human being of the twenty-first century. As such, I would commend him to read *Out of Place*. In fact, you don't need to be the President of the United States of America to find this book of interest. I comment *Out of Place* to everyone. It is an essential text for the postmodern twenty-first century!

1 Welcome

Jione Havea

Be Strangers, No Longer

Welcome to another book on subjects that are *out of place*.

Like other places and homes, this book is a site with several sectors or rooms (read: chapters) that have been constructed according to the imaginations, personalities, orientations and commitments of different designers (read: authors). The bookish confines of this construction, with words, memories, stories, struggles, desires and objections, create the expectation that visitors (read: readers) will enter at the front then roam into the other sectors, one at a time, according to the order in which they are lined up. Hence, this chapter: it aims to welcome you, as readers, to this site. I welcome you not to be detached voyeurs but interested visitors who enter in order to be engaged, visited, touched, inspired, troubled, humoured, irritated, and haunted, by voices and bodies, subjects, from *out of place*.

The ensuing chapters are the creations of persons from different locations – from Africa, Asia, Oceania and the Americas – addressing various *subjects* that are out of place. The subjects are individuals or groups of persons, but also memories and identities, textual characters and social struggles, ways of thinking and theologizing, and so forth. The subjects vary and differ, and are complex, but they share a common lot: they are *out of place* where they are. Their place is *out of place*, some because of fate; some because of choice, exclusion, discrimination, oppression, and so forth. Some of these subjects might not be strangers to you, so I in advance beg your pardon and patience.

In giving attention to subjects that are out of place, this book echoes another book by the same title, Edward W. Said's *Out of Place*. The chapters of this book are political and theological "memoirs" in the sense that they are biographical, both of and through the authors, who write in order that out-of-place subjects are not forgotten. I thus welcome you to consider this book as if it is a companion to Said's, which he wrote in anticipation of his passing on (he passed away in 2003), peace be upon him, without seeking to put one or the other out of place.

The authors of the following chapters seek to bring *out-of-place subjects* into place by embracing their presences, amplifying their voices and enabling their subjectivities to influence how one reflects, relates and performs, theologically or otherwise. In this regard, I welcome you to also explore this book as one that shares the same drives with two other books: Fumitaka Matsuoka's *Out of Silence* and *Still at the Margins* which R. S. Sugirtharajah edited. This book also hears subjects out of silence, with the awareness that margins still exist and marginalization still continues.

This book is therefore not a lone and strange voice in the wilderness, out of place, but a site where other works intersect. Together, these works seek to bring into place subjects that are out of place, with the awareness that this involves dislocating and making those subjects vulnerable, at least in your readerly eyes. Together, also, these works redress the ways in which theology, as a discipline, and theological reflection, as a practice, have been *out of place* in several locations, nations, communities, churches, disciplines, institutions, and so forth. For theology and theological reflection to transform and be transformed, they need to come out of place and embrace what has thus far been out of place.

In the next section, I welcome you to a straightforward reading of this book. This involves introducing each of the chapters to you and to each other, for it is at this site that the chapters have come into, under, the same cover. Then, in the following section, I welcome you to *out-of-place* kinds of reading, which one might call, in other words, queer eyes for straightforward readers.

Reading Chapters into Place

Four basic convictions lie behind this book:

1. our theologies are shaped by the place in or for which/from where we theologize (all theologies are rooted and rooting, and potentially uprooting);
2. and no theological statement can encompass the complexity of all places (locally and globally);
3. so we are challenged to allow our theologies to intersect and supplement each other;
4. and to engage subjects that have thus far not been (fully) acknowledged, expressed and entertained.

The following chapters emphasize the fourth conviction, that we need to account for subjects that are out of place. The book flows in the expected pattern, with a chapter that establishes why we need this kind of study, followed by chapters that are more theoretical in nature, then shifts to ones that are more organic. Of course, none of the chapters is purely theoretical or completely organic. There is integration in each chapter, hence the book is not divided into "parts" but the chapters are kept together within the same unit, as a whole, so that the *out of place*-ness of each can complement others into place.

Peter Matheson ("A Woman Out of Place: Argula von Stauff") sets the stage with a discussion of gender issues in the life of one woman who was *out of place*, Argula von Stauff, and probes the relationship between hermeneutical and gender perspectives. Whatever else, the Reformation represents a seismic shift in the understanding of Scripture. Yet little attention has been paid to the ways in which this was paralleled by an upheaval in attitudes to marriage and celibacy. How did a new look at the Bible during the Reformation affect traditional attitudes to gender? How did the understanding of what it meant to be *coram Deo*, before God, affect one's "in placeness"" in human society?

Joerg Rieger ("Alternative Images of God in the Global Economy") attends to a subject that is out of place in many theological circles outside of Latin America, namely, economics. Rieger begins with the assumption that the world of economics is based on its own kind of theology – a theology that is mostly hidden, *out of place*. How might we theologize in a world in which the "trickle-down" theory, according to which wealth accumulated at the top trickles down to the impoverished classes, does not work? The growing wealth produced by the global economy has not trickled down; rather, the economic production of the lower classes has aggregated into a flood of wealth upward. In this context, Rieger suggests that theology needs to take into account the complexity of solidarity among humans. This is one possible way of being *coram Deo*.

Vítor Westhelle ("Displacing Identities: Hybrid Distinctiveness in Theology and Literature") digs into the attentions to hybrid identity and argues that transgression of purity is at the root of Christian "identity" ever dissimulated in the search for genealogies and pristine origins but never successfully evaded in the history of Christianity. Hybridity is at the very core of a distinctive Christian doctrine of incarnation. Attempts have been made in recent theologies to conceptualize incarnation as Christian hybridity, as did the early Fathers in their own contexts. Westhelle reviews some of these, then addresses contemporary issues in hybridity, and concludes by taking up recent Latin American literature as an example of hybrid dislocation that expresses this template of impurity. Hybridity, Christian identity, incarnation and impurity are *out of place*, actually, and this is not problematic.

Clive Pearson ("Out of Place with Jesus-Christ") revisits Jung Young Lee's hyphenated Jesus-Christ theology, which is based on a theory of marginality and in his experience of dislocation as an Asian-American, which is *out of place* in well-disciplined systematic theologies. Lee's doctrine of incarnation, which posits Jesus-Christ as an emigrant, a hybrid if one appeals to Westhelle's chapter, is a trustworthy ally for diasporic theologies and for persons who are out of place in Australia and beyond. Pearson's attention to hyphenated identities has to do with the doctrine of incarnation in relation to the person of Jesus-Christ and also in relation to the Christologies that hyphenated migrant theologians (in Australia) develop.

Fumitaka Matsuoka ("Holy Amphiboly: Prolegomena of Asian-American Theology") addresses the common stories of Americans of Asian descent, both hybridized and hyphenated, who live in a racialized society, which testify to the renewing power of the Spirit in a community that is being continually reformed and reforming. The convergence of three decisive forces drives Asian American theological practices: their emerging subjectivity and self-representation as Asian Americans in a racialized society, their diasporic spirit of dissonance and dissent, and their particular faith orientation, the irresoluteness of faith, or the "Holy Amphiboly." The permutation of these powerful forces in the lives of Asian Americans frames and drives their theological articulations of Christian faith.

Namsoon Kang ("Out of Places: *Asian* Feminist Theology of *Dislocation*") examines the lot of an Asian feminist theologian: one has to think as if one is without home. Taking *dislocation* as a metaphor becomes an element in staging "the feminist" in extreme patriarchal cultures, and being a Christian theologian in multi-religious societies, where Christianity is still regarded as a *foreign* religion and feminism is disregarded due to its "foreign" origin. Thus, an Asian feminist theologian is constantly *out of places*. The three components of Asian, feminist, and Christian theologian lead Asian feminist theologians to a peculiar space of uprootedness and dislocatedness, requiring one to reside simultaneously in more than two worlds, constantly in exile even in one's home country. Kang's hope is for "homecoming" in a space of resistance, solidarity and compassion.

Hisako Kinukawa ("Re-covering, Re-membering and Re-conciling the History of 'Comfort Women'") focuses on the "comfort women" who were forced into prostitution during the Second World War by the Japanese government. As a Japanese woman, from the belly of the Empire as it were, in solidarity with the abused women of Asia, Kinukawa writes in support of an alternative history in which the future generations of Japan, and beyond, will both re-member and re-concile the violence committed against "comfort women" in the name of the empire. Kinukawa calls for both solidarity and responsibility on behalf of the *out-of-place* comfort women.

Albert W. Jebanesan ("Integration and Disintegration of Tamils in London Diaspora") draws attention to a group of people *out of place* at another Empire: the Sri Lankan Tamil refugees in London. They are children of the war, who carried the war within themselves into their new homes. After overcoming the shock of disintegration of their families and villages, they find themselves in London in a state of "culture shock." There is a conflict between their expectations of the new reality, and the expectations of the new social reality around them. Prolonged without a satisfactory solution, this has led to their anomic state. In London, the centre of their lives has shifted or totally removed. They have tried to create that centre but it is impossible to do so individually, hence the longing and quest for community.

Gerald O. West ("Newsprint Theology: Bible in the Context of HIV and AIDS") re-examines a particular Bible reading methodology, known as Contextual Bible Study, a form of studying the Bible that is done in community and is community forming. In this chapter, West is concerned with persons in the *out-of-place* context of HIV and AIDS. HIV and AIDS are substantially impacting on the South African context in every way, including how to read the Bible and do theology. West examines in particular the demand for dignity, the embodied nature of dignity's demand for presence, and the role of the socially engaged biblical scholar in bringing dignity's demand for presence into articulation. Contextual Bible Study is helpful in dignifying persons infected with HIV and AIDS even in their *out of place*.

Jacqueline Grey ("Isaiah 53 and the Suffering-less Servant in Australian Pentecostalism") explains how prosperity changes the way Isaiah 53 is read in Pentecostal circles. Pentecostalism appeared on the Australian scene in the early nineteenth century and was met with resistance from society and the established denominations. It was a movement led mainly by women and its academically un-educated membership was *out of place* in conservative Australian societies, both religious and general. In the early days, Isaiah 53 was understood as pointing towards the suffering of Jesus, but as the movement prospered and turned evangelical, Isaiah 53 became the pattern for responding to suffering, grief and loss.

Anastasia Boniface-Malle ("How can we Sing the Lord's Song in Africa?") writes in places where suffering is displacing and very pain-ful. Boniface-Malle starts with Psalm 137, in which Israel lamented the senselessness of having to sing the Lord's song in exile, and borrows the question for her African contexts: How can we sing the Lord's song *at home*, where we are *out of place*? How can Africans sing the Lord's song in Christian circles that discourage lamentation, even though the Church is encircled by death and dissymmetry? The way forward, Boniface-Malle suggests, is to revive the spirits of lamentation, in Africa and all over.

Joseph Mathew ("Retelling Tamar's Story [2 Sam. 13:1-22] in Postcolonial Terms"), somewhat shadowing Kinukawa's agenda, appeals to the complex project of historical and psychological "recovery" in postcolonial theory. For Mathew, with regard to Tamar's story, what is needed is resistance to both the violence committed and the tendency to ignore Tamar's story. Shadowing Namsoon Kang, Mathew reads *dislocation* in the story of Tamar. In these regards, Mathew invites Tamar to hold together subjects who are *out of place* in many locations.

Mercedes L. García Bachmann ("What is in a Name? Abishag the Shunnamite as *sokenet* in 1 Kings 1:1-4") explores the ways in which names and titles hide the importance of women in biblical stories. Women characters are not always presented as full characters, but agents in supporting roles. Such is the case with Abishag, the young woman brought in to warm up the cold and dying David. García Bachmann argues that Abishag is not completely *out of place,* for as *sokenet* (usually understood to be an "attendant" or "personal assistant") to David (or was it to Bathsheba?) she served a crucial role in the story of David and Solomon. The narrator needs Abishag only as a bedfellow, but García Bachmann shows that as *sokenet* she was most significant.

My bookend piece ("Return, Medium of En-dor") is a farewell chapter in which I revisit the story of another woman, a Medium, who was *out of place* because of the decree of an *out-of-place* man, Saul, a king, who came for her assistance (1 Sam. 28). If you persevere to my chapter, I shall leave you with an invitation to honour the complexity and richness of subjects who are *out of place*.

Now that you have an idea of how this site is set up, I welcome you to read the chapters in a different order. Each of the chapters, as a sector or room, to follow the metaphor, is a point of entry and exit. I welcome you to move freely, back and forth and around, and from side to side.

Reading *Out of Place*, Back, Outside, to the Cover

How might you read this book, this construction, if you take the painting on the cover seriously? If the painting has not already caught your interest, please turn back and read it into your imagination.

The painting on the cover invites you to expect a scuffle, represented through the face-off between a protestor and a riot policeman. The protestor comes bearing only a placard on which the words (demanding workers' rights) are blurred, and he appears to be gaining position over a riot policeman who comes with a shield and a baton, and the support of colleagues around him. The protestor comes with words and determination, almost prophetic, almost Davidic (see 1 Sam. 17:45-47); the riot policeman comes with full gear, but his baton is not as massive as the shaft of Goliath's spear (see 1 Sam. 17:4-7). The painting represents a point of tension between a protestor and a protector and representative of the authorities, and invites you to take sides. Even before you open this book, to enter this site, the cover queries: For whom are you entering? The protestor? The riot police? Whose side are you on, already?

The chapters of this book will put you on the spot, as if pushing you to take sides, but be warned, none would invite you to side with the authorities and the power keepers. This is because the chapters are about subjects that are *out of place*, rather than those that control spaces and protect authorities. If any of the chapters invite you to side with the authorities who keep and protect "the in," as the riot police does in the painting on the cover, then that would be out of place in this book. How ironic!

The painting on the cover manifests the kind of scene one would witness in places where activism is strong; and activism is and needs to be strong in places where authorities are corrupted and senseless. Whether it manifests in the streets of Bogotá or Manila, Canberra or Nairobi, and beyond, activism is necessary as long as subjects are *out of place*. How can one be impartial when confronted with such a struggle?

On the cover, actually, is a painting by the Filipino activist and theologian Emmanuel Garibay, *Jacob Wrestling with God*. It foregrounds a protestor, to the left, who represents Jacob, raising a placard (which looks like a shovel that has been flattened out) with his right hand while his left hand reaches to the shield of a riot policeman, who represents "the man" that wrestled Jacob, and whom Jacob saw as G*d (Gen. 32:22-32). The riot policeman wears a helmet that shields his face from the viewer, as if to undermine Jacob's explanation for why he named the place Peniel: "For I have seen G*d face to face, and yet my life is preserved" (32:30b). The painting raises critical questions: What face of G*d did Jacob see? What does the face of G*d look like? Who knows what G*d is like? Who owns G*d?

The constructors of this site are not too interested in what G*d looks like. They are more interested in subjects whom the gods press. Those *out of place* subjects include "comfort women" (chapters 8 and 14); slaves of the global economy (chapter 3); ones infected by HIV and AIDS (chapter 10); feminist women in Christian circles (chapter 7); exiled Tamils in London (chapter 9); persons in diaspora (chapters 5 and 6); Pentecostals (chapter 11); mourners (chapter 12); the raped (chapter 13) and used (chapter 14); and, in general, women (chapter 2) and Christians (chapter 4).

Each of the chapters is a point of entry, so you could start reading at different places, depending on where your interests lie:

- If *migration and relocation*, see at least chapters 5, 6 and 9;
- If *gender and women*, see at least chapters 2, 7, 8 and 12–15;
- If *identity*, see at least chapters 4, 6 and 7;
- If *economy and prosperity*, see at least chapters 3 and 11;
- If *Christian movements*, see at least chapters 11 and 12;
- If *Incarnation and Christology*, see at least chapters 4 and 5;
- If *empire*, see at least chapters 8, 9 and 13;
- If *biblical criticism*, see at least chapters 2 and 10–15;
- If *solidarity*, any of the chapters will work!

Of course, each of the chapters says more than I represent here, but they all share the courage to resist and rebel. Resistance comes out strongly on the cover, as well as in each of the chapters.

The figure of the protestor in the painting leans over the riot policeman, giving the impression that he is winning the struggle.

This is a fair reading of the Jacob story, for even when his hip was put out of joint (32:25-26) he had the upper hand and it was he who decided when to let his opponent go. It was G*d who asked to be released from Jacob, but not the other way around. Though disjointed (the marks between the legs of the protestor in Garibay's work is suggestive), Jacob held on and demanded a blessing. In this perspective, the giving of the new name and the blessing were G*d's way of surrendering to Jacob.

As Garibay sides with the disjointed Jacob of Genesis 32, so do the authors of the following chapters side with disjointed, out-of-place, subjects in their various settings. Such kinds of solidarity deserve places.

Works Cited

Matsuoka, Fumitaka (1995). *Out of Silence: Emerging Themes in Asian American Churches*. Cleveland: United Church Press.

Said, Edward W. (1991). *Out of Place: A Memoir*. New York: Knoff.

Sugirtharajah, R. S. (ed.) (2008). *Still at the Margins: Biblical Scholarship Fifteen Years after* Voices from the Margin. London: T & T Clark.

2 A Woman Out of Place: Argula von Stauff

Peter Matheson

Exile, physical or spiritual, is part and parcel of the Christian experience. Prophetic statements or actions have regularly been regarded
as being "out of place." Behind such condemnations lurk unquestioned assumptions about what is "in place." Whole peoples such
as the Jews or the Gypsies, for instance, have been regarded as "out
of place"; they were seen as threatening because they were rootless
wanderers, homeless and untrustworthy. Much of the hostility that
the Primitive Church's apostles encountered may be attributed to
such suspicions.

Today's culture may, on the face of it, be more tolerant, less censori-
ous of dissenting views and actions. A modern city such as Melbourne
"makes place" for countless different cultures. The cross-cultural and
highly mobile nature of such cities combines with a degree of moral
and spiritual relativism to foster a culture of openness.

Frequently, however, tolerance appears to be only skin-deep.
Profound anxieties about identity and "belonging" lie just under the
surface. Mobility itself can encourage such anxiety. Newly arrived
immigrants in Australasia can provide fertile ground for those spreading racist stereotypes about indigenous people precisely because
they want to adapt themselves as fully as possible to the dominant
culture. A perceived moral "mobility," similarly, can be profoundly
alarming to many religious people and may be part of the explanation why they perceive such a threat from particular groupings such
as gay people.

The paradox that the eschatological community of the Church
frequently attracts the most traditionally minded in our Western society may prompt us, therefore, to rethink radically what it means
for a Christian to be "in place," or "out of place." Could it be that
only those with a strong bonding with tradition are able to entertain

troublesome new ideas and initiatives? If so, the fault-line between "liberals" and "evangelicals" in the Church is a dangerous and misleading one. It obfuscates the commitment to catholicity. Neither "liberals" nor "evangelicals" may of themselves have the resources to resolve who and what is "in place."

This chapter looks at gender issues from one specific historical perspective, probing the relationship between shifting hermeneutical perspectives and gender perspectives. Whatever else, the Reformation(s) represented a seismic shift in the understanding of Scripture. Yet little attention has been paid to ways in which this was paralleled by an upheaval in attitudes to marriage and celibacy. How did a new look at the Bible affect traditional attitudes to gender? How did the understanding of what it meant to be *coram Deo*, before God, affect one's "in placeness" in human society? The question has countless ramifications, but here we will restrict ourselves to the relationship between women and men.

Margaret Forster's *Good Wives,* recounting the travails of the wives of such notables as David Livingston, Robert Louis Stevenson, and Aneurin Bevan (the great Labour leader in post-war Britain) poses the question of a woman's "place" very sharply, as does the recent study of the partners of some of New Zealand's greatest literary and artistic figures edited by Deborah Shepard, *Between the Lives: Partners in Art* (Foster 2002; Shepard 2005). The wives or partners of prominent men may of course lead particularly fraught lives, with the unspoken demand that they sacrifice themselves for the greater Other. One's place, however, is always dependent on that of one's neighbour or partner.

Gender perceptions vary momentously with country and culture and time. Yet our very best imaginative writers such as Christa Wolf in her evocative and heart-breaking novel, *Medea,* set in ancient Corinth, remind us that there is a stubbornly persistent conviction that the unforgivable sin for a woman is to live by what she believes, to state openly what she thinks, and especially if she manifests this not only in words but in her whole "attitude," the way in which she moves and dresses and even holds her head high (Wolf 2003).

Gender perceptions relate to the understanding of men as much as women. Very tardily, I fear, historians in my own specialist field of early modern Europe are beginning to realize that masculinity is as much a variable as femininity. When is a man "out of place"? While Foucault and others have taught us that gender roles have strong correlations with the location of power, control and authority, we need to recognize that other factors – economic, social, cultural, political and not least religious – are coiled together here. So raising in any company, at any time, the question of what is in or out of place has always had the potential to create what Luther called *uffrur*, uproar, for it menaces our elemental need to belong, our own sense of identity.

Until quite recently most societies took for granted hierarchies of virtually absolute immutability in society. One knew whom to look up to, and who one could look down upon. There was great comfort in that. Shakespeare assumes structured "estates" in society as much as the most conservative churchman of his time. The father ruled the home, the magistrates or prince were the fathers of their people, and God as Father in heaven ruled the world. As late as nineteenth- and twentieth-century Europe many good Christians took for granted the concept of "orders of creation," which were God-given, or based on natural law. It was the threat to such orderliness that lurked behind much religiously sanctified anti-Semitism and racism. It could be rather illogically yoked at times with Social Darwinism. The "primitive" are an unnecessary brake on the upward march of progress. It is a sobering exercise to read the novels, text-books and newspapers of early twentieth-century Europe and realize the extent to which it was drenched in such prejudices.

Class, race, caste or generational roles, then, were as clearly demarcated as gender. Everyone knew their place. Much of the bewilderment in today's conservative and reactionary church circles rests on a yearning for such lost certainty and security. This may also explain the stubborn refusal to distinguish between culturally conditioned gender roles and sexuality itself. The very idea that sexuality varies with time and place is deeply upsetting. The prevalence of the metaphor of "plumbing" in the discussion of gender issues today, even among those who should know better, is only the most overt indication of this intellectual and emotional blockage.

As important, moreover, as any analysis of who was "in place" or "out of place," is the question of how people learned to "move on," of what strategies have been historically successful in raising consciousness, loosening up hardened mind-sets, gaining leverage with the opinion-makers, exerting pressure on the gate-keepers? Those who feel contentedly "at home" will never, of course, be able to empathize with the exile. As Heidegger's ruminations suggest, there may be no more dangerous concept than that of home, of *Heimat*. Yet is it not true that only those who are ultimately confident about their own belonging can open up "their place" to others?

Angst about our place in the great scheme of things may undergird one distinguishing characteristic of our generation: the deep pessimism about bringing about any fundamental political or structural changes, for example, in the relations of rich to poor. The papacy of Pope John Paul reminded us how deep the chasm can be between "liberals" who care about issues of individual freedoms and prophetic voices about war and social justice. Few seem to get it right across the board.

We may, then, profit from a dialogue with past attempts to subvert hierarchy and privilege. Almost invariably this has been done by those whose own words and actions have been regarded as "out of place." In their own defence, they have often gone onto the offensive, and turned the argument around, by pointing to a transcendent order of things which points in a quite different direction.

As a case study, I would like to introduce you to a Bavarian woman with a name improbable even to Germans, one who lived on the cusp of the early modern period. She was the daughter of two conservative aristocratic parents, and became a mother of four. Her husband was a featureless nonentity. She was probably the first European woman to be published in her own lifetime. Her supporters hailed her as a prophet in the line of Deborah and Huldah, and as a reincarnation of the St Catherine who dished a hundred eminent scholars in Alexandria and whose martyr's death is still celebrated today by Catherine wheel fireworks. Her opponents slammed her as a whore, a bitch, and much else, and plotted her speedy demise.

Her name is Argula von Grumbach. She operated (or flourished, as we used to say) in the early years of the Reformation, the 1520s (Matheson 1995). She would never have got a hearing if it had not been a time of turmoil, one in which vast, or even cosmic, change was on everyone's lips. She would never have found the resonance she did without the very recent invention of printing which side-stepped the monopolization of the public forum by princes, clerics and academics. Only in a "musical chairs world" has an individual like her the opportunity to change their own particular chair, to find a new "place."

Argula von Grumbach (1492–1556/7) was prodigiously "out of place," but she lived in a church and a society whose pillars were manifestly collapsing, whose values and institutions were turning topsy-turvy day by day. That takes nothing away from her courage, imagination and intelligence. The context of such apocalyptic expectations and unprecedented social upheaval needs, however, to be kept firmly in mind.

Women of her time were by no means without influence. Think of Elizabeth of England, or Teresa of Avila, and a hundred thousand less prominent women who were patrons of art, sponsors of avant-garde groups, heroic martyrs, and efficient business-women. Men may have shone like the sun, one of the leading authorities on the early modern era has noted, but women shone like the moon (Wunder 1998). No household could exist without their quiet control of everything from children's education to the family finances. They had their own spinning groups; they went to the market or to the baths together. They had their own places and spaces in which they talked their own talk and framed their own counsel. They were agents, and should not be perceived as victims.

Yet there were some emphatic "No, Noes" for the female sex. Women could not attend university, could not preach or become clergy, were unable to be citizens or to offer themselves for public office in the cities. Indeed many even of their traditional rights as owners of a craft or business were being progressively curtailed. Their nunneries were soon to be shut down in Protestant lands, and strictly enclosed in Catholic ones. If women misbehaved it was often the husband who was punished because legally women just didn't figure (Wiesner-Hanks 2000; see Wiesner-Hanks 1993 and McKee 1998 concerning the role of women).

Behind these legal restrictions lurked a whole universe of assumptions which are profoundly alien to us today, but which we need to grasp if Argula von Grumbach's initiatives are to be understood. Classical and allegedly biblical authorities were cited as proof that women were inferior. They were, compared to men, of an inherently "damp" disposition (doctors pronounced their breasts cold and damp), were inclined to hysterical and emotional outbursts and generally were incapable of the cool, analytical reflection at which men excelled.

As the sinful daughters of Eve their God-given "place" in society was a submissive one. As daughters they were to be obedient to their fathers, as siblings to their brothers, as wives to their husbands, as widows to their guardians, and in property matters often to their sons as well. They had a public role at the side of their husbands on secular and religious occasions, one far from purely ornamental, but they had no voice in public. Exceptional women, as in the early Church, could sometimes attain to the status of "honorary men."

As children needed the rod for their own good, so did women. The current phrase "a rule of thumb," reminds us that it was permissible to beat them provided the stick was not thicker than one's thumb. On the whole, though, there was no need for such beating. Women knew better than to endanger their honoured and secure standing at home, church and in communal life by foolhardy words or actions. Here then is a tightly spun net of medical, philosophical, cultural and theological conceptions within which women were caught. Contemporary art and poetry, however, suggests that the relationship between the sexes was an area of constant tension.

Argula von Grumbach gained fame and notoriety by challenging many of these assumptions about what a woman can or cannot do. Her importance for us today lies not only in the pioneering nature of her initiatives, the persuasive biblical justifications she gave for them, and the remarkable resonance her writings found in the reading public, but because she signals the possibility of quietly subverting a universe of repression from within.

She did not argue from a "rights" perspective. Rather she burrowed into Scripture and engaged honestly and prayerfully with her own inner conflicts and those of her friends. She cared more about maintaining humility than about her own personal "space." As we seek to come to terms with the clinches and clichés about Scripture and authority and sexuality in our contemporary church there may be much to learn from this curiously indirect, highly personal approach.

A word about her life. She grew up as the privileged daughter of Bernhardin von Stauff and Katherina von Thering, and to the end of her life signed herself, "Frein," or baroness. The family was a proud one, involved in fierce, abortive skirmishes with the centralizing Bavarian state. Both parents died of the plague when she was still young, so she had to learn to cope on her own in the distant Munich court. She imbibed the family's love of chivalry, the ancient dreams of the pursuit of the Holy Grail – she and her siblings were all named after characters in the knightly romance, Parsifal – and she shared its passion for education. Her father presented her with a costly, beautiful printed German Bible on her tenth birthday.

The Munich court, where she spent some ten years as a young woman, was a lively one; it was open to Italian and French influences, to the charms and acids of humanism, and to the rich mystical piety of Johann Staupitz, so influential on Martin Luther. One role model for her was the formidable Duchess Kunigunde, her mistress, who had no truck with superstition and on one notable occasion exposed a charlatan in Augsburg who had claimed that the consecrated host was her only sustenance. A peephole in the wall revealed all!

In 1516 her influential uncle and guardian, Jerome von Stauff, was arraigned for treason, tortured and executed. Kinship mattered intensely at this time. Argula will have felt that everything that happened to von Stauff also happened to her. She left the court shortly afterwards to marry Frederick von Grumbach, a nobleman from Franconia. The Franks lived just to the north, but were very different in mores and dialect from the Bavarians. He was administrator of the little town of Dietfurt for the Bavarian dukes. Argula set up her little household there. This happened one year before Luther burst on the scene with his 95 Theses. Soon her first children were being born.

When we wake up one morning and find the world around us has suffered a sea change we speak of cognitive dissonance. We have the same eyes, senses, routines, values, treasury of experience as before but none of them make sense of the new landscape. Argula had already experienced such dissonance with the simultaneous death of both parents from the plague and then the final humiliation of her uncle. Jerome von Stauff's public execution informed all and sundry that the days of the independent Bavarian nobility were over for ever. It will have been no coincidence that Argula and her

traditionally "out of place" family were predisposed to welcome the
dissonance of what we have come to call the Reformation.

We know little about her actual transition to evangelical views,
but can infer from her lyrical writings that she thrilled to the liberating élan of Scripture. It meant for her a new song, a new birth, a
new dawn, a new freedom. She fell in love with it. Her vernacular
German Bible enabled her to roam over the whole of Old and New
Testaments, comparing and contrasting and collating stories and
insights and texts, a rare privilege for lay people. Most only pos-
sessed single books of the Bible. She homed in on the Psalms, Isaiah,
Jeremiah and Joel, Matthew's Gospel, Paul, and 1 Peter.

Lay reading of Scripture was the rage in humanist circles all over
Europe at this time, of course, from Colet's London, to Lefèvre's
France, to Pole's Italy and Zwingli's Switzerland, often with a special emphasis on Paul. The wild horse of Scripture was fast slipping
its domesticated reins. Outstanding city preachers such as Paul
Speratus in Würzburg and Andreas Osiander in Nuremberg appear
to have fired her imagination. Like thousands of other lay people,
however, she also devoured the smudgy pamphlets that poured
out of Wittenberg. She was never a "Lutheran," she averred, but
Luther's translation and interpretation of Scripture was a catalyst for
her own intense "study" of its contents. So far the Munich court had
been her "university." Now she benefited from the open university
which printing had created. Her tutorials were made up of friends
and relatives, who were soon drunk with the same wine. Scripture
"replaced" traditions. Christ "replaced" the saints. Brother and sister
"Christians" "replaced" a clergy-dominated Church.

The profound Christ-centred faith which emerged made sense of
her previous agonies of body and spirit at bereavement and humiliation. Almost overnight she jettisoned the entire freight of the traditional piety we know from her childhood prayers: the adoration of
the saints, the priestly channelling of grace through the sacraments
of penance and the Mass, purgatory, the authority of the papacy
(for a collection of her prayers see Matheson 1997). But simultaneously she sewed together for herself a holistic vision of Scripture,
one which was quintessentially her own. She negotiated her way
from the prophets to the Gospels to Paul and back again. She formulated her own canon within the canon. She was indebted to Luther,

undoubtedly, but remained very much her own woman (for her hermeneutic see Matheson 1996).

It was not, however, this transformation of her personal spirituality nor even her emergent social and ecclesiastical analysis which branded her as "out of place." Anticlericalism, apocalyptic expectations, and biblicism were widespread. Even at the Munich court there was no love lost for the traditional structures of the Church; and much impatience with a privileged and somewhat indolent clergy. There was definite openness to humanist flair and methods. In the early 1520s confessional loyalties remained highly confused.

The crunch came, however, in 1523. A young student from Munich, one Arsacius Seehofer, who had studied at Wittenberg, returned to his Alma Mater at Ingolstadt full of the ideas of Melanchthon and Luther. He had acted as a courier for Argula in her contacts with Wittenberg, no doubt bringing her news, letters, and some hot-off-the-press pamphlets. After rumours spread that he was infecting students with his heresies his rooms were searched, and after incriminating material was found he was interrogated, day and night, and what we would call today a show trial was staged. The university, then as now, was in part instrument and symbol of state authority, and dependent on ducal patronage (though the Bishop of Eichstett also had a look in) and the powers-that-be in Munich wanted to make it crystal clear that Ingolstadt was under their control; it was not going to become some heretical seminary.

So the eighteen-year-old Seehofer was publicly humiliated before a solemn gathering of the entire university, and forced to recant his views. Bible in hand, he denied what he believed and affirmed what he now passionately rejected. He dissolved into agonized tears, to the evident amusement of the professoriate, and was then shunted off to confinement in Ettal monastery.

"So what?" one might ask. Most did just that, either shrugging a cynical shoulder or keeping their cool to fight more winnable battles. Not so Argula von Grumbach. When she heard a first-hand report the very next day she became very emotional, no doubt conforming to the gender clichés: "Yes, when I reflect on this my heart and all my limbs tremble." But the reason was biblical: "You lofty experts, nowhere in the Bible do I find that Christ, or his apostles, or his prophets put people in prison, burnt or murdered them, or sent them into exile" (Matheson 1995: 76).

The symbolic abuse of the Bible was indicative, for her, of a University, a Church and a State that had totally lost the plot. Universities were supposed to be about the pursuit of the truth. Why weren't Arsacius's views properly debated? The Church of Jesus was supposed to be a community of love. What did this incident demonstrate but the primacy of coercion and the threat of death on the stake for anyone who dared to think differently? The prince was supposed to be our Christian brother, sworn to uphold justice. But here he was being led around like a chained monkey by the clerics. Worst of all, Christ and the Word of God were being smothered. The princes and professors were trespassing on sacred territory. They had no place there.

Why then was no one pointing all this out? Why were the constituted authorities silent, betraying their stewardship, those "in place" to guard such legitimate frontiers? Why were the intelligent men who were supposed to understand such matters keeping their light under convenient bushels?

Argula von Grumbach knew what she thought. She knew how she felt. But she also knew, as St Paul had said, that it was not the place of women to speak in church. She knew what Aristotle had to say about women. She knew about the humble but important role which society assigned to women, and that it did not include speaking out in public. So, as she said, "heavy of heart," she did nothing.

But she prayed about it and was propelled by the outrageous behaviour of the University to comb Scripture again, flitting, as she said, from text to text. Isaiah 59 testified to God's being appalled that none had spoken out against evil. She noted that repeatedly, in times of crisis, the Holy Spirit spoke through the unlikeliest of people. Even through Balaam's ass!

Joel 2's prediction that the Spirit would be poured out on all flesh, and Israel's sons and daughters would prophecy stuck in her mind. She noted the countless examples of women activists and prophets in Scripture: Judith's decapitation of Holofernes, for example, was depicted in countless carvings, sculptures, paintings, and broadsheets of the time. But Deborah, Jael, Philipp's daughters also occurred to her. Jesus himself had not chosen academics for his disciples, but simple fishermen. Above all, she kept going back to Matthew 10, with its insistence on a mutuality of witness. Christ witnesses to us as we to Christ. Every baptized Christian is called upon to admonish, to speak out. To be a Christian is to open your mouth. From the roof-tops.

This is no proof-text reading of Scripture. 1 Timothy 2, she concluded, had to be read in the context of what for her as a Christian woman was the centre of the Gospel. She surrendered neither to her emotions, nor to traditionalist exegesis.

Once she was clear about her duty she moved straight to action. She prepared herself meticulously. Acting at great speed, and as a mother with young children, burning the midnight oil, she gathered together her arguments and her courage and sped off to Nuremberg, where she was advised by the reformer Osiander. Within ten days she, who had never written anything more than a personal letter before, had composed two substantial booklets. One was directed to the University, another to Duke William of Bavaria.

To this day, they remain impressive and moving documents (English translations in Matheson 1995: 56–112). The first, peppered with Scriptural quotations, argues coherently against the use of coercion in religious matters. A disputation is easily won when one argues with the weapons of fear. Positively it puts the case to the theological faculty for an attentive reading of Scripture. The second argues that the prince, a childhood companion and friend of hers, should lead a much needed reform of the Church, education and the law. His generous patronage of Ingolstadt University had been abused. If she were persecuted for writing in this way (any support for Luther had been proscribed) she was ready to face the consequences. She knew that a hundred other women would spring up in her place.

She sent off these letters, and handwritten copies soon began to circulate. Indeed the demand was so great that she agreed to them being published. Within a year, fourteen editions of her letter to the University had appeared, all over Germany, as far as Basel. A reasonable estimate is that some 34,000 copies of her seven pamphlets appeared, and one has to remember the duplicator effect at a time when books were read out aloud.

She was an instant sensation. Woodcuts appeared portraying her as a female Luther, confronting the theologians, Bible in hand, as

Luther had confronted the Emperor at the famous Diet of Worms in 1521. What caught the public imagination was that she, a woman, had actually challenged the theologians at Ingolstadt to a public debate, and in German, before the assembled university and the princes. Scripture alone would decide who had the right of it. This time it would not be a cowering eighteen-year-old boy, but Argula von Stauff, Frein.

This was a woman "out of place" with a vengeance. Women could not even attend University. She had no Latin, the language of instruction. She had no theological training at all, apart from her own private "study" of Scripture. And here she was, a layperson, daring to take on John Eck, one of the most formidable debaters in Germany in public! Enthusiasts for her saw it as heralding a new age. Her opponents included one anonymous type who wrote a foul poem suggesting she longed to bed the young student, Seehofer. Others suggested she should get back into the kitchen, take up spinning, have her fingers chopped off to inhibit further incursions into writing, should be walled up permanently, or quietly rubbed out.

Despite the real threats to her life and reputation five more pamphlets appeared from her pen, including a spirited poem that she wrote to refute her anonymous traducer. None of them was acknowledged by the addressees. Her husband lost his job. Anyone who couldn't control his wife clearly had no role in public life. As Luther noted he took it out on her. Significantly, too, his loss of gainful employment was to be catastrophic for the family finances in the years to come.

The story of her later life deserves a chapter of its own (see Matheson 2000 and 2005). It was characterized by enormous grit and guts. Move out of place and you pay for it! The devastation and terror generated by the Peasants' War triggered a conservative reaction not unlike that to the September 11 attack on the Twin Towers. All religious innovation was branded as incendiary.

There was personal tragedy. She had to cope with the death of her husband, then of her second husband, the early death of two of her children and the murder of a third. Even by sixteenth-century standards, these were devastating blows. Yet she continued in tiny obscure villages, Lenting and Burggrumbach, to work away quietly in her estates and among her friends, building up a network of support, founding churches, ensuring the best possible education for her children.

Effectively she was in exile, "out of place." Though overlooked by historians, she made a significant intervention at the crucial Diet of Augsburg in 1530, when Lutheranism gained public recognition, encouraging the Protestant princes to stand firm, and facilitating a much-needed dialogue between South and North German Protestants on the vexed issues around the Eucharist. She even advised Luther's wife, Käthe, how to wean her children!

Her time, however, of public prominence was exceedingly brief, just two years. In later life she found a *modus vivendi* in hostile Ingolstadt, and made friends with moderate Catholics. She died in her bed at the ripe old age of sixty-four. Her memory has been successfully suppressed until recently with rare exceptions such as the odd eighteenth-century Pietist.

Here, then, was a woman very much "out of place." She admonished eminent Catholic theologians as if they were naughty children, and attempted to get Protestant theologians to see beyond their differences about the Eucharist. She founded churches and pioneered a new evangelical lifestyle at the local level.

How are we to read her writings and her life? How would she "read" us today? We began by noting that she signed herself by her proud family name. Radicals can spring from surprising loins and wombs. In some ways, her actions were possible because of a family tradition of dissent and noblesse oblige. Yet her concept of Christian brotherhood and sisterhood subverted all hierarchies, and her letters finished with a very sincerely meant "Humbly yours, Argula von Grumbach." Like all women in her time, she had to deploy a "rhetoric of humility." But she was entirely genuine about it. Humility was a fundamental value for her, the narrow road to the very heart of the Gospel.

She never spoke of her "right" as a woman to speak out. Rather, she embraced the duty incumbent upon all who had vowed in baptism to renounce the Devil and serve Christ to do just that. Like the classical prophets of every time and age, she had felt compelled to speak. It is unhelpful to use a modern label such as "feminist" for her (cf. Classen 1991). There is absolutely no doubt, however, that she saw herself as an advocate for other women. She championed the cause of widows who had been scandalously treated by their male relatives. She had no patience with male arrogance and ignorance, and considered that women generally gave more time to reading and reflecting, not least on Scripture. She insisted that her daughter Apollonia be properly educated.

Ultimately she was "out of place," because, she believed, the righteous God of the prophets and the gentle God seen in Christ's life and ministry were "out of place," out of kilter with the regnant values of the time. In the last resort, *coram Deo*, in the presence of God, she saw herself as "in place," seeking to reflect God's vision for the world, one in which coercion had no place, in which "chivalrous" values prevailed, in which young Christians were not threatened with the stake, and widows were not abused by their male relatives. The transcendent authority in Scripture showed how everything could be put in its proper place, and fellowship in the body of Christ afforded a sense of belonging that nothing could shake.

We find this sensibility reflected in the naïve words of her children's letters, which express their awareness that they are born into this world not for their own good but for the sake of God and their neighbour. Perhaps we should close on that rather touching note: Argula von Grumbach's defiant assertiveness is not self-motivated. Her undermining of conventional gender roles was directly related to her tunnelling into Scripture, which she understood in highly personal, dynamic and apocalyptical terms. Baptism, so easily seen as a passport into civil society, was interpreted as an intimate covenant between herself and Christ, binding her to her brothers and sisters in Christ.

She again and again found herself pushed "out of place," and having in consequence to tackle bishops, princes and professors in unexpected, public and confrontational ways. At great cost to her life she came forward with a public theology. Her dream of a comprehensive reformation for the Bavaria she loved so much was not to be, but her words continue to reach us, and the little villages where she spent most of her life, many of them Catholic, have been proud to adopt her as their own. She has won her place there. Finally.

Works Cited

Classen, Albrecht (1991). "Woman Poet and Reformer: The 16th Century Feminist Argula von Grumbach." *Daphnis* 20: 167–97.

Foster, Margaret (2002). *Good Wives? Mary, Fanny, Jennie and Me 1845–2001*. London: Vintage Books.

McKee, Elsie (1998). *Katharina-Schütz-Zell: The Life and Thought of a Sixteenth-Century Reformer*. Boston; Leiden: Brill.

Matheson, Peter (1995). *Argula von Grumbach: A Woman's Voice in the Reformation*. Edinbugh: T & T Clark.

Matheson, Peter (1996). "A Reformation for Women? Sin, Grace and Gender in the Writings of Argula von Grumbach." *Scottish Journal of Theology* 49.1: 39-56.

Matheson, Peter (1997). "Angels, Depression and "the Stone": A Late Medieval Prayer-book." *Journal of Theological Studies* 48.2: 517–30.

Matheson, Peter (2000). "Contours of Daily Life." In *The Imaginative World of the Reformation*. Edinburgh: T& T Clark.

Matheson, Peter (2005). "Form and Persuasion in the Correspondence of Argula von Grumbach." In *Women's Letters Across Europe*. Aldershot: Ashgate.

Shepard, Deborah (ed.) (2005). *Between the Lives: Partners in Art*. Auckland: Auckland University Press.

Wiesner-Hanks, Merry (1993). *Women and Gender in Early Modern Europe*. New York: Cambridge University Press.

Wiesner-Hanks, Merry (2000). *Christianity and Sexuality in the Early Modern World: Regulating Desire, Reforming Practice*. London and New York: Routledge.

Wolf, Christa (2003). *Medea. Stimmen*. Munich: DTV Verlag.

Wunder, Heide (1998). *He is the Sun, She is the Moon: Women in Early Modern Germany*. Trans. Thomas Dunlap. Cambridge, MA: Harvard University Press.

3 Alternative Images of God in the Global Economy

Joerg Rieger

Why would theologians feel the need to address matters of the economy?[1] Most of us do not have formal economic training, and we are not experts in the nitty-gritty operations of the economy. Theologians are nonetheless becoming increasingly aware of overlaps in the areas of concern to theology and economics. These overlaps are not new. New economic developments, particularly rising economic pressures and hardships for many people around the globe, are pushing us to take a closer look. In this context, overlaps between theology and economics have become matters of life and death, urging us to realize that economic matters can no longer be fully grasped without theological input and vice versa.

In the United States and Latin America, critics argue that the world of economics is based on its own kind of theology, which is mostly hidden (see Galbraith 1992: 82 and Hinkelammert 1991). This insight, proposed both by economists and by theologians, does not necessarily imply a negative judgment on economics (as if the existence of theological underpinnings would make economics less serious or less scientific and rational by default), but it implies a new and broader perspective and challenges us to search for what is still mostly hidden.

Arising in this new perspective are basic questions: On which authorities, powers, and energies do we rely? What is it that gives us ultimate hope and provides reasonable levels of security? Such questions are not always easy to address because the answers usually lie below the surface, in the realms of what might be called the "economic unconscious" (Fredric Jameson talked about the political unconscious). In times when the global economy is moving from one slump to the next, and when even the top economists do not really seem to know what to do, perhaps these questions will get more of an airing, with a chance to bear fruit.

The basic problem for an engagement of the overlaps of theology and economics is whether we rely perhaps on the wrong authorities and powers. This problem poses itself not first of all in terms of abstract theoretical or theological matters but in terms of the practical consequences of contemporary economics, particularly in terms of the constant and growing inequalities of rich and poor. These inequalities persist and grow no longer only during times of economic stagnation, but also during times of strong economic growth, as was the case during the 1990s in the US. In these situations, one of the basic images of hope for many economists, the so-called "trickle-down" theory – according to which wealth accumulated at the top trickles down to the impoverished classes – has not worked. The growing wealth produced by the global economy has not trickled down; rather, the economic production of the lower classes has aggregated into a flood of wealth upward.[2]

God and the Market

In the US, notions of God and of the free-market economy are closely related. It is common for the president of the nation and the presidents of corporations to make public reference to God. Devotions and public prayers are common both in the White House and in the board meetings of big corporations. Even most of the churches go along with this trend. Although not all preach the "gospel of success" (i.e., that God and the Christian faith guarantee economic success), few see the need to question the intricate relation of faith and economics. While the separation of church and state is commonly assumed – even though it is not necessarily realized – there is little concern for similar distinctions when it comes to church and economics. While there has traditionally been some concern for the distinction of faith and politics, for the most part the distinction of faith and economics is not even recognized as a problem.

Robert Nelson, a professor of economics at the University of Maryland, has shown the connection of religion and the free-market economy in two of his books (Nelson 2001 and 1991). Reflecting on his experiences as an economist in the US Department of the Interior, he points out that the job of the chief economists was not to provide formal economic calculations. Their main job was to preserve key economic values and actively promote those values in politics through collaboration with politicians (Nelson 2001: xiv, 8).

While these key economic values are not necessarily presented in explicit theological terms – economists may or may not refer to God openly when they promote their values – there are some efforts to do so. One of the most prominent supporters of a self-proclaimed "Christian" theology of economics in the US is Michael Novak of the American Enterprise Institute. Though he disclaims an explicit connection between theology and economics, he finds close connections between his conception of God and of what should be preserved in the economic status quo. According to Novak, the incarnation of Jesus Christ, for instance, challenges us to accept the world as it is and not to expect the reign of heaven on earth.[3] In other words, the status quo, particularly the economic one, should not be challenged since this is the way God intends things to be. The logical conclusion is that God, in the incarnation of Christ, has also sanctioned the capitalist free-market economy.

Theological justifications of the status quo are usually not that explicit, even in the US; however, the connections between God and the free-market economy are presupposed and few critical questions are raised. This shows us how deep-seated the matter really is and how successfully it is able to remain at work under the surface. In fact, just like the implicit theology on which it rests, the principles shaping economic functioning remain for the most part unchallenged. Continued economic difficulties and growing economic hardship for many become the ground not for seriously questioning the free-market economy but for an even stronger belief in its principles.

Economic hope derives from what might be called an "other-worldly" perspective. Economic indicators that would demand changes in the actual course of economics take a back seat. What rules is limitless faith in the reality of unstoppable progress. Hope, even in the midst of severe economic crises, is built on the faith that "things" will somehow take care of themselves and that "things" will eventually get better if the reign of free-market economics is affirmed. This hope in the "otherworldly" reality of progress also covers up the role of human failure in the creation of economic decline and hardship. CEOs of corporations, for instance, are rarely challenged, except in cases of crude moral failure or grotesque malfeasance. The thought hardly occurs that even key figures in the world of free-market economics, such as Alan Greenspan, the well-known chairman of the US Federal Reserve, could be somehow at fault in the current economic crisis. Some sought to hold President Bush accountable during the elections of 2004, but the result of the elections has shown that most people, including many of those most economically challenged, do not perceive the weak US economy to be the fault of the government, its policies, or its leaders. In the US, the focus on both economics and politics continues to be on otherworldly conceptions of reality: i.e. matters of faith.[4] In this light, the insight of theologian M. Douglas Meeks must be affirmed that economics cannot exist without some sort of divine or otherworldly sanction of its norms (Meeks 1989: xi).

The intensity of the entanglement of theology and economics is hard to imagine for those living outside of the US. In Europe, for instance, great care is taken not to refer to otherworldly matters in public, let alone to God. Even most of the churches are careful. When talking about economic matters, for instance, the churches rarely refer directly to images of God; they refer instead to general moral premises which they believe to be commonly acknowledged by everyone.[5] Nevertheless, the question needs to be raised whether even in Europe and other secularized places economic theories are based on certain embedded and unquestioned conceptions of God or of the divine.

One of the debates in economic thinking within Europe has to do with the question whether the free-market economy is a merely formal mechanism of distribution, which can be understood and predicted in mathematical and statistical calculations, or whether even in Europe the free-market economy is guided by other sets of values that cannot be considered to be "purely" economic (cf. Hays and Kreider 2001: 166). In the current situation, it seems to me, the latter position is closer to the truth. While the values that guide free-market economics in Europe are not always easily discerned, they become more visible in situations of tension.

The processes of economic privatization may serve as an example. When the German postal service was privatized at the beginning of the 1990s, the shape of the new postal system did not emerge, as one might have expected, out of empirical observations and analyses of the local markets. Frequently, American economists and CEOs were flown in to promote their values and ideas about privatization and in order to spark the imagination of their German disciples. General economic values such as deregulation and rationalization were far more important in this process than economic analyses and studies, and those values determined the questions that were raised and the answers determined.

Nevertheless, more is at stake than just the question of the role of values versus the role of formal calculations in economics. There is a theological component at work, as the following example will demonstrate. The German *Handelsblatt* reports that in 2002 the incomes of the board members of the thirty largest companies rose, despite severely falling values of their stocks. The Daimler-Chrysler corporation set the record: the incomes of its thirteen board members rose by 131 per cent, while the corporation lost 39 per cent of its value in the stock market.[6] Nevertheless, even those seemingly overrated German CEOs are still lagging behind their American colleagues, who in 2001 earned on average 531 times more than their workers.[7] This phenomenon, which is certainly challenged more readily in Europe than in the US, can certainly not be explained if economics were ruled by purely mathematical and statistical calculations. Yet there is still more at stake than can be contained in the question of specific sets of economic values: what is at stake is *what is of ultimate value*, and of course questions of ultimate concern are of theological import. We are approaching here the theological question of God.

Consider Martin Luther's response to the question "what does it mean to have 'a god,' or what is 'god'"? God is that, according to Luther, "to which your heart clings and on which you depend – that is really your god" (Luther 1964: 22).[8] In this sense, even the field of economics has a god to which it clings and on which it depends. This can be demonstrated most succinctly in situations of economic failure and in terms of the question of accountability for it. If the market on which we depend is rooted, consciously or unconsciously, in some godlike "otherworldly" reality, then it transcends the effects of actions and decisions taken by the leaders of the economy, including their calculations and their values. Accordingly, we cannot hold them accountable for disappointing results, any more than we hold priests responsible for "acts of God" such as earthquakes and tsunamis. This might help understand the otherwise very strange fact that in the US and elsewhere CEOs and other prominent economic leaders are often the last people to be held accountable for economic failure. It is quite common that in cases of economic failure no one is blamed at all. Not only are the leaders of the economy not held accountable for failure, they are rewarded for not giving up hope and for reassuring us of the transcendence of the market. Their usual message, repeated over and over again in slightly different words, is that the market has never been in a slump for very long and that progress is inevitable. At stake is much more than simply the values of the market; at stake is the transcendence of the market. The market becomes thus part of ultimate reality. We revere this transcendence of the market when we revere its highest representatives. Could it be that in paying homage to them with ever growing salaries and incomes we are trying to please the transcendent?

Against those who would prefer to see economics as a purely formal and mathematical science, I am arguing not only for the inclusion of the question of values but also for the inclusion of the question of God, which has been operating covertly. It is well known, for instance, that Adam Smith has talked about the "invisible hand of the market" (see Smith 1904: Book IV, Ch. II, par. IV). To be sure, this reference to a transcendent factor is not so much a theological leftover of outdated worldviews inherited by Smith but a theological principle that remains one of the foundations of free-market economics. Even at present, the free-market economy assumes the existence of this transcendent "invisible hand." This theological principle guarantees that human self interest – considered as one of the strongest sources of energy of the free market – is transformed into common interest, thus benefiting the community as a whole. Here, the theory of the free market touches the transcendent. Of course, this transcendent entity does not necessarily have to be called "God"; one might also call it the "nature of the world"[9] or the "order of things," or simply that "which keeps the world together at its core." But, using Luther's language again, it is this invisible hand to which our hearts cling and on which we depend, even in the midst of the most severe economic crises of the global economy.[10] This economic hope is not unlike what the Apostle Paul once called "hoping against hope" (Romans 4:18); this sort of hope can be guaranteed only by a transcendent power.

The Role of Theology

If it is true that even in secular Europe the free-market economy displays covert theological (and not just ethical) foundations, surely we can benefit by – at the very least – making these theological conceptions overt. More positively, I believe theology, understood as critical reflection on images of God, can make substantial contributions to economic debates, particularly when we cultivate a certain level of insight about where certain images of God come from and where they lead us.[11] In addition, theology might help us identify alternatives which are today thought to be scarce and, in the case of the remaining ones, are often suppressed.[12]

Those uncomfortable with overtly theological conceptions in economic debates might argue for more pointed ethical reflections instead; but ethics often tends to short-circuit the debate. Since Adam Smith, for instance, economists have regarded self-interest as a positive factor which drives the economy and contributes to common interest and progress.[13] In common ethical opinion and in most ethical debates, on the other hand, self-interest is usually critiqued and rejected as a negative factor which can only lead to selfishness. Robert Nelson considers such general ethical prejudices as among the biggest hurdles for students of economics. The task of economics, which strongly depends on concepts such as self-interest, is therefore first of all to overcome such common ethical short-circuits. Free-market economists do this, for instance, by trying to demonstrate that the free markets work successfully and are thus able to channel self-interest in support of common interest and the common good (Nelson 2001: 331). Here we enter the realm of theology.

The work of Nelson supports my argument for theology when he points beyond the ethical to the religious dimensions of economics. The free-market economy, in his opinion, is based not only on an ethics but also on a religion which is able to provide an appropriate framework for the pursuit of self-interest (Nelson 2001: 9). Nevertheless, Nelson does not raise the question of God. Going beyond Nelson, we need to ask about the images of God presupposed in such a religion. What are the foundations of our hope? Here, theological reflection can help to search and dig deeper, and to investigate how solid those foundations are. As we shall see at the end, theological reasoning can also help us develop a fresh perspective on issues such as self-interest that follows neither the common ethical rejections nor the unilateral economic endorsements of the concept.

An increasing number of theologians are beginning to realize that talk about God is always contextual. Even apparently abstract and general dogmatic-theological statements and confessions of faith are rooted in particular contexts. When 1 John 4:16 claims that God is love, for instance, the reference is not to love in general but to a particular history of love which is closely connected to how the authors of the passage have experienced God's love in their own world. Theological trouble emerges particularly in situations where the contextual nature of our talk about God is repressed. When context is thus neglected, we end up with absolute images of God that can no longer be debated and adjusted, and which are therefore easily misused. Church history is full of examples of such misuse of absolute images of God. The most severe trouble emerges when such images of God operate below the surface, as an *invisible hand,* without being recognized. This is the case in and – I am prepared to argue – one of the central problems of the global free-market economy.

What might be the basic hope, the most basic image of God of this global economy, and what is its context? The matter of self-interest, as introduced above, is merely a symptom, pointing to a deeper hope. Self-interest points to another "who is to come" (Matt. 11:3). In the work of Adam Smith self-interest points in the direction of the basic ideas of growth and progress. Taking up the standard, Nelson notes that scientific progress is the most vital religion of modernity and that economists are the modern priest-hood of the religion of progress (Nelson 2001: 329).

The task of critical theological reflection challenges us to search for the contextual roots of these images of God and of this hope in real life. Although adherents of the gospel of the global economy expect much to be taken on faith, their message is still rooted in a particular contextual reality, and this reality needs to be raised to the level of consciousness so that it can be addressed. In a nutshell, the contextual roots of the image of God as the one who guarantees progress can be found in certain people's real-life experience that the market economy works for them and that they can expect prog-ress to be the inevitable result of market dynamics. This particular contextual experience is then universalized in economic theory and applied to humanity as a whole (Nelson 2001: 330).[14] Those who continue to doubt can be presented with the visible successes of the market economy, though not all doubts can be cleared.

At this point, however, a new question needs to be raised. Is it true that the global market economy works always and everywhere – and for everyone? Is it true that the god of free-market econom-ics, the god of inevitable and unstoppable progress, is the true God of all? Obviously, there are some people who appear to have been richly endowed by the grace of the god of progress, those who sub-stantially benefit from the meanderings of the free-market economy. The stories of those people, of the economic elites and of those who enjoy economic success at the moment, are well known and well publicized by the media. Even the representatives of the mid-dle classes of the so-called "first world" are made to believe that the global market economy works for them and are taught to gaze admiringly upward rather than to the side at their struggling peers, much less down to their drowning fellow citizens.

Nonetheless, it is here that the first doubts emerge. In many "first world" countries there are new generations of the middle class who are fully aware that their own standard of living is, and most like-ly will remain, significantly below that of their parents. If we look below the middle class, things are much worse yet. The economic progress of the last century has not benefited most of humanity, not even in the "first world." The considerable economic progress of the 1990s has not stopped the problem, as those who believe in the universality of progress should have expected, but exacerbated it. In the US, for instance, economic disasters for the lower classes have rapidly increased during those years – exemplified by a steady downward trend for the weakest members of society, represented in the trauma of falling real wages, growing debt, growing rates of child poverty, and increasing rates of child homelessness – the latter representing a phenomenon that does not even exist in most industrialized countries.[15]

This perspective challenges us to question the images of God presupposed by the global free-market economy. The most important question has to do with "blindspots" (see Rieger 2001). What is repressed and overlooked when we follow the god of progress? What about the billions of people who do not benefit at all from economic progress and growth, but on whose backs progress and growth are produced – often achieved through ultra-low wages, low valuation or usurpation of their land, their raw materials, etc.? We constantly need to remind ourselves that in many places around the globe and particularly in the so-called "third world," poverty has not been reduced but continues to grow, despite decade-long efforts at "economic development" and "economic aid."

This is the place where theology needs to enter into a critical dialogue with economics. Of course, theology itself cannot render judgment "out of nowhere," as if it were part of a completely different context; rather, theology itself needs to be judged according to its own interconnections with growing global suffering and the all-pervasive logic of free-market economics (compare Long 2000). Even the kind of theology which intends to be purely "traditional," working exclusively with classical concepts, needs to be examined for how it is now shaped by the current ideology of the market. Of course, since this influence is located mostly at the subconscious level, theologians are not usually aware of it.[16] Even the most classical theological confessions, for instance the confession that "Jesus is Lord," can become confessions of the market; the notion of Jesus' lordship is easily subverted and assimilated to that which rules the free-market economy, without anyone noticing the heresy. Absolutized images of God create problems both in the life of the church and in the life of the free market – not only can they not be critiqued but they can even function as Trojan horses which activate their cargo in secret, making them more powerful and dangerous. Absolute images of God lead to an absolute church and an absolute market, and to institutions that can no longer be questioned and challenged.

Another Theology

If theology has a place in the discussion of global economics, we need to consider what the theological alternatives are. As I have argued, the question is not whether there are images of God in economics and whether this is appropriate or not. The problem is whether those images of God are supporting life. As a Christian theologian, I am particularly interested in determining whether these images of God match Christian ideas of the reality of God as the one who offers life to all, including the "least of these" and the weaker members of society.

The basic question in this regard is whether the current economic theology of progress merely sanctions and sanctifies the status quo or whether it contributes to a better life for all. Robert Nelson, for instance, finds the basic contribution of Adam Smith to the history of economics in his efforts to convince economic losers that they need to accept their fate without revolting against it (Nelson 2001: 289). In this approach, the status quo is sanctioned without particular consideration of those who are crushed by it. At stake is not the question of honest belief in the market (this seems to be a given), but the question of awareness of the lives of those who at present do not benefit from the market, and the role of this awareness in economic theory. Most serious economists, I would submit, honestly believe that they have found the most effective solution – if not the only viable one – for the problems of the world and thus firmly trust that in the end even the sacrifices of the losers contribute to the common good. Their deep faith in the progress created by the free-market economy keeps them on track even if the economic reality looks dismal for more and more people and – if nothing else, this matter should give us pause – even if billions of lives are lost. In sum, such deeply held faith in progress actively interferes with the potential of developing a deeper awareness of the suffering of other people.

What happens when the question of God is posed not from the perspective of the economic status quo but from a perspective which includes all of humanity? What happens when the economy is viewed not exclusively or primarily from the perspective of the select few at the top but from a perspective which includes the billions of people at the underside? What gives hope and comfort to all those who are being crushed by the economic success of some? I seriously wonder whether the kind of "natural theology"[17] built on the status quo, which trusts in the "invisible hand of the market" without much consideration of its effects on diverse groups of struggling people, has anything to offer to the majority who do not benefit from free-market economies. If the current extreme economic imbalance does indeed display the real nature of the world, as many contemporary economists seem to believe, there is very little hope for those who find themselves on the underside. Their lives will continue to be miserable.[18]

An alternative perspective might take a cue from alternative theological approaches that – in the midst of the catastrophes of the early twentieth century – have developed resistance to the "natural theology" of the status quo. These theologies of resistance talked about God as the "wholly Other."[19] God was described as Other not because God is located in some isolated transcendent realm, far removed from the world, but because the true God is Other than the familiar gods of the status quo. God is Other than the authority and power of those on top, the elites, those whom we commonly consider to be in control and who seem to determine the order of things. This God comes as a surprise, because this Other God is in solidarity with those who suffer, with the weak, the widows and the orphans of the Old Testament and with those on the margins of society in the New Testament. In short, God is in solidarity with those on the underside of life and of the economic system.[20]

Here is one of the most crucial challenges posed to the global economy by Christian faith, a challenge deeply rooted in many of the multiple voices that come together in the biblical sources, from the Old Testament to the Apostle Paul; the latter even includes an awareness of the suffering of non-human creation (Rom. 8:21). Even in the earliest beginnings of the Jewish-Christian heritage, God could be found choosing solidarity with the small, insignificant people of

Israel, which did not hold a place of honour among the empires of its day and which was frequently enslaved and exiled by them.

There is one more step that critical theological reflection needs to take. It is not easy for those of us who benefit from the global economy to step outside the economic theology of progress, even if we honestly intend to do so. This is true not only for professional economists but also for professional theologians and for mainline Christian churches. If God as Other remains merely a pious idea that does not interfere directly with the economic system, not much will change. In order to resist the almost inevitable accommodation to the status quo of those who benefit from the free-market economy, the awareness of God as Other will have to be tied very closely to an awareness of people as other, and anchored there. Those other people to whom I am referring are those people who are designated as "other" by the logic of the free-market economy, perhaps because they cannot compete in the market or because they are prevented in various ways from performing at what counts as superior levels of success. In building relationships and ties of solidarity with these other people, we have an opportunity to gradually develop greater respect for that which is other, respect which ultimately will also shape our images of God as Other (see also Rieger 2001).

The main goal of this critical theological reflection is to discover and make use of new impulses and energies that can reshape our images of God – whether those subconsciously held by economists or those consciously held by theologians – and lead us in new directions.[21] What guides and reinforces our hope in this new paradigm is no longer an absolute and abstract image of economic progress, but a tangible world of real people which includes "the least of these," a world in which all cannot only survive but also live a decent life. In this new paradigm, the now ubiquitous preference for individual wealth would be replaced by a preference for those who have been severely crushed by the economy (see Rieger 2003).[22] This new type of preference is related to biblical notions of God's own concern for those who suffer and are crushed by the powers that be, from the "oppressed poor" and the "crushed needy" mentioned by the Prophet Amos (Amos 4:1) to the "low and despised" mentioned by the Apostle Paul (1 Cor. 1:28). This preference emerges also as the central issue when we consider the question whether all can survive and live (cf. Rieger 1998).

These theological considerations lead us back to ethical and economic matters. One of the biggest surprises in this respect might be that we can now claim a new place for self-interest, one of the key terms for free-market economics since Adam Smith. Rather than demonizing or sanctifying self-interest, as ethicists and economists are wont to do, we need to realize that self-interest is part of life and of survival. When we encounter God as Other, however, we begin to see self-interest in a new light. Self-interest that is becoming aware of the challenge of otherness does not necessarily have to lead to the exploitation or the exclusion of the other; it can also lead to new kinds of relationship with the other and the other's inclusion. Even in the thinking of free-market economics, of course, self-interest includes some awareness of the other – but what if self-interest came to include particularly those others whom we do not notice at present and those who, in terms of the dominant economic system, do not seem to be of much use to us? Jesus' commandment, "love your neighbour as yourself" (Mark 12:29-31, with roots in Lev. 19:33-34), reminds us that self-interest is always tied to others, whether we notice them or not. At stake here are not primarily special acts of support or the distribution of alms, but the recognition that the neighbour is a part of ourselves, even when we are not aware of it. This goes in the face of common economic (and theological) wisdom.

That the neighbour is part of who we are is not religious idealism or wishful thinking. This is the (still mostly hidden) truth of the global economy. Our neighbours are always a part of ourselves, even though we may never know them and even though we often might prefer not to get to know them. Unfortunately, that the neighbours are part of ourselves today often means first of all that we are developing our own economic advantages on their backs; they are part of ourselves because we benefit directly or indirectly from their exploitation – if only because we can buy certain goods very inexpensively and because certain services are cheap. But in the midst of these oppressive relationships other connections are created, connections that might be seen as a different and unexpected kind of "surplus" which cannot be measured with current economic tools. This different kind of "surplus" has nothing to do with economic gain but with a potential for alternative relationships among people welded together by the economic system; these relationships might lead to a kind of solidarity that typically emerges only under pressure, when people begin to realize their true common interests (cf. Rieger 1998: 79). As the Apostle Paul realized long ago, "if one member [of the body] suffers, all suffer together with it" (1 Cor. 12:26). As a first step, we need to become aware of these connections already in place and realize the true complexity of our relationships.

Without seeing this complexity of our connections to other people, including their distortedness, we will never be able to transform them in more life-giving ways. In this regard, seeing the complexity of our connections to the divine Other might be of help, too; more hopeful and life-giving alternatives emerge where the pressure is greatest and where the divine Other enters into our predicament, rather than remaining at the lofty tops of comfortable progress for the few. Is this not part of the Christian message of the incarnation of Jesus Christ – in a manger and under persecution (Luke 2:7; Matt. 2:16)? When we thus more fully realize our complex location between other people and the divine Other, might we not have a better chance of becoming fully human and of developing a more human economy?

Works Cited

Carsten Herz, Siegfried Hofmann (2003a). *Handelsblatt* Nr. 070, April 9, 1.

Carsten Herz, Siegfried Hofmann (2003b). *Murrhardter Zeitung*, May 22, *Leitartikel*.

Galbraith, John Kenneth (1992). *The Culture of Contentment*. Boston: Houghton Mifflin.

Hayek, Friedrich A. (1960). *The Constitution of Liberty*. Chicago: University of Chicago Press.

Hays, Donald A. and Alan Kreider (eds.) (2001). *Christianity and the Culture of Economics*. Cardiff: University of Wales Press.

Hinkelammert, Franz J. (1991). "Wirtschaft, Utopie und Theologie: die Gesetze des Marktes und der Glaube" In *Verändert der Glaube die Wirtschaft? Theologie und Ökonomie in Lateinamerika*, ed. Raúl Fornet-Betancourt. Freiburg: Herder.

Long, Stephen D. (2000). *Divine Economy: Theology and the Market.* London: Routledge.

Luther, Martin (1964). *Der grosse Katechismus.* Calwer Luther-Ausgabe, Bd. 1. Munich und Hamburg: Siebenstern Taschenbuch Verlag.

Meeks, M. Douglas (1989). *God the Economist: The Doctrine of God and Political Economy.* Minneapolis: Fortress.

Nelson, Robert H. (1991). *Reaching for Heaven on Earth: The Theological Meaning of Economics.* Lanham, MD: Rowman and Littlefield.

Nelson, Robert H. (2001). *Economics as Religion: From Samuelson to Chicago and Beyond.* University Park, PA: Pennsylvania State University Press.

Novak, Michael (1982). *The Spirit of Democratic Capitalism.* New York: American Enterprise Institute, Simon & Schuster.

Novak, Michael (1990). *Toward a Theology of the Corporation*, rev. ed. Washington, DC: AEI Press.

Rieger, Joerg (1998). *Remember the Poor: The Challenge to Theology in the Twenty-First Century.* Harrisburg: Trinity Press International.

Rieger, Joerg (2001). *God and the Excluded: Visions and Blindspots in Contemporary Theology.* Minneapolis: Fortress.

Rieger, Joerg (2002). "Theology and Economics. The Economy is Expanding: Theology to the Rescue." *Religious Studies Review* 28.3 (July): 215–20.

Rieger, Joerg (ed.) (2003). *Opting for the Margins: Postmodernity and Liberation in Christian Theology.* American Academy of Religion, Reflection and Theory in the Study of Religion. Oxford: Oxford University Press.

Rieger, Joerg (2009). *No Rising Tide: Theology, Economics, and the Future.* Minneapolis: Fortress Press.

Smith, Adam (1904 [1789]). *An Inquiry into the Nature and Causes of the Wealth of Nations*, 5th ed. London: Methuen.

Sung, Jung Mo (1991). "Der Gott des Lebens und die wirtschaflichen Herausforderungen für Lateinamerika." In *Verändert der Glaube die Wirtschaft? Theologie und Ökonomie in Lateinamerika*, ed. Raúl Fornet-Betancourt. Freiburg: Herder.

Sung, Jung Mo (1994). *Economía, tema ausente en la teología de la liberación.* San José, Costa Rica: DEI.

Wolman, William and Anne Colamosca (1997). *The Judas Economy: The Triumph of Capital and the Betrayal of Work.* Reading, MA: Addison-Wesley.

4   Displacing Identities: Hybrid Distinctiveness in Theology and Literature

Vítor Westhelle

Introduction

I start by avoiding an oxymoron: hybrid identities. Hybridity is the transgression of identities, of idios, of that which is *proper* to oneself and does not belong to another. Hybridity crosses the line between purity and pollution.

Hegel, the great philosopher of Western (European) identity, revealed in his youth a thought that was rather puzzling and way more interesting than his famous definition of dialectics as being the "identity of identity and non-identity" (Hegel 1970: 5:28). About a decade earlier, he wrote the following: "When the Absolute slips on the ground in which it strolls about and falls into the water, it becomes a fish" (Hegel 1970: 2:543). Fish – this creature inhabiting the waters that ecologists call the universal communicant – is exactly the opposite of what absolute (*ab-solus*) means, detached and abstracted from everything. When you fall from your place, you become something else, totally dependent of everything else, the opposite of being absolute. The Absolute, Hegel's "god," has become a hybrid. It slipped from its familiar environ of absolute detachment to be an organic living being, totally connected to everything else.

Let us leave Hegel and fish behind and take a mule as a typical case of hybridity. It is neither a donkey nor a horse, yet, in a sense, both. It does not have in the strict sense an identity, for to have an identity, something that is proper, needs to be passed on, to have some permanence, to have a lineage (mules are sterile) and their ascendancy is mixed. Without a lineage, and a genealogy, there is no identity. Hybrids do not have, strictly speaking, identities. Their "identities" are "impure;" they have been "corrupted" and displaced. Hybrids are out of place.

Hybrids are impure because they defy the either/or of propositional logic, the great maxim of western thinking: *sic aut non et tertius non daretur* (yes or no, and the third is excluded), as they settle neither for a *tertium datur*. They do not belong to either category but are both without being a synthesis. They cannot reproduce themselves, they only spawn further impurity. They are degenerative. Identity is to purity what hybridity is to pus. Pus: white cells and exuded necrotized bio-debris and tissue, shortly, displaced bio-matter.

Hybridity has migrated from its original use in genetics to ethnocultural studies. In fact, this is not new. In Latin antiquity, it was used not only to describe an offspring of different animal species, but also children begotten by a Roman man and a foreign woman, or by a freeman and a slave. In theology, it is only recently that it has become a significant issue of discussion. In fact, since the great syncretism of the first five centuries of Christian endurance until the twentieth century, Christianity, at least in the West, only solidified its own sameness. In *Glaubenslehre*, the monumental document that opens the door to the history of modern Protestant theology, Schleiermacher gives the most telling account of western Christian doctrinal purity. For him, "new heresies no longer arise, now that the church recruits itself out of its own resources; and the influence of alien faiths on the frontier and in the mission-field of the Church must be reckoned at zero." And then the great Berliner adds condescendingly: "there may long remain in the piety of the new converts a great deal which has crept in from their religious affections of former times, and which, if it came to clear consciousness and were expressed as doctrine, would be recognized as heretical" (Schleiermacher 1989: 96; 1960: 1:128).

North Atlantic Christianity, where about two-thirds of Christians were to be found until the beginning of the twentieth century, had insulated itself throughout the Constantinian age. One hundred years later, by the end of the millennium, the majority of Christians (roughly 60 per cent) were to be found in the Third World. Contrary to Schleiermacher's colonial view of mission, Christianity is not only growing in the South, but also, most importantly, growing precisely in areas, as in Asia and Africa, where it often is not a hegemonic religion, disputing spiritual territory with other faiths. The effect of this on the self-understanding of Christian theology is still to be seen. Different religious affections are bound to come and are coming into consciousness (see Jenkins 2002) and it is doubtful that they are going to be verified against Schleiermacher's law of purity to check whether they are heresies. This is a significant new development, but not unique in the history of Christianity, which from its very inception is soiled. In this lies its *dis-tinctiveness*, that which has either lost or has a different coloration (*dis-tinctum*).

The Reformation and a cascade of other ecclesial schisms were hardly more than caste affairs, an inside group-selection. H. Richard Niebuhr's chastising of denominationalism notwithstanding – that ensued from multiple schisms in the western Church – is hardly more significant than a symptom of a malady at the very core of Christianity itself. This symptom signals attempts to evade the embarrassing hybrid impurity that lies at the very core of Christianity (so in other religions). To use an expression coined by Derrida, this evasion is an archival malady (*mal d'archive*): the feverish recruitment of the past to justify the present (Derrida 1995). It is the search for a genealogy to establish a lineage. No better example can be given than Matthias Flacius Illyricus who in the name of true Lutheranism, gnesio-Lutheranism, published the *Magdeburg Centuria*, a collection of volumes which attempted to show that Lutheranism was the true expression of the non-adulterated and unbroken Christian faith throughout the ages. However, archives do conceal surprises. We might find dead ends rendering a genealogy irretrievable or else discovering that the search for a pristine spring well will find only a polluted puddle.

Origins can be very embarrassing. And the embarrassment comes not only because of debasement, but also because of impurity. Origins often fail to justify the present. In some rabbinic theology, much more than Genesis 3 (which Augustine inscribed as the master narrative for the human condition), it was Genesis 6 that accounts for human wickedness due to the intermingling of the sons of God with the daughters of humanity, who bore children to them. It is a tale about impurity. However, this narrative is the template for the account of Mary's pregnancy in the Gospels of Matthew and Luke.

In these accounts Jesus is not the Pauline second Adam, the eternal logos made flesh of John, or the anointed Galilean man of Mark, but the offspring of the second instance we hear in the Jewish-Christian tradition of divinities impregnating women. Nietzsche called the death of God "Christianity's stroke of genius" and Ernst Käsemann once remarked that if there was a historical proof of Christianity, it was that no one would have thought about grounding a religion in the shameful crucifixion of its founder. But Mary's bearing of God (*theotokos*) is on this background of impurity as much as disturbing, puzzling and a/mazing.

I am thus suggesting that hybrid transgression of purity is at the very root of Christian "identity" ever dissimulated in the search for genealogies and pristine origins but never successfully evaded in the history of Christianity. Hybridity is at the very core of a distinctive Christian doctrine of incarnation. Attempts have been made in recent theologies to conceptualize incarnation as Christian hybridity as did the early Fathers in their own contexts. I will briefly review some of the current attempts and then address contemporary issues in hybridity. To conclude I will take up recent Latin American literature as an example of hybrid dislocation that expresses this template of impurity.

Mestizaje and Syncretism

In 1925, the Mexican philosopher and writer José Vasconcelos published one of the most celebrated, criticized and controversial books produced in the Americas in the past century: *La raza cósmica* (*The Cosmic Race*). With its idyllic idealism, the book suggests that in the Americas a fifth race was coming into being, the definitive, final, cosmic race that would unite the treasures of all the other races that have helped to form it. The first and theoretical part of the book is an attack on Gobineau, and social Darwinism, leading to Nazism, as he explained retrospectively in the preface of the revised second edition of 1948 (Vasconcelos 1961). In this context, he introduced a concept that only in the last couple of decades has been reclaimed and owned by theology: *mestizaje*, the mixture of races that was fashioning the cosmic race. In theology, the notion has been extended to include social and cultural intermingling.

Theologians, in particular Latin Americans and Latinos/as in the USA, have turned *mestizaje* into a fundamental theological concept. Virgilio Elizondo, Ada Maria Isasi-Dias, José David Rodriguez and Alex García-Rivera, among others, have fought valiantly to transpose the notion of *mestizaje* from its idyllic view of racial blending into a dynamic socio-cultural and theological concept. However, the problem of addressing societies that are profoundly multi- and inter-cultural, yet highly stratified and internally differentiated, remains.[1] As an example of this concomitance of interculturality and differentiation we have in Latin America more than a dozen categories to describe the offspring of a racial intermingling, depending on who the mother is and who the father is (American Indian, African, Asian or European, and all the combinations thereof). Difference is multiplied, even if more nuanced. And the same will be true for the cultural sphere from unexpected cuisine combinations to music and dance. What is tango or *capoeira* if not this "impure" admixture of heterogeneous forms of body-displaying techniques in combination with just about everything from waltz to martial arts? How else would one categorize Frida Kahlo paintings and cuisine? The cultural examples are legion. The same goes for the religious sphere (Canclini 1995).

Eduardo Hoornnaert, Hermann Brandt, Leonardo Boff, Andre Droogers, and a few others, attempted to tackle this phenomenon in Latin America in the 1970s and 80s. They proposed the notion of syncretism to address the intellectual effort in accounting for this observable fact in which there is intercultural overlapping, and yet difference is retained. Syncretism was thus rescued from its infamous association with sacral impurity and pollution, and also challenged were the pejorative connotations implied by "impurity" when used in ethnic, cultural or religious contexts. In this regard syncretism represents a qualitative step beyond *mestizaje* by providing a Christological grounding in the doctrine of the incarnation, and particularly its emergence at the time of "the great Christian syncretism" of the fourth and fifth centuries when the Chalcedonian dogma of the two natures and one person was conceived. Two transcending different entities are not only related to each other, but united while the difference remains in the union: *vere deus et vere homo.*

If *mestizaje* theory lifted up the cultural significance of ethnic miscegenation, syncretism was able to lift up a broader context that gave prominence to the social and religious dimensions of intercultural phenomena. However, categories are always haunted by their etymology that lingers on as a specter or a ghost, long after they are consciously remembered. And this is also the case with syncretism. We know that *syn-cretism*, for example, means to do it *like* or *along with* (syn-) the Cretans. But there is dispute over what this really means. What was it that characterized the Cretans? One explanation resorts to Homer who in the *Odyssey* makes mention of the supposed fact that the many towns in the island of Crete, often in strife with each other, would overlook their differences and unite when threatened by a foreign enemy (hence the prefix *syn-*). In this sense syncretism means a tactical and temporary move in order to defend a cause in the face of a greater enemy. Far from the embodiment of true difference, syncretism would only mean an occasional truce, but neither a true yoking, nor an organic unity (in Christology this would end up in Nestorianism).

The other more widespread interpretation moves in the opposite direction. It suggests that the island in the middle of the Mediterranean (the conceived centre of the earth, as the name of the sea implies: *medius terrae*) was a place where people from everywhere (Africa, Asia, Europe) would meet, creating a culture that blended elements as different as they were known in Mediterranean civilization of the classical era. In this sense, syncretism would be an indiscreet, or careless, amalgamation of differences; this is probably the sense that has equated syncretism, in its common acceptation, with the fusion of cultures and religious systems – an anything-goes sort of approach (in Christology, this would be a sort of monophisitism). The problem with these two etymologies is that one never really unites that which is different, while the other (as was the case with *mestizaje*) fuses all differences. The challenge is to find a concept that can simultaneously affirm union without forfeiting difference.

Hybridity

Theories of hybridity attempt to simultaneously affirm union and difference at the same time. Building on the insights that come from cultural, anthropological and theological re-appropriations of *mestizaje* and of syncretism, concerns have been raised and theoretical efforts developed to address issues not yet addressed explicitly either by the *mestizaje* or by the syncretistic approach. In addition to the ethnic miscegenation that *mestizaje* tackled and the cultural and religious intermingling that syncretism addresses, theories of hybridity encompass other dimensions also. The blurring of the line that divides the natural from the artificial is one among them. What follows offers some examples.

Donna Haraway, a historian of science at the University of California at Santa Cruz, trained as a molecular biologist and self-proclaimed theologian, wrote an article in 1985 entitled "A Cyborg Manifesto" (cf. Haraway 1991: 149–82). Cyborgs are organisms that have physiological and mental processes aided or controlled by mechanical and/or electronic devices. What was already common in science fiction, at least since Frankenstein, she turns into a strong philosophical claim, namely, that humans as well as other organisms have been conditioned and shaped by technology and artificial apparatuses that it is impossible and utterly idealistic to speak of human nature apart from technical, artificial and cybernetic devices that are part and parcel of our existence and survival. "It is not clear who makes and who is made in the relation between human and machine... Insofar as we know ourselves ... we find ourselves to be cyborgs, hybrids, mosaics, chimeras. Biological organisms have become biotic systems... There is no fundamental ontological separation in our formal knowledge of machine and organism, of technical and organic" (Haraway 1991: 177–78).

Cybernetic devices operate both indirectly and directly. Indirectly and externally they work through cultural and environmental means from which we cannot dissociate ourselves, like the tools we depend on, electrical gadgets, transportation, cyberspace communication (even the Amish community in the USA has a web page!) and so forth. Internally and directly they operate in a strict bio-organic sense. Our dependence on technologically enhanced drugs, surgeries, implants, prostheses, artificial organs, pacemakers, joint replacements, prophylactics, in vitro fertilization, cloning, etc. are examples. We are cyborgs, Haraway claims; we have crossed the boundary, transgressed and blurred the line that divides a presumed pristine nature from technology, the natural from the artificial. By overcoming this basic anthropological binarism other binary structures crumble, as in gender differentiation, for instance. We are cyborgs and have been so for a long time, only now it has reached such proportions that we can name it.

A theological argument for this cyborgian form of hybridization has been developed by the work of my former colleague Philip Hefner and his associates at the Zygon Center for Religion and Science in Chicago. The theological significance of this work is to reclaim and "update" for contemporary theology the notion of the *imago dei* in the tradition that can be traced back in its origins to Irenaeus' understanding of the human in the process of growing up to full maturity. The capability to grow up in God's providence is what *imago dei* ultimately means. From this particular tradition of interpreting *imago dei*, Hefner claims that human beings are "created co-creators" (see Hefner 1993). And this capability of co-creating is the endowment of God's *imago* to humanity. This would account for the emergence of the cyborg. Hence the cyborg is the intended prospective image of God. It is not the product of human ingenuity, but is rather our own self-generation, *autopoiesis*, or emergence. The *imago* is de-essentialized; it is not something we have inherited (our rational capacity, our bodily appearance, our moral disposition, etc.), but the capability of life self-generating itself in the process of transgressing boundaries between the humans and machine, and also between humans and other creatures.

In spite of this positive anthropology, it does not mean that there is a necessary evolution towards an increasing goodness and perfection. In the words of Haraway: "a cyborg world might be about lived social and bodily realities in which people are not afraid of their joint kinship with animals and machines." But, she continues, from another

> perspective, a cyborg world is about the final imposition of a grid of control on the planet, about the final abstraction embodied in a Star War apocalypse waged in the name of defense … in a masculinist orgy

of war. ... [The point] is to see from both perspectives at once because each reveals both dominations and possibilities (Haraway 1991: 176).[2]

There is indeed always "dangerous possibilities," the demonic, or the "many-headed monsters," as Haraway names them. The demonic, in the line of Tillich's interpretation of demonry, is the good turned upon itself (it echoes Luther's *incurvatus in se ipsum*) (cf. Tillich 1936: 77–122). But it is also the case that technology, in this perspective, is not essentially demonized. The point is to recognize in the cyborgs the magnification of the options between promise and disaster. Such interpretation of the *imago dei* lends a theological grounding for this mode of hybridization in which the divide between the natural and the artificial is transgressed without romanticizing pristine nature or demonizing technology.

Another dimension of hybridity questions the divide between humans and other animals. More and more of their interconnectedness are coming to the forefront, as the "genome project" shows. It reveals the little difference in the genetic mapping of humans in comparison to some other creatures, who are not only amazingly similar to us but often hold the key to our survival as can be illustrated by the Onco Mouse.[3] If the Cyborg transgresses the line between the natural and the artificial, the Onco Mouse questions the presumed divide between humans and non-human nature, and in a very radical way. (The very word used, "oncomouse," is in itself already an orthographic hybrid that mixes together the Greek prefix *onko*, which means mass or tumor, and the old English word *mus*, which comes possibly from the Latin *mus*, meaning rat or mouse.) The Onco Mouse is the name given to laboratory mice that undergo transgenic operations and are infected with an activated oncogene which will produce cancerogenesis in order to become experiments in the attempt at finding treatment for different sorts of human cancer. The Onco Mouse has become a symbol for the human immersion into the rest of nature to the point that a rodent that we trap and kill in our homes might hold the key for the survival of many humans if not eventually of the species. As a symbol it just heightens the growing awareness, not only of our interdependence with the rest of nature, but our utter immersion and dependence on it. Nature carries our genes; it is us. Nature not only provides for our sustenance (like in food, water and shelter), but even more, provides for our survival and regeneration insofar as we are *in* it, in the strongest, even genetic sense of it.

With this I have already suggested the theological implications of what the Onco Mouse symbolizes. Consider what in the fourth century Athanasius attested to by reverting the way we now conceive the chain of being that sets humans at the top of natural evolution. In his work "On the Incarnation" he says:

> Now, if they ask, Why, then, did [God] not appear by means of other and noble parts of creation, and use some nobler instruments, as the sun, or moon, or stars, or fire, or air [and I add: or a mouse], instead of a [human] merely? Let them know that the Lord came not to make a display, but to heal and teach those who were suffering... nothing in creation had gone astray with regards to their notions of God, save the [humans] only (Athanasius 1954: 97).

What this form of hybridity represents conveys that God's presence in a human goes to such low depths into depravity as to encompass the whole of creation, the cosmos, from the galaxies to mice, and even way down to humans for, as Gregory Nazianzen phrased it, "what is not assumed is not redeemed." Or in the words of the fifth-century Christian poet Cajus Caelius Sedulius of Achaia: *carne carnem liberans...*, the flesh is liberated through and by the flesh (quoted and translated by Martin Luther in Weimer Ausgabe 35, 150). *Cum grano salis*: mice save humans.

All of these dimensions of hybridity have profound theological implications. But here I would like to lift up a further dimension which not only has implications for theology but is theologically foundational in its very non-foundational hybridity. I am referring to the postcolonial consciousness' criticism of the assumption that a clear dividing line can be drawn between high and low culture, between accepted or hegemonic régimes of truth and those that do not meet the standards of the former, and are thus excluded and marginalized but which have the power of "insurrection" (Foucault), disturbing those régimes. As Homi Bhabha formulated it:

> Hybridity is not a *problem* of genealogy or identity between two *different* cultures which can then be resolved as an issue of cultural relativism. Hybridity is a problematic of colonial representation and individuation that reverses the effects of the colonialist disavowal, so that other

"denied" knowledges enter upon the dominant discourse and estrange the basis of its authority (Bhabha 1994: 114; original emphasis).

Here the distinctiveness of hybridity lies in the crossing and displacing of different cultural, semantic, economic ethnic or social spheres. What is crucial for hybridity is the act of transgressing these domains and not the unifying, blending, binary coupling, or assembling of different entities. Anyone can be a hybrid as it does not depend on any essential endowment, be it racial, cultural, ethnic, social or any other. Hybrids transgress. They are not beholden to any exclusive constituency. However, they don't surrender their own selves in the transgressive roles they play. If they would so do, they would egress existence as such and be only accessible in the tradition of the memory of the victims, of which we have plenty. They can pretend an identity which is not false but is intentionally and deceptively always something else, *dis-tinct*.

In providing a better example of such a hybrid tactic, I cannot hold a candle to the one offered by Luke in Acts 17, the account of Paul's speech at the Areopagus where he proclaims to know the unknown god of their worship to be the one who became a man that was killed, that is, the identity of the unknown is "revealed" only to be in the same act displaced. Karl Barth, in a not often seen praise of Luther, says that the genius of his understanding of revelation is not only that it is indirect, taking the form of a creature instead of the creator herself, but doubly so in that it expresses itself under utter sinfulness, Christ as the *maximus peccator* (Barth 1952, I/1: 171–80).

God out of Place: The Biblical Template

This last dimension of hybridity that transgresses the line that divides the high and the low, wisdom and madness, power and weakness (1 Cor. 1), the outer and the inner (Derrida called it "insideoutness") offers the most compelling reason for the hybrid character of displaced Christian "identity."

Let me start at the surface of Jewish-Christian narrative tradition, where we should always start. In the monumental commentary on the development of western literature from Greek antiquity to Virginia Wolf, *Mimesis*, by Erich Auerbach, the distinctiveness of the biblical literature, either the one written in Hebrew or in Greek, is presented as truly a unique hybrid product:

> [The] mingling of styles [is] inconceivable [in classic Greek literature], … [it] was rooted from the beginning in the character of Jewish-Christian literature … [from where] the principle of mixed styles makes its way into the writings of the Fathers from the Judaeo-Christian tradition… The sublime influence of God reaches so deeply into the everyday that the two realms of the sublime and everyday are not actually unseparated but basically inseparable … the King of Kings was treated as a low criminal, … he was mocked, spat upon, whipped and nailed to the cross – [here] a new *sermo humilis* is born, a low style, such as would properly only be applicable to comedy, but which now encroaches upon the deepest and the highest, the sublime and the eternal… In antique theory, the sublime and elevated style was called *sermo gravis* or *sublimis*; the low style was *sermo remissus* or *humilis*; the two had to be kept strictly separated. In the world of Christianity, on the other hand, the two are merged, especially in Christ's Incarnation and Passion, which realize and combine *sublimitas* and *humilitas* in overwhelming measure (Auerbach 1953: 72, 151).

This conflation of *humilitas* and *sublimitas* that, according to Auerbach, first distinguished biblical literature has been described by the early twentieth-century scholar Martin Dibelius as little or low literature (*Kleinliteratur*), which, Christians say, conveys nothing less than divine revelation (Dibelius 1959: 1–2). That the lowest can be the vessel of the highest is not a strong enough statement of what we are witnessing. More correct would be to say that only the lowest can encompass the highest.

That the highest gives itself to the lowest and is with it inseparable, is properly called a gift, for it cannot enter an economy of exchange or return, which is always a negotiation between two values (*do, ut des* – I give so that you give). This *divine* economy is the transgression of all rules of *our* economy, even as we try to define divine economy. Or else, why would God be found, of all places, nailed to a cross?

Hybridity in Latin American Literature

This template, introduced by biblical literature, dislocates rules of dominant discourse, and finds its expression throughout an inventory of Jewish-Christian theologies. But it finds also its imprint, as Auerbach has shown, in secular literature. As such, these secular texts entail a theological reading. To illustrate it, I will give some examples of recent Latin American novels, often classified as magic or marvellous realism, otherwise known as fantastic literature, as it has been defined originally by Alejo Carpentier and Gabriel García Márquez. Apart from the debate regarding the differences between the two descriptions, their common ground lies in the hybrid tactic move of crossing, displacing and transgression of semantic domains. The North American writer Barbara Probst Solomon in an essay that she wrote about the Venezuelan Teresa de la Parra and her magic realism and who precedes the literary boom in Latin America (as is also the case with Mario de Andrade or Borges), says it well: "while we North Americans frequently think of magic realism as exotic canaries flying through windows, its origins often had to do with displaced taboos and evasions" (Solomon 1999: 257). Indeed the best definition of such a displacement or transgression is given early in the twentieth century by Oswald de Andrade (*Anthropophagous Manifesto*, 1928) describing Brazilian culture: "the transfiguration of taboo into totem" (de Andrade 1971: 389). Under colonial or neo-colonial conditions the taboo is what demarcates the limit of the domain of the discriminated, subaltern subject, its social, cultural, economic, sexual, linguistic, ethnic or any other sphere that ought not be transgressed; their transfiguration or transvaluation evades by a constant displacing move the desire of colonial discourse to split it into alternate others. In the words of Bhabha, "hybridity ... enter[s] upon the dominant discourse and estrange[s] the basis of its authority" (Bhabha 1994: 114). The impossibility of locating the exact moment in which fact and fiction can be discerned is not a mere blurring of distinct categories but a perception of reality out of an engagement and commitment that sees with the eyes of faith, as Carpentier would say about Latin American and Caribbean cultures. Yet this displacement is tricky, for it does not postulate a third, as Bhabha observed, but keeps the undecidability, corroding any attempt to opt for a presence, to unequivocally re-present the world. In this sense, hybridity has been described as a parasitical tactic, which akin to a parasite, feeds on and embraces its host, but does not surrender to it. This happens in many dimensions of Latin American literature. For example: The crossing of ages as in the legendary Macondo of García Márquez, or in the conversation between Bolivar (in his novel *The General in his Labyrinth*) and this enlightened Frenchman who was trying to teach the general some lessons in history. The conversation ends with Bolivar saying: "Don't try to make us like you, don't expect us to do well in twenty years what you have done so badly in two thousand ... *carajos*, let us alone to do our own Middle Ages" (Márquez 1989: 129). The irony is that only from a European perspective can we even talk about Middle Ages. García Márquez makes Bolivar defend the autonomy and uniqueness of Latin America by parasitically using the very historical frame of European history, yet not being ruled by it. This is hybridity. And the novel, which is also biographical, gives no indication as to where the historical Bolivar ends and the fictional one begins. As he says in the bold epigraph to the first volume of his recently published memoirs: "Life is not what one lived, but what one remembers and how one remembers it in order to recount it" (Márquez 2002).

Hybrid indeed is Mackandal in Carpentier's *El reino de este mundo* (*The Kingdom of this World*) who crosses the line between the human and the animal in successive metamorphoses. Or as in the character of Vadinho in Jorge Amado's *Dona Flor and her Two Husbands* the barrier of death itself is crossed. Even gender crossing is seen in the character Diadorim in João Guimarães Rosa's *Grande Sertões: Veredas* (*Rebellion in the Backlands*). One of the most fascinating examples of multiple crossings in a myriad of dissimulations is presented in Mário de Andrade's *Macunaíma*. The very description of the main character as a "hero *without* character" betrays the elusive tactics of hybridity. Macunaíma, born black unlikely of a white mother in the core of the Amazon, migrates to São Paulo, the modern metropolis of South America. He eventually becomes a French mistress to seduce the giant Venceslau Pietro Pietra who had stolen his amulet. In the process even the divide between human and machine is crossed:

He couldn't come to any conclusion because he wasn't yet used to reasoning things out, but he was guessing – confusedly! – that the Machine could become a god out of man's control simply because it was not made in the form of a beautiful enchantress, understandable but hardly a reality in this world. Out of all the mixed-up thoughts churning around in his mind, just one shone like a ray of light in the dark: "It's men who are machines and machines who are men!" Macunaíma gave a great guffaw. He felt free again, and his spirits lifted enormously. He turned Jiguê [his brother] into the telephone machine contraption, rang up a night club and ordered lobsters and a selection of French tarts to be sent over (de Andrade 1984: 36).

Although more surreal than fantastic, in comparison with the Latin American authors that would come a generation after, Mario de Andrade's character is indeed the avatar of scores of people forging their hybrid identities as a survival tactic.

Ernesto Sábato, particularly in *Sobre heroes y tumbas* (*On Heroes and Tombs*), has made the reflection of Latin America's non-essentialist "impurity," or hybridity, probably the most self-consciously argued case. In a long discussion about the criticism a certain Méndez raises against Borges' lack of Argentine authenticity, Bruno, one of his characters, reflects: "What? They want a total and absolute originality? There is no such thing. In literature or in anything else … There is no purity in nothing human. The Greek gods were also hybrid and were infected (as a way of putting it) by oriental and Egyptian religions" (Sábato 1965: 181). Or, as we have observed, he could have said the same about the Christian God as a poor homeless man executed as a criminal.

As mentioned earlier, hybrids transgress. And theirs is a transgression where they don't cede their identity but one that is at the same time dissimulative and inimitable. In response to the accusation of Borges not being really authentically Argentine, Sábato's character Bruno says: "What could he be but Argentine? He is a typical national product. Even his Europeanism is national. A European is not an Europeanist: A European is simply European" (Sábato 1965: 180). In fact, one could say that Borges was a parasite of Europe … and beautifully so as an orchid.

All these characters are so fantastic and marvellous that, as Carpentier said, one cannot miss stumbling into them in almost every step of our pilgrimage in *nuestra America*.

Before Gustavo Gutiérrez's major work (*A Theology of Liberation*) reached the north Atlantic academy (and placed Orbis on the publishers' map), Latin American theology was and still remains largely a small or low literature, made up of leaflets and pamphlets, songs and poems developed for base communities, NGOs, and student circles. The same can be said about literature in Latin America. Before it evolved into world-class literature (dated from the so-called Latin American literary boom of the 1950s), it is there in the myths and legends preserved in the stories of the people where it has been culled from. Alejo Carpentier, reflecting about his experience in Haiti in the late 1940s, while collecting material for his novel *El reino de este mundo*, says what many others have since repeated:

> I was discovering, with every step, the marvelous in the real. But it occurred to me furthermore that the energetic presence of the marvelous in the real was not peculiar to Haiti, but the heritage of all America, which, for example, has not finished fixing the inventory of its cosmogonies. The marvelous in the real can be found at any moment in the lives of men and women who engraved dates in the history of the continent, and left behind names that are still celebrated... For what is the history of America if not the chronicle of the marvelous in the real? (Carpentier 1967: 98–99).

Until the more recent works of Rivera Pagán, Pedro Trigo, Antônio Carlos Magalhães and a few others, the connection between literature or fiction and theology remained unidentified. Rubem Alves, one of the pioneers in the field, abandoned theology presumably because in venturing into the fictional he did not feel that he was being well received in theological circles as a serious thinker.[4] Even Gutiérrez, whose friendship with the novelist José Maria Arguedas appears circumstantially in many of his writings (although he even wrote an essay on Arguedas), never really makes an organic connection between his theology and the novels of the author of *Los rios profundos* (*Deep Rivers*).

Latin American novelists and poets have been less scrupulous than theologians about transgressing the divide of literary genres while keeping the admixture, the conflation of the high and the low. From someone known more for his insistent sarcasm and invincible irony, Jorge Luis Borges, one can read a poem like this (Borges 1999: 130-31):

Luke XXIII

Gentile or Jew or simply a man
Whose face has been lost in time,
We shall not have the silent
Letters of oblivion.

What could he know of forgiveness,
A thief whom Judea nailed to a cross?
For us those days are lost.
During his last undertaking,

Death by crucifixion,
He learned from the taunts of the crowd
That the man who was dying beside him
Was God. And blindly he said:

*Remember me when thou comest
Into thy kingdom,* and from the terrible cross
The unimaginable voice
Which one day will judge us all

Promised him Paradise. Nothing more was said
Between them before the end came,
But history will not let the memory
Of their last afternoon die.

O friends, the innocence of this friend
Of Jesus! That simplicity which made him,
From the disgrace of punishment, ask for
And be granted Paradise.

Was what drove him time
And again to sin and to bloody crime.

Cross and paradise, shame and glory are displaced into each
other's domains. The same simplicity that led the robber into sin
and bloody fate was the one that made him ask and be granted
paradise, as the original so well expresses: *ese candor que hizo que
pediera y ganara el Paraíso ... era el que tantas vezes al pecado lo
arrojó y al azar ensangrentado.*

As in biblical literature where it says the lowest is the highest and
the last shall be first, those who Gutiérrez called (after Kafka (!) introduced the notion) nonpersons, become, as those fishermen from
Palestine two thousands years ago, the protagonists of the story (and
of history). One might only be reminded of some of the characters

in Latin American and Caribbean literature: Garabombo, Artemio Cruz, Makandal, Ti Noel, Clara, Alba, Cándida Eréndira, Eva Luna, Macunaíma, Diadorim, Santiago Nasar, Pedro Páramo and the list goes on. These so-called "nonpersons" enter centre stage and estrange its basis of power. These people become the incarnation of a destiny greater than them. In their apparent insignificance, marginality, they embody a graceful nobility that enriches all. The significance, the *sublimitas* of their existence is rooted in the simplicity of their own disgrace, their *humilitas*. This mode of hybridization, this gift that is poured from on high, which is a gift because it cannot be returned and can only keep on giving, is what we should in theological terms properly call grace. Or else, consider this passage from a short story by Mario Benedetti:

> There are those who die at dusk and others in the heat of noon. There are dead ones who simply lay down and others that rise as the sun. Adolescents who in their last smile invested all their faith in life and afterlife. Young women who gave birth to their sacrifice, gave them a name, and fed them in their breasts. And when the machine gun was heard, they covered them with their beautiful bodies so as to save them. And the sacrifice was saved. This is why in a misguided and gray county where no one seems able to give ten minutes or ten pesos, these immortal and sober men and women were capable to give their lives, this is why their defeat is rooted in the earth. And it germinates and is born again with flags and dreams in promises happily fulfilled (Benedetti 1980: 131–32).

This is marvellous realism: the triumph of the defeated (as the title of the story conveys: "Victoria de los vencidos").

Arguably no one has been able to articulate theologically this hybridity between the sublime and the lowly in recent theological literature better than Juan Luis Segundo in his interpretation of Chalcedon's notion of *communicatio idiomatum*, the communication of attributes between the divine and the mere human in Jesus Christ. Segundo calls attention that before it becomes a question of a metaphysical exchange of attributes it is a communication of different languages (idioms). In Segundo's terminology it is the hybrid result of moving between the semantics of digital language and iconic language, between a language that is ruled by strict logic of literal statements and another that is symbolically suggestive and metaphorically elusive. This hybrid semantics is something that we are very familiar with, for it is at the core of many jokes that rely on the mechanism of this very semantic displacement. And there is so much grace in a joke. In Spanish and Portuguese the word for "gracefulness" (*gracioso*) also means witty, humorous or funny. But here we are not speaking of jokes, but of the mingling of the sublime with the lowly. In the words of Benedetti, "the sacrifice was saved." These are fundamental theological categories to describe the brutal murder of people under military regimes in Latin America yet coupled with saving promises. So what is Chalcedon saying with this hybrid formula *vere Deus et vere homo*? In the words of Segundo, this affirmation of the divinity of Jesus "does not entail that which is not human in Jesus, but precisely his way of being human" (Segundo 1982: 663). And he continues showing that what Chalcedon accomplishes is not a metaphysics of exchange of abstract attributes, but: Jesus, in his limited human history, interpreted from a secular tradition in search of the meaning of human existence, reveals us the Absolute, the ultimate reality, the transcendent datum par excellence.

Finally he concludes the five volumes (in the English edition) of his Christology, asking the question: "What difference does Jesus make?" And answers:

> If there is a difference, and undoubtedly there is, it is not what Jesus added by himself from the pages of the gospels, but what step by step, the contact and commitment with the problems, crises, and historical conflicts [people encounter] … has contributed to the meaning of his good news (Segundo 1982: 980).

The very story of Benedetti has been such a contribution, as well as so much of Caribbean and Latin American literature. For what Segundo is saying is that, as he had said elsewhere, such texts *continue* the narrative of the gospel of Jesus Christ.

Grace: las finezas de Cristo

The one who originally has argued this very case was a poet, playwright and theologian whose voice comes to us from the very inception of Latin American theological flirtation with literature and also vice versa. In 1690 or 1691, the arguably greatest theologian that the colonial Americas has produced, Sor Juana Inés de la Cruz, wrote a long essay, entitled "Carta Atenegórica" ("Letter in an Athenian Style") in which she takes issue with a sermon from the one who was considered the greatest preacher of the time, the Jesuit António Vieira. The "Letter" is in itself the occasion for the most tragic turn in the life of Sor Juana, which makes some forget what the content of the text was. It is a daring and surprising argument written in the high baroque style that the author mastered as few ever have. The argument is about the greatest kindness that Christ has shown us, the ultimate gift that he has given (*las finezas de Cristo*). The Spanish *fineza* was common in baroque amorous writings, and appears frequently in Sor Juana's poetry. I would like to suggest that the debate with Vieira, about *las finezas de Cristo*, is about a particular understanding of what grace means. Sor Juana's rendition of the meaning of grace has found, consciously or unconsciously, echo in the two contemporary intellectual endeavours we are discussing and that she mastered as no one else, more than three centuries ago, literature and theology.

After discussing the opinions of Augustine, Thomas Aquinas, and Chrysostom, in this order, she goes for what she calls the Achilles' heel in Vieira's argument. The famous Jesuit preacher, diplomat and missionary had made the argument that the greatest kindness Jesus had shown was to love without reciprocity, of which the washing of the feet of his disciples would best illustrate. Radically inverting the argument, Sor Juana argues that although this is a gesture of kindness, the most graceful gesture of Christ was to absent himself so that we would not make bad use of what we receive, the gift, but will allow us to act out of what we have already received. And she concludes with the admonition "that to ponder about his benefits [should] not remain speculative discourses, but that it turns into practical services, so that his negative benefits become in us positive ones finding in ourselves proper disposition" (de la Cruz 1981: 827).

For Sor Juana the "absence" of God implied a messianic presence which happens not in what she called "speculative discourses" but in practice. The genius of her argument is that the gift we receive comes to us as sheer emptiness and absence. However, this is precisely what brings life, an indwelling hidden presence that is filled

by the meanings of the ongoing contribution to the evangelical narrative, to put it as Segundo did. The grace of absence (*apousia*) is
what allows for the fruition of the gift that indwells in and among
us (*parousia*). While the whole tradition of modern liberal theology
insists on the *pro nobis* of God's relationship to the world and while
the whole neo-orthodox tradition has insisted on the *extra nos* of
God, Sor Juana reminds us of the words of Jesus in the Gospel of
John: "It is to your advantage that I go away, for if I do not go away,
the Counselor will not come to you" (Jn 16:7). Sor Juana, in a crisp
and paradoxical way, reminds us of the third mode of God's relation
to us: *in nobis*. The absence of Jesus is the presence of Christ in us,
in whom his story (and history) continues.

Let me conclude with a short story by García Marquez that conveys well what I am trying to express. The story, published in 1968,
is called "The Handsomest Drowned Man in the World" (*El ahog-
ado mas hermoso del mundo*). He wrote this only some years after
the first military coups that would spread themselves all over Latin
America took place (Brazil in 1964, and Argentina in 1965) and carried out their practice of dumping enemies of the régime on high
sea. These bodies would eventually be washed ashore – before Chile
(after 1973) improved the "technology" by placing a large piece of
metal in the bowels of the victims before throwing them to the sea.
I don't know whether this was in Gárcia Marquez's mind when he
wrote the story. But taking license from the epigraph to his memoirs
I mentioned above, it does not matter what was in his mind, but the
memories it evokes.

In a small village of fishermen off the Colombian coast of the
Caribbean Sea a drowned man is washed to shore. He is found by
the villagers and brought into town. While the women start preparing his body for a proper funeral the men go around nearby villages
to see if someone is missing. The women were already imagining
places and experiences he has been through, filling that corpse with
a fantastic life, giving him a name, Esteban, and assigning him parents and relatives so that the whole village was through him related
to each other. When the news came that he did not belong to any of
the villages nearby, there was jubilation in the midst of tears among
the women preparing the body for the burial: "'Praise God,' they
sighed, 'he's ours!'" After preparing the body of the drowned man

who "was the tallest, strongest, most virile, and best built man they have ever seen" they return him to the ocean dressed in new cloth they had to tailor and fully adorned with flowers. And so the story ends:

> While they fought for the privilege of carrying him on their shoulders ... men and women became aware for the first time of the desolation of their streets, the dryness of the courtyards, the narrowness of their dreams as they faced the splendor and beauty of their drowned man. They let him go without anchor so that he could come back if he wished and whenever he wished, and they all held their breath for the fraction of centuries the body took to fall into the abyss. They did not need to look at one another to realize that they were not whole, and they would never be. But they also knew that everything would be different from then on, that their houses would have wider doors, higher ceilings, and stronger floors so that Esteban's memory could go everywhere without bumping into beams, ... they were going to paint their house fronts with gay colors to make Esteban's memory eternal and they were going to break their back digging for springs among the stones and planting flowers on the cliffs so that in future years at dawn the passengers on great liners would awaken, suffocated with the smell of gardens on the high sea, and the captain would have to come down from the bridge in his dress uniform ... pointing to the promontory of roses on the horizon, he would say in fourteen languages, look there, where the wind is so peaceful now that it's gone to sleep beneath the beds, over there, where the sun's so bright that the sunflowers don't know which way to turn, yes, over there, that's Esteban's village (Márquez 1984: 253–54).

Stories such as this are gospel parables flowing out of the experience of people with a God in the flesh who simply lived and keeps on living a dislocated existence in places and people where God is not supposed to be.

Works Cited

de Andrade, Mário (1984). *Macunaíma*. Trans E. A. Goodland. New York: Random House.

de Andrade, Oswald (1971). "Manifesto Antropófago." In *An Anthology of Brazilian Prose*, ed. R. L. Scott-Buccleuch and Mario Teles de Oliveira. São Paulo: Ática.

Athanasius (1954). "On the Incarnation of the Word." In *Christology of the Later Fathers*, ed. Edward R. Hardy. Philadelphia: Westminster.

Auerbach, Erich (1953). *Mimesis: The Representation of Reality in Western Literature*. Princeton: Princeton University Press.

Barth, Karl (1952). *Die kirchliche Dogmatik*. München: C. Kaiser Verlag.

Benedetti, Mario (1980). "Victoria del vencido." In *Letras de emergencia*. Mexico: Nueva Imagen.

Bhabha, Homi (1994). *The Location of Culture*. London: Routledge.

Borges, Jorge Luis (1999). *Selected Poems*. New York: Viking.

Canclini, Nestor García (1995). *Hybrid Cultures: Strategies for Entering and Leaving Modernity*. Minneapolis: University of Minnesota Press.

Carpentier, Alejo (1967). *Tientos y diferencias*. Buenos Aires: Calicanto.

de la Cruz, Sor Juana Inés (1981). *Obras Completas*. Mexico: Porrúa.

Derrida, Jacques (1995). *Mal d'Archive*. Paris: Galilee.

Dibelius, Martin (1959). *Die Formgeschichte des Evangeliums*, 3rd ed. Tübingen: J.C.B. Mohr.

Haraway, Donna (1991). *Simians, Cyborgs, and Women: The Reinvention of Nature*. New York: Routledge.

Hefner, Philip (1993). *The Human Factor*. Minneapolis: Fortress.

Hegel, G. W. F. (1970). *Werke in zwanzig Bänden*. Frankfurt a/M: Suhrkamp.

Jenkins, Philip (2002). *The New Christendom: The Rise of Global Christianity*. New York: Oxford University Press.

Márquez, Gabriel García (1984). "The Handsomest Drowned Man in the World." In *Collected Stories*. New York: HarperCollins.

Márquez, Gabriel García (1989). *O General em seu Laberinto*. Rio de Janeiro: Record.

Márquez, Gabriel García (2002). *Vivir para contarla*. New York: Alfred Knopf.

Sábato, Ernesto (1965). *Sobre héroes y tumbas*. Buenos Aires: Sudamericana.

Schleiermacher, Friedrich (1989). *The Christian Faith*. Edinburgh: T&T Clark [*Der christliche Glaube*, 2 vols. (Berlin: de Gruyter, 1960)].

Segundo, Juan Luis (1982). *El hombre de hoy ante Jesus de Nazaret: Las cristologías en la espiritualidad*. Madrid: Cristiandad.

Solomon, Barbara Probst (1999). "Teresa de la Parra." In *Mutual Impressions: Writers from the Americas Reading One Another*, ed. Ilan Stavans. Durham: Duke University Press.

Tillich, Paul (1936). *The Interpretation of History*. New York: Charles Scribner's Sons.

Vasconcelos, José (1961). *La raza cósmica: misión de la raza iberoamericana*. Madrid: Aguilar.

5 Out of Place with Jesus-Christ

Clive Pearson

Hyphenating and Backslashing

Towards the end of the last millennium Jung Young Lee made the case for a hyphenated Jesus-Christ (Lee 1995: 77–99). Lee set his thinking on Jesus-Christ inside a theory of marginality which saw itself in critical tension with centralist conceptions of culture, text and doctrines. His argument is rarely reproduced in the works of well-disciplined systematic theologians. Any references appear with an element of surprise attached to so "striking" a paradigm for theology (Newlands 2006: 153–54). The relative neglect of Lee's proposal in the ongoing task of Christology is not too surprising for its internal momentum is directed towards margins and edges. Its omission from standard texts is in keeping with its own logic, as is its appeal for those who live in a condition of diaspora, exile and rootlessness.

I have often made use of Lee's theory of marginality and his hyphenated christological hermeneutic. It has been employed – in association with a range of other options – for migrant-ethnic students wrestling with matters to do with identity, the myth of home, generational difference and a confusion of how two small pronouns in English, I and we, relate to each other and personal experience. Its attentiveness to the complex ways in which margins and peripheries relate to centres has also proved helpful in configuring strategies for minorities in coping with a dominant majority. Lee's theory has a capacity to energize and undermine the passivity so often associated with a rhetoric and loose practice of multiculturalism.[1] Some of those students have spoken of how Lee's Christology and theory of marginality have left them feeling "haunted," "wet eyed," and almost as if they had been reading their own personal story of dislocation: "we have the same virus" was one claim which bound together readers whose first homeland had been in Fiji, Tuvalu, Tonga, Vietnam, Myanmar, Solomon Island and Korea.

Lee's theological initiative was a little surprising insofar as a hyphen is not part of the grammatical structure of his first language – Korean. Its usage here reflected the primary audience for whom he was writing. Lee had come to the United States for purposes of study and had imagined that he was a "sojourner" who would return home – except that he did not. Lee became a Korean-American and, a little bit more broadly, a theological Asian-American. This hyphen, then, is not a western imposition or an arrogant naming by an/other. It is self-selected for purposes of identity and cultural differentiation with an eye to making a theological point. It emerges out of his recognition that "I was out of place" (Lee 1995: 38).

The origins of Lee's recourse to a hyphen lies inside the parable of a dandelion he constructs. Its purpose is to come to terms with how he could not simply slip into the conventional myth of the American dream come true. Lee compares himself with the dandelions which kept on popping up in his lawn after "the cold winter had gone" and which he strove to keep manicured and well-cut. The dandelion stood for himself. Where was it to "settle" and "root itself deeply in the soil"? Where was its place of belonging – on the lawn, or with the "wild plants" on the roadside? How might its flower resist the owner of the yard who did not appreciate this weed? Should the brightness of its colour be camouflaged and not be exposed? If so, then to what purpose? In the parable the dandelion decides the next year to show its golden and yellow flower and dream of the spread of its seed. Lee is the owner of the yard and his campaign against the weed is interrupted by the presence of his young son. Lee undergoes a conversion; rather than merely fitting in and not trying to draw attention to himself, the white seeds of the once-hated dandelion are allowed to sail high and "fall like parachutes over the rich green yards." Lee encourages them: "let them live; let them live anywhere they want. It is God's world, and they are God's creatures" (Lee 1995: 11–13). The dandelion represents the descent of the other into an alien soil and its desire for integrity and flourishing. It prepares the way for Lee's decision to be an advocate for hyphenated existences on a revitalized periphery.

Of critical significance for Lee's theology is his understanding of marginality. His personal experience of dislocation led him to critique received theories of marginality which saw it as a condition of a "failure of assimilation." Lee senses the need for an alternative which is resistant to notions of melting pots and a life established on the prepositions of "in-between." The dislocated migrant is hedged into a thin space at the edges of ethnicity and race and rather removed from the centres of two or more cultures. For Lee this space represents a negative view of marginalization informed by a double negative – neither one of us, nor one of them. It implies a third category of persons. The principal problem with this definition is the manner in which it is imposed by the dominant culture at the "centre of centrality" in the receiving society. Lee is also convinced that it lacks accuracy and sufficient precision. The theory of marginality he espouses is one which has room for the further prepositional mix of "in-both" and "in-beyond." Here Lee is "more than an Asian because an American" and "more than American because I am an Asian." That sense of alienation which comes from the first model is not something which Lee wishes to disown; it is part of his experience – it is real. What he wishes to do is place alongside it the possibility of this more positive reading and create a paradox. To be "in-both is as authentic as to be in-between." It is a simultaneous expression. To be "in-between" and "in-both" is also to be "in-beyond"; the marginal person inhabits a kind of immanence and transcendence. Lee's "hyphenated person" is in a creative space and is always "overcoming marginality without ceasing to be a marginal person." The hyphen which now links the "in" and "beyond" allows the hyphenated person to live in different worlds but without being bound by them (Lee 1995: 55–62).

For the purposes of constructing a diasporic identity Lee's mix of a hyphen and margins has enabled a role for Christology. From Gustavo Gutiérrez he has learnt that Jesus Christ is "the great hermeneutical principle" and the "basis and foundation" for all its theological reasoning (Lee 1995: 71). To that quest for meaning which the parable of the dandelion bears witness the hyphen inserts a critical concern for an identity in Christ alongside the markers of culture and ethnicity. It recognizes, in the first instance, that there is a liminal space in and in-between cultures. For Fumitaka Matsuoka this space is a place of "holy insecurity" which requires exploration and fearless speech (Matsuoka 1995: 64). From personal experience Martin Krygier knows the benefit of "two visions" and "public hybrid thoughts" that can come from inhabiting this potentially dislocating space. Lee writes of what it is like to live in a setting of both/ and rather than either/or where one side of the hyphen is likely to overcome the other in an invasive linear progression. Lee knows that the term culture itself has a complex history and is subject to reinterpretation (Tanner 1997). This quest for meaning is aware that Lee's hyphen can seem to join two essentialist understandings of culture, in a way which is misleading to the hybrid nature of ethnicities as well as their variations of gender and age. Lee is not naïve with respect to this matter.

From the outset of his argument, Lee weaves his reading of hyphens and margins into an autobiographical method of doing theology. In the performance of such Lee makes use of a practice which has become a stock strategy in diverse forms of an Asian-American hermeneutic. It is a tactic also used to good effect by David Ng under the name of a "life story"; Peter Phan manages to hold the autobiographical in tension with a recovery of providence in order to show how he has stumbled into becoming an "accidental theologian" while being "between and betwixt" (see also Phan and Lee 1999). Lee prefers to think in categories of theology as a "a story of my faith journey" and "how God formed me, nurtures me, guides me, loves me, allows me to age, and will end my life." This autobiographical reference point here is not the same as saying theology is autobiography. Lee's thinking should not be dismissed on that count. Rather, that story of faith is "a basis for theology."

Coming from a cultural background that is more accustomed to think and act along the lines of a corporate "we" – *Oori* – migration has led Lee to consider the importance of "I am." The prominence given to the subjective in the story of "my faith journey" is a diasporic discovery but Lee is careful to underline the relational nature of personhood. The autobiographical is not a passport to individualism and a singular expression of will to unitary power over others. Lee delights in how his life is related to the lives of many. His "I am" becomes "I-am" and is pluralistic (Lee 1995: 1–2). It bears the character marks of others. Lee is well aware of how each one of us are in relationships where we possess centres and margins.

The autobiographical is thus set inside the "complex patterns" of Asian-American experience and is ever mindful of the risk of stereotypes that "still hurt." His life is indeed like "a small drop of water in the stormy ocean of Asian experiences in America" (Lee 1995: 10). It is "vital" that he is placed within the history of that context for the sake of his theology. This shift into the territory of the relational "we-are" turns attention to the vocation of the theologian. For whom is he or she writing? What model of a representative self is at work in the diasporic scholar? Where are the lines of allegiance and attentiveness? It is far from self-evident.

There is a fertile analogy here with the life and work of poetry and prose. Through his autobiographical method, Lee exhibited a variation on themes identified by the Chinese author, Ha Jin, on his recent lecture series on *The Migrant as Writer* (Ha Jin 2008). Ha Jin was born in Liaoning but now teaches in Boston. He has published anthologies of poetry, short stories and novels. He has won a number of prestigious writing awards in the United States while much of his writing – in English – is set in China. Ha Jin is a pen name which, of course, invites a consideration of which self is being presented to which audience and why.

In his *Migrant as Writer* Ha Jin has had to wrestle with perceptions of why one migrates to the world of the "materially privileged" and what kind of ironies that might release. There is the need to engage with the subject matter of the "anachronic fear" of uncertainty and the absence of clarity that can mark, even debilitate, the displaced person. What is to be done with the yearning, a nostalgia, for what no longer exist as it once did and where the one who aspires is not the same person he once was? Is the task then to forego the security of a homeland and look towards a journey towards an unknown arrival rather than a backward glancing point of departure? Is the writer to be the "fortunate one," perhaps speaking on behalf of the unfortunate? Does the writer become the "tribal spokesperson" through her composed stories – or is that a temporary state of mind which will need to be shed because the tribe may be able to do without that voice? What happens if there is not effective recognition after which the spokesperson is "hankering"? Ha Jin raises the most awkward of

questions: from whom does migration then alienate the self? Is the
answer closer to home, within the family itself, rather than the more
obviously external other, the stranger? There remain a host of questions for the literary as well as the theological writer: which language
becomes the vehicle for one's art? How are various audiences being
served? Ha Jin must also deal with mood. Is he writing in anger, for
instance, and if so, at whom and is it justified – or is it self-serving
and condescending, a kind of reverse colonizing? In this new world
how "cunning" and "resourceful" must the writer be?

Lee is not as self-conscious of the many dilemmas which pockmark
the calling of the diasporic writer. He is not a poet like Ha Jin. His
"story of my faith" is not a short story; it is servicing a more technical discipline, though it knows well about harassment, discrimination,
humiliation and rejection based on racial and cultural bias (Lee 1995:
27). The matters Ha Jin raises are there in the shadows of his text,
nevertheless. Lee is under no illusions about the risks of his autobiographical method. He recognizes that he cannot write theology for all
Korean-Americans; the most he can do is write out of his own experience and hope that it may "resonate" with others and acquire a kind
of representative role, though not an exclusive one. His negotiation of
the rite of passage from sojourner to settler means that he is not writing for a Korean audience back home in his birth-land; his commitment to a specific people, an aggregate of that mix of I and we caught
up in a hyphen, also distances him from primarily thinking within a
global flow of maybe "fortunate" elites communing with one another.
His focus is before him and it so for Christ's sake.

From the perspective of an Australian site for a diasporic theology
Lee's hyphen reflects a long-standing and current practice. It has often
been used by migrant-ethnic communities seeking to orient themselves in a new land. The most recent employment of the hyphen has
been the work overseen by Ghassan Hage on being Arab-Australian
(Hage 1998). It is a label which is sometimes used in a rather eclectic
and overly generic fashion. The point worth noting, though, is its employment. Its usage may not always meet the strictures and demands
of the best diasporic and postcolonial thinking; it is a little rough and
ready, admittedly – but, nevertheless, the practical reality is its existing
function in personal and social life. The hyphen here is like a signpost,
an assistant, marking out an alternative, an "other" condition of being

which does not wish to be subsumed in a master narrative of "we are all Australians" and who is "one of us" without some sort of qualification. It is a site of resistance. This hyphen needs to be seen within the context of Australian history and the various manifestations of multiculturalism. This act of grammar belongs inside a cluster of words, like assimilation, integration, accommodation and resistance, each one of which has a history. This signifier is embedded in time and place. This hyphen is not detached and circulating in a global flow of ideas devoid of specificity. It is well practised. Now and then the hyphen is cast aside for studies of the Germans, Italians, Jews, Greeks, Chinese and English *in* Australia. Now and then it is replaced by a backslash – like, for instance, alter/Asians – which is admittedly performing another, but related, task. Here the backslash and the use of the "alter" is designed to refer to Asian generations born in Australia conscious of their difference to those who belong to their ethnicity back in the "first homeland" and the dominant majority in the new.

In terms of a politics of identity the hyphen in this particular sociopolitical location is a highly charged grammatical convention best viewed out in the open rather than one buried beneath a postcolonial preference for hybridity. The hyphen has been regularly put to use ever since the term Anglo-Celt was used to describe its dominant "core imaginary." This title is more frequently and peculiarly used in Australia than it is in other colonized societies such as Canada, the United States and Aotearoa-New Zealand. Here it represents a kind of strategic ethnofusion; it identifies the first wave of migration and settlement over and against indigenous and subsequent ethnicities. The hyphenated term is a short-hand way of describing English and Irish influences without necessarily pointing too much attention to differences and the tendency for one to be protestant and other catholic. For Miriam Dixson this core imaginary should constitute a "holding pattern" while Australia undergoes the process of becoming a more pluralist, polycentric, polycultural nation (Dixson 1999). For much of the time this particular form of the hyphen is actually out of sight, quietly assumed, but its power, even in its hiddenness, is considerable. This hyphen lies at the heart of Lee's readings of centres and margins. For the sake of equity in this practical context this hyphen – as well as those other hyphens which punctuate the identity of migrant ethnic-communities and those who sometimes feel themselves to be "Australien" – should be rendered visible. There is a politics at work here which is not well served by a reluctance to become involved with this small grammatical dash. Back in his own context Lee's hyphen establishes a bridge between a reading of American culture and some primary doctrines of the Christian faith. Here he differs from the more widely known icons of postcolonial and marginalized readings of cultures and faithful texts. The likes of Fernando Segovia and R. S. Sugirtharajah, for instance, only ever skirt around the edges of a more systematic agenda in theology. What might seem to be a criticism here is not intended as such. The benefits of a diasporic optic or hermeneutic of Scripture and place are assumed and warmly commended (see Sugirtharajah 2005: 535–52). What is being intimated, though, is that the frequent reference to interdisciplinarity in such studies has seldom looked sideways to consider what a seemingly formal discipline like a systematic theology can do. Perhaps this way of organizing Christian belief is conceived as being too bound to the promotion of orthodoxy and has been the vehicle of a colonizing faith couched in an antique language. The counter-response begs the question: is that really so? Are biblical and cultural critics of this fundamental disposition succumbing to a "frozen" moment in time which is no longer up with the play in a related discipline?

The Divine Emigrant

Through a reading of the doctrine of the incarnation, Lee posits the idea of Jesus-Christ being the divine emigrant. Rather than follow the more conventional line back to Chalcedon Lee cites, in support, the prologue from John and the hymn to Christ's humiliation in Philippians. The purpose of this biblical appeal is not so much a postcolonial disregard for metaphysical theories of the two natures of Christ expressed in and through the categories of a Greek philosophy. The textual narratives themselves embody a storyline of dislocation which resonates with the life and experience of those on the theological and cultural margins. Lee is writing self-consciously on their behalf. His hermeneutical perspective was one of marginality which was distinguished from a "centralist" exegesis.

That dislocation or alteration of place is reckoned to be an episode in divine marginalization and a form of *kenosis*. These "well-known" stories from John and Philippians are read in sequence. The prologue describes how this marginalization is "initiated" in creation and subsequently "actualized through Christ's rejection by his creation." For Lee, creation is an act of divine immanence which is extended through the "creative presence" of Christ himself; he is the "agent of creation" through his participation in and affirmation of this world. The incarnation itself then becomes a story of Christ's own marginalization, his removal or re-location, from the divine centre. This transition is conceived on a cosmic scale. Read in association with the Philippians hymn the prologue lends itself to a further step into the process of becoming marginal. Through the act of divine *kenosis* – a "self-emptying process" – the incarnation enables a further transition in the move from divine nature to human nature. The humiliation of Christ here is, in effect, twofold. The incarnation, whatever form Christ might then have assumed, is an act of marginalization; it is compounded through divinity assuming the "lowly human occupation" of being a slave. Through the incarnation the divine emigrant becomes "the margin of marginality by giving up everything he had" (Lee 1995: 81).

The pivot of Lee's hyphenated Christology lies in these two texts. The hyphen binds and ruptures the divine and the human. The manner in which the hyphen does not then dig deeper, and explain how its bridging function works itself out in process, is likewise synonymous with how Chalcedon refuses to spell out in detail the relationship between the two natures of Christ. One of the extra benefits of this hyphen is how it effects a loop back into the ministry of Jesus. The standard complaint often directed towards the Chalcedonian solution is that it preserves the generic humanity of the Son of God, the second Person of the Trinity, but at the cost of losing the specificity of Jesus of Nazareth. Where Lee's hyphenated Christology avoids this prospect is initially through his recourse to how the gospels describe the background of Jesus' birth. Through critical readings of the infancy narratives in Matthew and Luke, Lee identifies a series of sympathetic "marginal episodes":

Conceived by an unwed woman, born far from his hometown, sheltered
in a manger, visited by Eastern wise men rather than by the elite of his
nation, and flight into Egypt: these are all inklings of what would be his
life-long marginality (Lee 1995: 78–79).

This linking of birth narratives with the condescension of Christ falls
within the scope of an account of what are sometimes called the
"dogmatic episodes" in the "career of Christ," "Christ the creature"
or the humanity of God. The orthodox concern is expressed here
through viewing the incarnation from the Godward side; it is likely
to fasten upon the more creedal episodes to do with pre-existence,
the birth of Jesus, his baptism and temptations, the transfiguration,
his abandonment on the cross, the resurrection, the descent of Holy
Saturday and the climax of the ascension. What this line of approach
does not do is engage with the horizontal relationship between Jesus
and those whom he encounters in the course of his ministry. It skirts
around what Colin Gunton has described as the "material determi-
nateness" and "genetic inheritance" of who this Jesus was (Gunton
1992: 41).

The strength of the more explicitly hyphenated aspect of Lee's
Christology lies in the areas of pre-existence and birth. It allows him
to think of the incarnation as an act of divine emigration from eter-
nity to temporality. The myth of migration also enables an analogy
with the experience of hyphenated persons in their new land. The
reference back to the second humiliation of Christ, of becoming
like a slave, resonates strongly with the fate of those who once held
professional-level positions in their birth land but now are "janitors,
launderers, cooks, and other marginal workers." Lee does not wish
to push the analogy too far; it is limited and does not stand alone in
his thinking on the person and work of Christ. For him the incarnation and career of Christ must embrace the life of Jesus which he sees
as a "paradigm of a new marginality." The device of the hyphen is
preparing the ground for a subsequent frame of reference reliant on
the rhetoric of margins, peripheries and centres. For a liberation theology the emphasis frequently falls upon the public ministry of Jesus,
a bias to the poor and his proclamation of the kingdom of God. That
link back into pre-existence and birth is often underplayed whereas
Lee intentionally weaves them together.

Lee extends then his marginal hermeneutics into the balance of Jesus' life and death. The shape of this Christology falls into several distinct stages which possess an escalating momentum. It almost seems as if, at first, Lee is keen to keep to the more formal route of episodes, careers and the humanity of God. The act of baptism is where Jesus is "symbolically placed in-between the worlds, belonging neither to heaven nor earth." Lee's reading of pre-existence and birth is that Jesus no longer "belongs to heaven because he left there." Through his submission to baptism he does not belong to the world because he renounces its ways. His rising from the water and his confirmation through vision and the voice of the Spirit is tantamount to his becoming a new person "who lives in-beyond by integrating and harmonizing both the total negation (neither/nor) and the total affirmation (both/and) of two different worlds." This embrace of marginality is confirmed through his rejection of options which characterize those who aspire to be at the "centre of centrality" through wealth, glory and dominance (Lee 1995: 84–86).

Rather than follow this trajectory through to the cross via the transfiguration, Lee takes time over the public ministry of Jesus. It is the omission of such which led Jürgen Moltmann in his *The Way of Jesus Christ* to call for a missing clause to be inserted into the creeds. For Lee this particular focus does not lead into a discussion on options arising out of the quests of the historical Jesus: should we think in terms of an apocalyptic or sapiential Christ? Nor is there a debate over whether it is better to think of "where is Christ to be found?" along the lines of Sugirtharajah and, more recently, Clive Marsh (Marsh 2006). Lee likewise ignores the case that a liberation theology will make for Christopraxis over Christology, though it is more than likely he would have been sympathetic to Sugirtharajah, Marsh and Jon Sobrino. Instead he makes a distinction between the healing and teaching/preaching ministry. In the midst of this distinction Lee identifies a Jesus who is homeless, like a beggar, a servant, but able to minister in a mode which is one of a neither/nor exclusion but is both/and. His public ministry demonstrates a complementarity where the marginal are included and those at the centre with power are presented with an option for reversing the way things are.

For Lee the principle of love and how it lends itself to life in-beyond is critical. This principle is contrasted with a passion for justice which might at first glance seem surprising. The desire for a reversal of alienation could lead to a rhetoric of human rights – or maybe an imitation of Terry Eagleton's recent wrestling of the question as to whether Jesus was revolutionary (Eagleton 2007: vii–xxx). The discourse of love can appear sentimental and lacking in prophetic fire. Lee is determined with respect to the case he makes on behalf of his theory of marginalization but it comes with a politics of gentle strength. Talk of justice and rights in an "I am" culture can so often lend itself to an individual assertion that can marginalize another. Lee's way of thinking has, not surprisingly, a more eastern flavour: it is anticipated in the text through an emphasis on humility, an intimation of harmony, and a quick detour through the poetry of Rabindranath Tagore and the life of Kuan-yen, Bodhisattva, "who often appears as a beggar or a poor old woman to assist others in need" (Lee 1995: 88).

One of the gifts of a diasporic theology is the *entrée* it provides for ideas and axioms to emerge from more than one culture. The impetus lies not in a global supermarket of hermeneutical options but is there, residing in the heart and experience of Lee's hyphenated new migrant. In this instance he draws upon a way of seeing which is at times more Asian than American. For a western reader Lee's way of coming to the cross, for instance, is initially a puzzle. The subheading is one of "the loneliness of Jesus" rather than his crucifixion or suffering *per se*. It is not as if the cross is absent. It is the "epitome of negative marginality" (Lee 1995: 91).

The episode of the cross, with other events within the passion narrative, falls within a reading of rejection and abandonment. For Lee the most bitter of afflictions is loneliness and humiliation. Here he stands in the line of Kazoh Kitamori's *A Theology of the Pain of God*, with which he had previously been in conversation with reference to divine passibility. For cultures established within the bounds of the "we" and codes of shame, loneliness is the ultimate signifier of rejection. The death of Jesus-Christ on the cross comes when loneliness and rejection reach their maximum. This point is the "margin of marginality" and Lee cites the song of the suffering servant from Isaiah. Lee is privileging the rhetoric of desertion, rejection, denial and accusation. The despairing cry of God-forsakenness leads to a "cosmic loneliness" where Jesus-Christ is "hung in-between belonging neither to heaven nor earth." The cross is the "nadir of everything"; it is the "bottomless abyss" where the hyphenated Jesus-Christ is both human and divine, and torn between the two (Lee 1995: 93).

Throughout his Christology Lee punctuates his narratives with occasional illustrations of dilemmas in life faced by migrant settlers living in liminal spaces. Lee knows that his analogies are rough and ready, and are limited. Their effect is to create a hook by which experience and a quest for meaning is bound in with talk about Christ. The hidden presence hovering over and within the hyphen which holds in tension two cultures is Jesus-Christ. There is a sense in which he is Emmanuel, God-with-us, in the midst of this upheaval and re-creation. That claim has a structure of plausibility because this Jesus-Christ has plumbed the depths of rejection, loneliness and marginalization; he knows homelessness and the concern for his hyphenated identity is expressed via questions to do with who do people say that he is.

The hope that Lee discerned in and through his parable of the dandelion flourishes through the resurrection. Once again Lee diverts attention away from the stock questions to do with whether it was a physical or spiritual resurrection; was it an historical or eschatological event? Nor is there a desire to compare resurrection with the immortality of the soul, reincarnation or resuscitation. For Lee the resurrection is the confession of Christ-Jesus becoming a "new marginal person," a "new creative core," who lives within the domain of the "in-beyond by affirming both worlds." This creative core is not the same as the "centre of centrality" after which established systems of power and dominant cultures aspire. That centre is one which we create in our diverse searches for security, power, solid belief and ideology. This new core emerges instead out of the act of divine marginalization. This creative core is where the relational triune God is present. It is the "authentic centre where God reigns over the world." The distinguishing features of this new core is the way in which this particular centre marginalizes that all too human quest for the centre of control; its desire is for peoples to place their "centre in God" who through the incarnation knows rejection and the periphery. The invitation is to reconciliation, the possibility of a "genuine pluralism; and a capacity to live in-beyond for Christ's sake (Lee 1995: 96–99).

Out of Place …

This Christology of divine marginalization and the loneliness of Jesus has its origins in the confession of a hyphenated Asian-American. His overriding concern is not the performance of competing cultures and ethnicity so much as a desire to answer the question posed by Jesus: "who do you say that I am?" Far too often the answer given solidifies the centre. Here it leads into talk of Jesus-Christ in a way that is unusual. Lee's Christology does not wrestle with theories of atonement and the finality of Christ. It shows little interest in conciliar decisions, historical quests, the witness of multiple Christologies in the New Testament, the ascension and a pneumatic Christology. It lacks the refined thinking on matters of ontology and kenosis to be found in Oliver Crisp's thinking on Chalcedon and the two natures of Christ (Crisp 2007). From the perspective of a classical Christology, Lee's thesis is likely to be categorized as harbouring functionalist tendencies. There is such a close link between Lee's idea of Jesus-Christ and the experience of being hyphenated oneself. This Christology could easily fall under the criticism Gunton made of those readings of Christ which succumbed to the "Scylla of idealizing Jesus" and allowing one's own face to be "reflected back from the bottom of a deep well" (Gunton 1992: 41). Lee's thinking on Jesus-Christ, "the hermeneutical principle" of the Christian faith, is "out of place" in a line-up of standard Christologies.

The logic of the case Lee mounts on behalf of Jesus-Christ is not to disengage with those Christologies he has identified as belonging to the "centre of centrality." There is a demand for radical inclusion in his thinking of a life which is in-between, in-both and in-beyond. For the present purpose, though, Lee's intention was to talk of faith, identity, Christ and the Christian life for those who were dislocated through the act of migration. Lee is not under illusions. His work is incomplete: a theology of emigration is never finished and, in a way, his parable of the dandelion foreshadows further steps. Once the flower has whitened with seeds the common practice is to blow upon them and let them scatter where they will.

For students in Australia Jung Young Lee has been a most helpful textual ally. His work is regularly cited, along with others. His autobiographical method of doing theology has been permission-giving. One of the habits that has emerged in this context had been the desire for migrant-ethnic communities to tell stories, release telling tales and exhibit a poetics of witness. The autobiographical has represented a "coming out of silence," a finding of voice, an encouragement for others and a way of allowing theology to become an acoustic, listening discipline. That aspect of the theological and biblical disciplines is underplayed at the best of times. The manner in which the public recital of that story has been expressed in the providential categories of faith and not just cultural theory has touched the emotive regions of the heart identified by Kosuke Koyama. It has enabled the personal story to be told in a mode that is able to direct the focus onto the self in relationship to others, multiple cultures and the transcendent.

Aeryun Lee (2004), for instance, has written of "who is Jesus Christ for Korean migrant women in Australia?" In a modest way the account of her story reflects the project of Jung Ha Kim in her writing on the hyphenated roles of *Bridge-Makers and Cross-Bearers* (Kim 1997). What is it like for particular Korean women to live in a new society where the birth culture is now in the margins? The telling of that story weaves in others and also becomes representative. The tale is subjective but it is also more than this for it is a testimony, in a manner of speaking. It is inviting a hearing and a resonating echo in others who discern similarities of experience as well as "yes, but" moments of difference. The tale is not simply personal or cultural, however. What we have here is not a quest for identity that is confined to the referenced cultures on either side of a hyphen.

That organizing question, "who is Jesus Christ for ... ?" is derived from Dietrich Bonhoeffer's *Letters and Papers from Prison* and, less directly, from his lectures on *Christology*. For Bonhoeffer the question posed by Jesus to his disciples – "who do you say that I am?" – is the one question that is truly transcendent. Even when now lost in the status of cliché, it stands over and apart from our speech and all our "how" questions. It has the theological priority of the

Logos which speaks into our silence. This question has the capacity
for those formed in this particular narrative to seek us out. It invites
a response and, in making reply, we disclose a great deal of who
and what we are / not. It is no accident that diasporic theologies
are inclined to address first the question of Jesus Christ – what do
you make of me?, reckons Eagleton – before any other doctrine. For
Gutiérrez, Jung Young Lee and a host of others, how we think about
Christ is the hermeneutical key to the Christian life and Christian
identity.

What Jung Young Lee has done is furnish a model of a hyphenated Jesus-Christ for those like himself who felt "out of place."

Works Cited

Baber, H. E. (2008). *The Multicultural Mystique: The Liberal Case against
  Diversity*. Amherst, MA: Prometheus Books, 2008.
Crisp, Oliver D. (2007). *Divinity and Humanity*. Cambridge: Cambridge
  University Press.
Dixson, Miriam (1999). *The Imaginary Australian: Anglo-Celts and Identity,
  1788 – to the Present*. Sydney: University of New South Wales Press.
Eagleton, Terry (2007). *The Gospels: Jesus Christ*. London and New York:
  Verso.
Gunton, Colin (1992). *Christ and Creation*. Carlisle: Paternoster; Grand
  Rapids: Eerdmans.
Hage, Ghassan (ed.) (1998). *Arab-Australians Today: Citizenship and
  Belonging*. Melbourne: Melbourne University Press.
Jin, Ha (2008). *The Migrant as Writer*. Chicago and London: Chicago
  University Press.
Kim, Jung Ha (1997). *Bridge-Makers and Cross-Bearers: Korean-American
  Women and the Church*. New York: Oxford University Press.
Lee, Aeryun (2004). "In Search of a Christ of the Heart." In *Faith in a
  Hyphen: Cross-Cultural Theologies Down Under*, ed. Clive Pearson,
  88–94. Adelaide: Open Book & Sydney: UTC Publications.
Lee, Jung Young (1995). *Marginality: The Key to Multicultural Theology*.
  Minneapolis: Augsburg Fortress.
Marsh, Clive (2006). *Christ in Practice: A Christology of Everyday Life*.
  London: Darton, Longman and Todd.
Matsuoka, Fumitaka (1995). *The Color of Faith: Building Community in a
  Multiracial Society*. Cleveland: United Church Press.

Newlands, George (2006). *Christ and Human Rights: The Transformative Engagement*. Aldershot and Burlington: Ashgate.

Phan, Peter C. and Jung Young Lee (eds.) (1999). *Journeys at the Margin: Toward an Autobiographical Theology in Asian-American Perspective*. Collegeville, PA: Liturgical Press.

Sugirtharajah, R. S. (2005). "Postcolonial Biblical Interpretation." In *The Modern Theologians: An Introduction to Christian Theology since 1918*, ed. David Ford with Rachel Muers, 535–52. Oxford: Blackwell.

Tanner, Kathryn (1997). *Theories of Culture: A New Agenda for Theology*. Minneapolis: Fortress.

Tavan, Gwenda (2005). *The Long, Slow Death of White Australia*. Melbourne: Scribe.

6 Holy Amphiboly: Prolegomena of Asian-American Theology

Fumitaka Matsuoka

> As scholars concerned with … responsible constructive work for Asian American communities, it is imperative that we frame our analyses in conjunction with the very communities that determine and define Asian American religious identities.
>
> – Rudy Busto

> It is important not to ignore the alternative paradigms rooted in Asian American dispositions. We should not sacrifice non-Western paradigms thoughtlessly or quickly for the dominant paradigm, which measures religious value in different terms.
>
> – Rita Nakashima Brock

The heart of the matter is a shared story of a displaced people, Americans of Asian descent, who live in a racialized society; their story testifies to the renewing power of the Spirit in a community that is continually reformed and reforming. Historically speaking, diverse voices arising out of multiple origins, places and times comprise genealogical characteristics of Christian faith. These myriad voices flow into the river of tradition-making, *actus tradendi*, which constitutes the very fabric of a larger Christian identity. What contributions do the Christian faith communities of Asian diaspora in the US make to the flowing stream of Christian tradition-making? In what ways do these communities practise and articulate their experiences of faith?

The convergence of three decisive forces drives Asian-American theological practices: our emerging subjectivity and self-representation as Asian Americans in a racialized society, our diasporic spirit of dissonance and dissent, and our particular faith orientation, the irresoluteness of faith, or the "Holy Amphiboly." The permutation of these powerful forces in the lives of Asian Americans frames and drives our theological articulations of Christian faith.

Contrary to the historically shaped Christian orthodoxy of *credo ut intelligam* and its *a priori* character of historicized monotheistic cosmology, the revelatory orthodoxy of Christian faith does not always serve as the foundational referential point of the faith understanding and practice for Asian Christian diaspora in the US. In our experiences and in the shared stories that cohere us into a community, the taken-for-granted Christian revelatory monotheism is sometimes submerged into symbolic and ritualized expressions of the communities' self-representation amid the societal forces that have historically made such a representation ignored and devalued. In our attempt to claim our own subjectivity, the dominant revelatory identity of Christian faith is at times mutated into something different from its previously familiar and "orthodox" historical expressions. As those forces – the claim for subjectivity, the diasporic spirit of dissonance and dissent, and the irresoluteness of faith – swirl in and around Asians in the American diaspora, they characterize the practice of faith and theology in Asian-American Christian communities. These forces help form distinct expressions and practices of faith thereby serving as a frame of reference for life amid the disruptions and adversities that we have been experiencing in society. In this way, the Christian faith practices of Asian Americans challenge and transform the historical Abrahamic faith affirmation of the monotheistic divine being as the ultimate referential point of life. In fact, an amphibolous co-existence of divergent cosmologies and life orientations is a real historic and existential reality for Asian Americans. The historically shaped revelatory foundation of Christian faith becomes truncated in the practice of faith in Asian-American communities leaving irresolute and tantalizing questions about the reality of faith. The *actus tradendi* thus becomes highly disjunctive and often historically disruptive in the Christian faith experiences of Asian Americans vectoring the traditioning process of Christian faith to yet an unexpected and uncharted direction.

Asian-American Identity: The Spirit of Contradiction

In recent years, self-definition and self-representation have become a decisive factor for the participation of various communities of colour in North American theological discourse. Asian Americans' participation in the conversation is no exception. Self-definition and self-representation may sound so obvious in a democratic society. And yet they have proven to be one of the hardest endeavours for historically underrepresented groups of people in North America. Those who are in the position of dominance often prescribe the definition of people of colour on our behalf. Our own attempts to define and to represent ourselves have been met with dismissal. In the arena of Christian faith and practice, the dominating power that claims the singularity of a Christian past has ignored and dismissed our faint voices as a deviation from the orthodoxy thereby diminishing the vitality and wealth of the Christian faith that come from the participation of voices reflecting "different mirrors" (Takaki 1993) in both theological discourse and practice. Until recently, theological language was largely bequeathed and represented to us through totalizing conceptions of a particular cultural, philosophical and cosmological tradition and its notion of truth that originated in the North Atlantic basin. This totalized history of Christianity is, furthermore, racialized, politicized, "colonialized" in the American context. It has been oppressive to underrepresented people, particularly of colour. The totalized history of Christian faith is brittle, often too narrowly confined and does not speak to those of us whose existence and voices have been dismissed or ignored and are just recently beginning to claim our own agency and representation in today's world. It is especially problematic on two interrelated accounts: its particularized definition of faith canonized and universalized, and its use of particular religious and philosophical paradigms being construed as definitive.

Asian Americans and our faith communities are likely to employ a distinct paradigm that is shaped by our responses to the racialized treatment of our beings and communities by the larger society, the religious impulses of our particular existence as a displaced people, and distinct worldviews and value systems that flow out of our own life experiences and our ancestral heritages of Asia. We "resist the formal abstraction of aestheticization and canonization" of historically particular experiences (Lowe 1995: 54). To reclaim the genealogical and cumulative identity of Christian faith, as well as to participate in its collective and genealogical "traditioning" (cf. Irvin 1998) movement, the theological voices of Asian diaspora in the US provide different vantage points, distinct readings, and perhaps new insights that have not previously entered the Christian theological discourse.

A radical departure from the past theological tradition is a serious challenge to the notion of the *a priori* nature of the historicized revelation of a monotheistic divine being that has been considered the pillar of Christian orthodoxy. However, the priority of the monotheistic divine revelation over human experiences is not necessarily believed or practised in Asian-American communities. The faith expressions reflected in our shared stories, literature, scholarly discourse, reported life-shaking events, attest to this. The primary reason for the disruption of the *a priori* notion of the revelation is due to the discordant experiences of Asians in North American societies and our inheritance of the embodied cosmological orientations and heritages from Asia. The more the acts of "disidentification," "decolonialization" and "displacement" are practised, the less persuasive is the all-consuming and heavy-handed approach of the historical *analogia fidei* for Asian Americans. Even the notion of *analogia entis,* the meaning of life and truth disclosing itself through nature or history, becomes questionable for its tacitly assumed *a priori* reference to the revelation of the monotheistic divine being. For the lives of Asian Americans shaped by experiences of contradiction, dissonance and dissent in the North American societal context, the revelatory event of Christ often reminds us of the unresolved questions we face in life as much as being the anchor point of faith and life. Christian faith is lived more ambiguously and irresolutely in our faith communities creating an alternate outlook of life which is consistent with our diasporic experiences but is contrary to the traditional equation of faith and "salvation." In other words, the practice of faith for Asian Americans is likely to place us in an unresolved state of continuing discordance as we experience ourselves as displaced people and community. How do we represent ourselves in our practice of faith and how do we articulate what faith means to us? This chapter is an attempt to articulate our own representation in the flowing stream of *actus tradendi* of ecumenical Christianity.

Asian-American Identity: An Amphibolous Existence

Who are Asian Americans? Asian Americans are culturally and racially marginal groups of people in the United States who emanate core values and ideals of the nation. Historian Gary Okihiro defines Asian Americans this way: "In their struggles for equality, these groups have helped preserve and advance the principles and ideals of democracy and have thereby made America a freer place for all. Herein lies the true significance of Asians in American history and culture" (Okihiro 1994: ix–x).

Sociologically speaking, Asian Americans are portrayed as middle-person minorities in the racial landscape of America who are crucial components of a split labour market. Historically speaking, they are sojourners and perpetual foreigners at home. However, in the highly radicalized American society which is often framed in terms of black and white bipolarity, Asian Americans have often been identified with European Americans, at the same time, confronting invisible ceilings and visible anti-Asian violence from both ends of the polarity. In other words, we are amphibolous members of American society in our own self-definitions as well as in the perceptions of other racial groups. The symbolic images of the "yellow peril" and "model minority" are two enduring images of Asian Americans. The amphibolous character of Asian Americans are reflected in these two images. The "yellow peril" is a negative image that portrays Asian Americans as a threat to the nation's body politics whereas the "model minority," though presented as a positive image, indeed pits Asian Americans against other racially underrepresented groups by unjustly elevating our economic and educational status. Asian Americans constantly negotiate our identities between these images, between our own insistence for self-definition, self-representation and the perceptions imposed upon us by the racially dominant groups, and among a myriad variables existing within our own communities.

The invention of Asian American identities is intimately related to the question of how the American quest for empire has historically influenced definitions of race and ethnicity (Kramer 2003). The language of international relations reveals, and is even based on, racial and gender prejudices, argues Emily S. Rosenberg, historian at Macalester College (Rosenberg 1982). Christina Kleine of Massachusetts Institute of Technology points out, for example, that Hawaii presents a fascinating kind of borderland, an Asian Pacific borderland. During the Cold War, the US "had to define itself as a global power in a big way. As part of that, it had to define itself as a racially inclusive nation back home" (Kleine 2003). So, in the 1950s, Hawaii was cast as a paradise of racial tolerance. US officials hoped that image would reassure Asian nations dubious about American expansionism. They talked of Hawaii as a bridge into Asia, and described its statehood as a sign of mainland American's acceptance of Hawaii's large Asian population. James Michener's novel, *Hawaii* (1959) was published in the same year that statehood was granted. The novel showed a Hawaii becoming more tolerant, and told classic, ethnic-immigrant stories of overcoming hardships. The reality was not so rosy, however. The racial and ethnic make-ups of the Hawaiian population are much more complex. The economically and politically based power hierarchy of Hawaii was closely tied with the intricate ethnically defined groups competing with each other. But the romanticized image of Hawaii served as a powerful instrument of US foreign policy against the backdrop of the Cold War.

The formation of America, particularly in the last century, has had everything to do with "westward expansion" across the "Pacific frontier" and the movement of Asians onto American soil. Historically, the amphibolity of Asian-American identities has to do with a great wall between "Asian" and "American" when the two threatened to merge. Stanford scholar David Palumbo-Liu (1999: 54) argues:

> [M]odern Asian America should be read within a context of multiple subjectivities whose multiplicity can be depathologized through a close and critical reading of Asian, American, and Asian/American history, *and* that the unity presumed to be enjoyed by "America" is in fact better read as a set of adjustments and reformations that disclose the fact that America is

always in process itself. And a large part of this process in the twentieth century has *particularly* involved Asian America [original emphasis].

The amphibolity of Asian-American identities also extend to the roles gender and sexuality play in both our self-representations and imposed definitions of who we are. The heart of recognizing diversity within Asian American, gender, sexual, as well as national, generational and class locations, is a particular notion of subjectivity. J. Craig Fong, a gay Asian American, reflects (cited in Mendez 2000: 357–58):

> *Being Asian and being queer are a different set of interests and balances. I'm not saying that it's easier or harder. But it's different. How you deal with those differences is something you look to other Asians to help you with because white folks don't understand* [original emphasis].

What is different for Fong is the Confucian and Buddhist roots of the Asian cultures that impinge upon the issue of sexuality for Asian-American gay persons.

> *... you are nothing until you become an ancestor. If I don't make my father an ancestor – what that means is giving him a grandson. So that when my father dies, my son will grow up remembering and revering his grandfather.... And you don't become an ancestor until you have people alive today worshipping you when you are dead. So the idea, even for me, a fourth generation Chinese American, that I will never be an ancestor. Why? Because I don't have kids. Who will burn incense on my grave?*

Fong recalls a Holocaust poster he once saw hanging on the office wall of a friend that depicts signs commemorating persons who died of AIDS with a candle surrounded by barbed wire. The inscription reads: "Who Will Say Kaddish For Me?"

> *That's exactly it. Who is going to say Kaddish for me? Who is going to burn incense at my grave? It's not about the future. It's about the past. It's about maintaining a link to the people who came before you. When we try to explain that to the mainstream gay and lesbian community, they don't get it. And that is the Asian equivalent of "Who Will Say Kaddish For Me?... You become brave. You remind yourself that it is not so much whether or not your family burns incense at your grave. You condition yourself to remember that the honor and memory to who you are lives on in those who continue after you... And those people who remember your contribution are those who will symbolically burn incense at your grave.*

And those are the people you need to cultivate now. Because most of us, as Asian gay men and lesbians, will not have children.

For Fong, a hybridized notion of the sacred, Confucian and Buddhist roots of Asian cosmologies, coupled with the Jewish practice of saying Kaddish, is the context in which the discovery of the "being an ancestor" is made.

I would say what is probably the best lesson to be taken away from this, is that finding your identity is an exercise in great courage. It is particularly so for marginalized people, for minorities, for people doubly marginalized.

The notion of self as non-unitary and amphibolous stands in sharp contrast to the coherent and unitary identities that find expression in recent discussions on diversity, such as the idea of the unity in diversity. Asian-American feminists and gay writers remind us that the subjectivity claim is often fraught with diffuse, shifting and often contradictory forces. Furthermore, the matter of sexuality for Asian Americans points to the state of marginalization of Asian Americans more acutely than any other forces that shape our identities. "[G]ay Asian organizations are not likely to view themselves as a gay subculture within Asian Americans any more than they are likely to think of themselves as an Asian American subculture within gay America," says Dona Takagi of University of California at Santa Cruz (Takagi 1994: 1). Marginalization is not as much about quantities of experiences as it is about qualities of experience. "Identities whether sourced from sexual desire, racial origins, languages of gender, or class roots, are simply not additive," reminds Takagi. Just as US policies in Asia are interrelated with the construction of Asian Americans as a racial category, gender and sexuality are closely intertwined with the notion of race. A significant issue that arises out of these intersections is the fluid and dynamic ways we need to consider the qualities of our amphibolous experiences.

Who are Asian Americans? The answers historically given to this question are fraught with many assumptions and categories that need to be questioned and destabilized. Scholars of Asian-American studies affirm the articulation of "Asian-American" identity while simultaneously warning us of its overarching, consuming and essentializing dangers. But the one thing that can be said about the identity of Asian Americans is that Asian Americans are not an exception to the very make-up of American society. The main representative values and ideals of America historically emanate from the underrepresented groups who occupy the margins of society. Asian Americans play a role in shaping these values and ideals. The split, fluid and contradictory self is the one who can interrogate the prevailing positionings. The amphibolous ones can help construct and join rational conversations and fantastic imaginings that could change history, that is, if the culturally and racially dominant groups of people would acknowledge the strength of marginality.

Faith and Race: The Locus of Asian-American Theological Discourse

A "different mirror," as Ronald Takaki, professor of ethnic studies at University of California at Berkeley, describes the racial and ethnic diverse landscape of the US population that sets the locus of Asian-American theology (Takaki 1994). A different mirror is a particular image of life and its meaning that racially underrepresented and underprivileged groups of people see as reflected in American society. What Asian Americans see in the mirror is the inseparable relation between our racial and religious identities. The question of "what is it that attracts people to each other?" leads to the question of the ways Asian-American religious communities have been formed around the meaning of race in the United Sates (Jeung 2005: 6). In order to talk about faith experiences of Asian Americans we need to pay attention to the matter of race and how race has impacted our lives. Race is to a large measure the locus in which faith talk takes place for Asian Americans. Race as it is reflected in the "different mirror" reveals how our faith experiences are lived, and our lived faiths give us a clue as to the question of how we experience race. Our racial formation in the history of the United States points to the heart of the matter for Asian Americans' faith experiences as a "People on the Way," an exilic people (Omi and Winant 1994; Ng 1996).

Historian Gary Okihiro poses the question "Is Yellow Black or White?" (Okihiro 2000: 63–78) which reflects not only the ambiguous role Asian Americans hold in this racialized society and its future but also pertains to the question of American identity as a whole and the nature of America's racial formation.

> By seeing only black and white, the presence and absence of all color, white renders Asians, American Indians, and Latinos invisible, ignoring the gradations and complexities of the full spectrum between the racial poles. At the same time, Asians share with Africans the status and repression of nonwhites as the "Other" and therein lies the debilitating aspect of Asian-African antipathy and the liberating nature of African-Asian Unity (Okihiro 2000: 75).

To be sure, the irreducibility of race applies appropriately to African-American experiences of racism because of their history of forced slavery, their involuntary introduction to the US. It is also necessary to note that the ambivalence associated with the positioning of Asian Americans in the US landscape of race, the "foreigners within," originates from how we have been treated in the history of racial formation in the US. There are periods in the history of the US when both African and Asian work forces were seen related insofar as they were both essential for the maintenance of white supremacy. "[T]hey were both members of an oppressed class of 'colored' laborers, and they were both tied historically to the global network of labor migration as slaves and coolies" (Okihiro 2000: 68).

At the same time, Asian Americans were paradoxically classified as whites, sometimes in order to insulate whites from African Americans. For example, in the post-Civil War South, Asians were considered as replacements for African Americans precisely because they were not African Americans. The contemporary notion of the "model minority" perception of Asian Americans maintains its underlying assumption that Asian Americans are "near whites" or "whiter than whites," even though in this minority stereotype we continue to experience racism like African Americans and other racially disfranchised groups of people in educational and occupational settings. Such an amphibolous state of race classification of Asian Americans has resulted in a confused image of who we are in the racial hierarchy of the US and, simultaneously, created opportunities for an alliance with other racially oppressed groups of people.

The question "Is Yellow Black or White?" reveals its complexity for Asian-American racial identity and our place in society. "The question is only valid within the meanings given to and played out in the American racial formation, relations that have been posited as a black and white dyad," cautions David Kyuman Kim (cited in Okihiro 2000: 75). Race, as it is formed and expressed in the state of US history, symbolic interactions, social structures of the society, as well as conflicts that arise out of both interactions and structures, is highly complex. Posing the question of race in terms of a black and white dyad dismisses the gradations and complexities of the full spectrum between the racial poles and a larger question of the nature of American identity and racial formation. Thus, the locus of theological reflection is not merely the amphibolous state of racial classification for Asian Americans. The locus needs to be seen in a wider context of the history of racial formation and its future for all Americans.

Asian-American communities, increasingly their faith communities, have been engaged on at least two fronts throughout the history of this society. They have sought access to full citizenship rights in the civil community and to confront the apostasy of the dominant civil and religious establishment with respect to publicly stated national values. This is the real meaning of the hybridization process of Asian Americans. Religious and theological symbolization and reflections take shape in narratives of common struggles and aspirations in these hybridized institutions. In other words, in our experiences within this racialized society, the legacy of "American Orientalism" as Henry Yu characterizes it, is where we find the "sacred texts" of Asian America that are "the stories and articulate silences of families and communities, of diaspora, immigration, discrimination, racism, and other struggles for survival," thereby exposing the limit of the national myth and simultaneously contributing to the shaping of a more honest and robust national identity as Americans (David Kyuman Kim in Okihiro 1994: 333).

The meaning of revelation, then, is no less than the narratives told by those who are compelled to speak of what they know by telling the story of these racialized events and experiences that compose the history of racial formation in the United States. Paul Ricoeur's appropriation of the Aristotelian notion of *mimesis*, the

"the imitation of an action" or, more accurately, the representation of activity through language, is helpful for Asian-American narrations of the racial formation in the US and their place in it (Ricoeur 1984–88).[1] Narrative is defined as the form of *mimesis* that represents a particular human experience through time. Narrative is always a form of representation. It does not coincide with reality as it is publicly told. In one sense, it is continuous with it, but in another, it is discontinuous and disruptive of the past trajectory. By the very nature of narratives of racial formation, narratives of Asian Americans introduce a different reading of reality, an alternative reading to the prevalent and "public" reading that dominates life in the US. If the spirit of dissent is the religious impulse in collective identity-making for Asian Americans, racial formation functions as the locus of the reflection on the "movement" of the spirit in time.

Asian-American narratives of racial formation are a "form of self-definition. It tells us who we are, because it reveals where we come from and where we've been" (Raboteau 1986: 115). Narrative recounting of the racial formation as *mimesis* represents our experiences through time. By remembering and representing what was experienced, the historical narratives of racial formation in which Asian Americans situate ourselves tie the present to the past in order that self-definition or identity can be sustained. Theology for Asian Americans is thus a re-examination and reconstruction of the very American national identity, re-inscribing our past, positioning our work from within the harsh realities of the American material context, and deploying the tools of critical scholarship to accompany the prophetic visions and dreams to form the national community for all. "The images of the past arranged in chronological order, 'the natural order' of social memory, arouse and transmit the remembrance of events worthy of preservation because the group sees a unifying factor in the monuments of its past unity, or what amounts to the same thing, because it derives from its past the confirmation of its present unity" (Bourdieu 1992, cited in Le Goff 1992: 124). Asian-American narratives as *mimesis* challenge this reading of the myth of the unity. The narrative accounts of racial formation not only entail rendering an account of the past in a manner that is intelligible, so as to render intelligible self-definition and identity in the present, it also entails changing conditions in the present, liberating participants of the lived history of which they are a part from structures or conditions that oppress them. To accomplish this task Asian Americans claim our self-representation by creating our own institutions, both within and outside our communities, in order to claim our rights to interpret the reality we share with the majority and to contribute to the stream of the narration of the national history and identity.

The revelatory witness of faith for Asian Americans, then, has to do with building an equitable and just life that takes into account the history of racial exclusion and oppression in the US.

> Race divides and race makes similarity. Some of the most telling differences, however, are not the blatant and obvious ones that so often lead people to generalization but those subtle variations between people who are seemingly alike. They promise us again and again that the wonder of humanity lies not in the discernment of patterns or either similarity or differences but in the infinite varieties of human experiences (Bourdieu 1992, cited in Le Goff 1992: 204).

Witnessing to the wonder of humanity in reference to the revelatory event of Christian faith within the context of the racialized society of the US is the central task of theology for Asian-American Christians. This task, however, calls for further exploration of forces that drive Asian Americans, that is, the diasporic dissonance and the embodied cosmologies of "disorienting subjects" that go beyond the prevailing Abrahamic notions of monotheism. Asian Americans' experience of race along with our diasporic life raises questions about the normativity of the monotheistic claim of the Judeo-Christian faith traditions and its significance for our lived faith experiences.

The Diasporic Life: A Shared Pathos of Dissonance and Dissent

The next subject to be treated in this chapter is the diasporic life of Asian Americans as it triggers certain religious impulses. The central issue is the distinct spirit of diasporic dissonance and dissent that provides us with an angle of vision and associated religious impulses to engage in theological endeavours and faith quests. These impulses are ritualized in actual practice in order to be traditioned into a reliable cultural referential point within our communities. Religious impulses arise out of a cultural identity which is shared experiences and histories of contradiction that we hold in common.[2] Cultural identity is a conscious *positioning* of our beings in society, not an essence, but a wilful acknowledgement that a continuous frame of reference and meaning underlie any historical disruptions we have been experiencing, awaiting excavation and retrieval. Acts of imaginative rediscovery of these referential frameworks are the significant, though tenuous, glue that binds us together as Asian-American communities. These acts carry the memory of a rehabilitative meaning both in regard to ourselves and in regards to other socially and culturally familiar referential frameworks, uncovering "hidden histories" that fuelled the emergence of important social movements of the time. In this sense, the spirit of diasporic dissonance and dissent is both equally subversive and constructive. It is a powerful driving force to move us towards the future as a "people on the way," exilic and diasporic (Ng 1996).

A shared experience of pathos shapes the collective sense of cultural identity. In such a shared experience can be heard a deep expression of longing and the plurality of vision that kindles the religious impulses of Asian Americans. This pathos is "a bridge, where 'presencing' begins because it captures something of the estranging sense of dislocation and the relocation of the home and the world – the unhomeliness – that is the condition of extra-territorial and cross-cultural initiations" (Bhabha 1994: 9). Dislocation, relocation of the home, and one's refusal to despair in the condition of predicament are interrelated one with another. Dislocation, or the sense of being racially other, reminds us that certitude is not really certain, that privileges are fleeting commodities, and at the same time, dominant powers are increasingly ineffective. Existing institutions seem less and less able to deliver what they intended and have been long counted upon. Even the relocation of the home does not seem to create a new social possibility. We are still being "perpetual foreigners" at home. Home is not really home. At-homeness is an unattainable goal. Sadness, rage and loss are operative feelings. To make the situation even worse, this society lacks ways of thinking and ways of speaking that can give us remedial access to this predicament.

How does one avoid despair so as not to be defeated in life? *"In him I can see my heritage. My soul in me He can see his youth His life."* Communities, particularly religious communities, are formed to mitigate raging racism and to avoid despair. Some refuse to accept the impossibility of change and strive towards social and racial justice. This is Asian Americans' experience of diaspora.

A diasporic life is an alternative to the institutions that dominate modern life. It is "strangely compelling to think about but terrible to experience," says Edward Said (Said 2002: 173). It is terrible to experience because we really do not have home to go back to and, at the same time, we are not totally at home in the place we choose to live. It is "part of morality not to be at home in one's home," as Theodor Adorno ironically puts it (Said 2002: 184). It is "strangely compelling to think about" because it accords a person a particular angle of vision to see reality in impermanence, liminality and dislocation. And yet the life of diaspora also offers a glimpse of freedom, intimacy, and possible originality of vision.

How do we frame the understanding of diaspora as a constitutive force of our collective cultural identity, of an ambiguous and tenuous attachment to each other as Asian diaspora in North America? The mediating factor is the capacity of diaspora to view the world through what W. E. B. Du Bois calls a "double consciousness" that makes the originality of vision possible. It is Wallace Stevens' notion of "'a mind of winter' in which the pathos of summer and autumn as much as the potential of spring are nearby but unobtainable" (Said 2002: 186). This realization results from a diasporic person longing to be rooted in some secure place, "the most important and least recognized need of the human soul," as Simone Weil noted (cited in Said 2002: 183). And yet, remedies we seek for overcoming this quest for security are often just as dangerous and stifling as they are supposed to quench our thirst for being rooted. Often these remedies not only tame one's sensibility to the vicissitude of life but, more importantly, they can alter one's life perspective.

> To be unhomed is not to be homeless, nor can the "unhomely" be easily accommodated in that familiar division of social life into private and public spheres. The unhomely moment creeps up on you stealthily as your own shadow and suddenly you find yourself with Henry James's Isabel

Archer, in *The Portrait of a Lady*, taking the measure of your dwelling in a state of "incredulous terror" (Bhabha 1994: 9).

This is the predicament of Asian diaspora that we share as our cultural identity creating a rapport beyond a politically motivated confederate alliance of ethnic and national differences. Moreover, "Asians have been admitted into the U.S. nation in terms of national economic imperatives, while the state has estranged Asian immigrants through racialization and bars to citizenship, thus distancing Asian Americans, even as citizens, from the terrain of national culture" (Lowe 1996: 176). Due to this ironic paradoxical status, Asian Americans come together because there is an awareness that we are together in choosing not between two opposite poles of racial and ethnic identities, not between the pure and the despoiled, but that our identity has to do with its impermanence, "a state of 'incredulous terror,'" and a choice we have to make about what degree of "unhomely," in-betweenness, which of the innumerable possible combinations, an expression of hybridity we will bring into being. This is the texture of the spirit of dissonance and dissent. Attorney Angela E. Oh expresses this texture as an "openness." "What has been the greatest gift in my life is openness. In this, I have found both pleasure and pain, inspiration and disappointment, laughter and tears. In short, I have found a way to grow. I recognize the gift of being blessed" (Oh 2002).

This realization of "transcendental unhomelyness" constitutes the major driving force for religious impulses and theological reflections for Asian Americans. Located particularly in a society where values are clear, identities stable and unquestioned most of the time, and disinherited middle-class people seek to construct a new world that somewhat resembles an old one left behind, the catch 22 situation in which a diasporic person finds oneself of not being at home in one's own home, "distance from the terrain of national culture," speaks of the religious and spiritual condition and consciousness of Asian-American experience. Some seek to overcome this paradox by identifying themselves with and affiliating with the mainstream parties, mass institutions that dominate modern life, whereby diminishing critical perspective, of intellectual reserve, and moral courage are diminished. Others, sensing an urgent need to reconstitute a restored community, resort to a jealous and resentful isolation by creating an exclusive community of their own. Yet even those who romanticize a solitude experienced outside of the dominant group risk trivializing the radical nature of the very solitude, the habit of dissonance. The question is this: What would it mean to consider collective identity formation in light of diaspora as religious and spiritual enterprise? This is the question regarding the veracity of faith communities for Asian diaspora in North America.

The Holy Amphiboly

The emerging subjectivity and representation of Asian Americans in a racialized society and our diasporic spirit of dissonance and dissent form a particular faith orientation and practice of faith, or the "Holy Amphiboly." The "Holy Amphiboly" is located in the fissure between the Abrahamic faiths and the Asian cosmological orientations that are transported into a new land and transformed into embodied experiences of a dislocated people.

In the novel, *Picture Bride*, novelist Yoshiko Uchida describes a predicament that a character in the novel, Kiku, experiences about her religious orientations and affiliations (Uchida 1987: 13):

> Kiku confessed that she rarely went to church on Sundays because she could not sit through Reverend Okada's sermons. She had a small Buddhist shrine in her living room, however, and occasionally lit incense there to pray for her ancestors. "I guess I'm part-Buddhist, part-Christian and part nothing at all," she laughed.

The monotheistic cosmology of Christian faith in this and other similar stories is placed on an equal par with other cosmologies that are inherited from Asia and then mutated within the Christian faith practices of diasporic Asian Americans. The cosmologies and worldviews also continue to evolve in the practices of Asian-American communities creating hybridized and distinct expressions in the midst of our struggle to claim our own subjectivities in a racialized diasporic life.

Theresa Hak Kyung Cha in her book *Dictee* also describes an experience of the "Holy Amphiboly." In the section "Calliope" which was written from the perspective of a Korean American returning to South Korea in the place where the dictatorial regime once suppressed student uprisings, Cha recalls her naturalization into the United States. Her language, history, national origin, race and gender are at odds with the formation offered by the promise of citizenship. Her identity and subjectivity are

> multiply determined but also that each determination is uneven and historically differentiated, leaving a variety of residues that remain uncontained by and antagonistic to the educational, religious, colonial, and imperial modes of domination and assimilation (Lowe 1996: 52).

In her visit to her place of origin after eighteen years, Cha describes her displaced situation as a Korean American immigrant. The pathos of the "Holy Amphiboly" is the loss of contact with the solidity and the satisfaction of earth. Homecoming is out of the question. "They take me back they have taken me back so precisely now exact to the hour to the day to the season in the smoke mist in the drizzle..." And yet, when she turns the corner, "there is no one. No one facing me. The street is rubble." Still, in such a state of displacement and ambiguity exists a real drive for life, crying "freely." The tears well up out of life. Two children with their arms around each other are crying, dissolving seamlessly between life and death. Cha refuses to acquiesce to the official account of the event that privileges insurgencies, containments and violence that are central to both US neocolonialism and South Korean nationalism. But in claiming her own subjectivity she is also aware of the simultaneous existence of the irresolution of the painful historical past and her yearning for restoration. This is Holy Amphiboly.

The term "amphiboly" connotes an acknowledgement and acceptance of the givenness of such amphibious and amphibolous experiences of life, the life lived in two sets of life orientations, often contradictory to each other, but nevertheless co-existing in one person. The amphibolous state of life is not to be essentialized. It exists in a highly charged historical circumstance of the material construction of life. As Simone Weil reminds us, to be rooted is perhaps the most important and least recognized need of the human soul; to exist in the state of insecurity and amphiboly could result in resentment of those who live in material security and in

rootedness of location. Yet it could also be an opportunity for affirming life's meaning. That is why an amphibolous existence is
holy suggestive of the mystery of the depth of life. To be sure, to
live in the state of holy amphiboly is a jealous state. There is a longing for that which cannot be attained. And yet the unattainability
of security and rootedness of one location is precisely the source of
life, the reservoir of life's vitality. The truth of faith in such a state is
not an objectively verifiable ahistorical matter, but something that
is wrestled over in the midst of daily life. There always exists in
any conviction an element of uncertainty and ambiguity that can
negate an assurance, permanence and certainty. Truth is acknowledged not as a result of indubitable proof but as a result of power
or rhetoric. Values are formed out of such uncertainty.

The sensibility expressed by the term, "Holy Amphiboly," is not
a privilege but an alternative to the mass institutions that historically
dominate Christianity. It is fundamentally a discontinuous state of
being, a solitude experienced outside the dominant and dominating
group. It is driven by a need to reconstitute broken lives by those of
us who find ourselves living amid the power of the dominant ideology but whose existence is on the fringe. The crucial thing is that
those whose faith is amphibolous are desirous of freeing themselves
from the dominant ideology and are driven by the desire to reassem-
ble their broken history into a new whole. Those who embrace the
"Holy Amphiboly" of faith are, at the same time, aware that such a
restoration, to become a restored people, is often unattainable given
the histories of failed attempts of the past to establish a restored
subjectivity by such communities as Native Americans, Palestinians,
as well as Asian Americans. Thus faith exists in a precarious state of
being without any assurance of a glorious future, but we still insist
in "planting an apple tree even if the world comes to its end tomorrow." The pathos of the "Holy Amphiboly" indelibly etches its mark
on the lives of Asian Americans.

The participation of Asian diaspora in the US in the "traditioning"
genealogy of Christian faith communities is simultaneously politicized,
racialized and inextricably bound to the material contexts of immigration and labour history, racism, and stereotyping. The participation
arises out of the ongoing cultural identity formation as a displaced
people. The traditioning is politicized because it claims and insists on

our own representation in the ongoing theological discourse of the wider Christian faith community, as well as in our institution-building efforts for the sake of making such a representation possible and credible in the wider theological circle. It is, at the same time, racialized because such a claim is in large measure driven by societal forces that resist Asian Americans' representation. The driving force for the traditioning of Christian faith by Asian Americans is the shared history and values that are dynamically emerging among us as people of diaspora. This complex matrix of forces that are combined with the "passing on" of the Christian past and the "crossing over" of our hybridized cosmologically and diasporically formed life perspectives constitutes the context of theologizing for Asian diaspora in the US. Only in this context are our faith experiences theologically reflected, described, and our participation in and contribution to the genealogical movement of the whole Christian *oikumene* understood.

"Asian American theology" is an incarnate expression of the common spirit of life that flows as a historical stream whose contour is shaped by the banks of our own historical, religious and cultural experiences and corresponding values and worldviews that are emerging out of them as well as through a plurality of historical churches (Troeltsch 1923: 103–29). As such, it is no more and no less distinct than any other theological expression. It is a voice among multiple theological voices of both the past and the present that in turn pave a way for multiple options in the future for the *actus tradendi* of Christian faith. What is at stake is that the very reality of its underrepresentation in the Christian *actus tradendi* reveals its contributing characteristics. The life of underrepresentation with its tenuous and often transitory bearings in a society that values certitude and geographical locatedness sets the tone of Asian diaspora's theological reading in the US.

The Asian-American voices may not objectively share a common language or a particular faith tradition but they often share a symbolic narrative in that they come to believe in their common roots. The commonality is expressed in terms of a racialized political interest and a shared unique relationship to each other as a diasporic people. Nazli Kibria's notion of the development of an Asian-American collectivity as an emerging ethnic group is instructive in this regard. She states that those Asian Americans she interviewed, second-generation

Chinese and Korean Americans, reported feeling neither authentically ethnic nor truly "American." Instead, these respondents only maintain core ethnic values in the form of a "distilled ethnicity." While Asian Americans may retain their ancestral values such as filial piety, hard work and education, they identify more with the common racialized ethnic experiences of other Asian Americans with whom they interact and intermarry. For them, being Asian American is "another possible way, besides ethnonationally, 'to be ethnic,' to think about and define one's ethnicity" (Kibria 2002: 196).

No matter where the voices are spoken from, what is being said by these voices, the act of "breaking tradition" as poet Janice Mirikitani describes, often defies the familiar reading of Christian faith that prevails in the existing theological literature of the North Atlantic basin. Lisa Lowe claims that the study of Asian-American literature disrupts the assumptions of what constitutes a literary canon, and by its very existence resists appropriation by traditional academic disciplines (Lowe 1995). The same can be said of the study of Asian-American faith practices. It is inextricably bound to its material contexts of racism, lived cosmologies, social history, and trans-locality. Rudy Busto, quoting Buddhist scholar Bernard Faure's insight that "all religious, ideological, or scholarly standpoints are eventually reinscribed in new, complex, and at times conflicting strategies," calls for an "open" approach to the study of Asian-American religions (Busto 2003: 9–28). These voices, represented in this study, also counter the very acculturalized assumptions behind the Christian faith that we are used to – exclusivity, certitude, visibility, clarity, receptivity and progress. In their places, these voices of Asian diaspora in the US speak of ambiguity, unresolvedness, silence and transience amid the assumed dominant cultural and cosmological values of the society thereby transgressing these prevailing accepted values. "Ultimately, revealing is always hiding; any insight generates its own blindness; any deconstruction is always already a reconstruction," says Faure (1993: 151). Contradictions are not readily resolved but are seen as the very source of life's vitality and the very texture of faith understanding. Asian-American theology is thus disruptive of the past shaping of the *actus tradendi* of Christian faith, vectoring it to a previously uncharted direction.

Does the act of "breaking tradition" by Asian Americans fundamentally challenge the historical understanding of the meaning of revelation? How does the "room of open window" contribute to the tradition-making process of the Christian faith? An answer to this question awaits the unfolding of the story.

Works Cited

Bhabha, Homi K. (1994). *The Location of Culture.* London and New York: Routledge.

Busto, Rudiger V. (2003). "Disorienting Subjects: Reclaiming Pacific Islander/ Asian American Religions." In *Revealing the Sacred in Asian and Pacific America,* ed. Jane Naomi Iwamura and Paul Spickard, 9–28. New York: Routledge.

Faure, Bernard (1993). *Chan Insights and Oversights: An Epistemological Critique of the Chan Tradition.* Princeton: Princeton University Press.

Le Goff, Jacques (1992). *History and Memory.* New York: Columbia University Press.

Hall, Stuart (2000). "Cultural Identity and Diaspora." In *Diaspora and Visual Culture: Representing Africans and Jews,* ed. Nicholas Mirzoeff. London: Routledge.

Jeung, Russell (2005). *Faithful Generations: Race and New Asian American Churches.* New York: Rutgers University Press.

Kibria, Nazli (2002). *Becoming Asian American: Second-Generation Chinese and Korean American Identities.* Baltimore, MD: Johns Hopkins University Press.

Kleine, Christina (2003). *Cold War Orientalism: Asia in the Middlebrow Imagination, 1945–1961.* Berkeley: University of California Press.

Kramer, Paul (2003). *The Blood of Government: Racial Politics in the American Colonial Philippines.* Baltimore: Johns Hopkins University Press.

Lowe, Lisa (1995). "Canon, Institutionalization, Identity: Contradictions for Asian American Studies." In *The Ethnic Canon: Histories, Institutions and Interventions,* ed. David Palumbo-Liu. Minneapolis: University of Minnesota Press.

Lowe, Lisa (1996). *Immigrant Acts: On Asian American Cultural Politics.* Durham: Duke University Press.

Mendez, Carlos (2000). "A Fighter for Gay Rights." In *Asian Americans: Experiences and Perspectives,* ed. Timothy P. Fong and Larry H. Shinagawa. Upper Saddle River, NJ: Prentice Hall.

Mirikitani, Janice (1988). "Breaking Tradition." *Ikon* 9. *Without Ceremony: A Special Issue by Asian Women United* (1988): 9.

Ng, David (1996). *People on the Way: Asian North Americans Discovering Christ, Culture, and Community.* Valley Forge: Judson.

Oh, Angela E. (2002). *Open: One Woman's Journey.* Los Angeles: UCLA Asian American Studies Center.

Okihiro, Gary Y. (1994). *Margins and Mainstreams: Asians in American History and Culture.* Seattle and London: University of Washington Press.

Okihiro, Gary Y. (2000). "Is Yellow Black or White?" In *Asian Americans: Experiences and Perspectives*, ed. Timothy P. Fong and Larry H. Shinagawa, 63–78. New York: Prentice Hall.

Omi, Michael and Winant, Howard (1994). *Racial Formation in the United States: From the 1960s to the 1990s.* 2nd ed. New York and London: Routledge.

Palumbo-Liu, David (1999). *Asian/American: Historical Crossings of a Racial Frontier.* Stanford, CA: Stanford University Press.

Raboteau, Albert J. (1986). "Africans in the Diaspora." *Princeton Theological Seminary Bulletin* 7.2: 115.

Ricoeur, Paul (1984–1988). *Time and Narrative*, trans. Kathleen McLaughlin and David Pellauer. Chicago: University of Chicago Press.

Rosenberg, Emily S. (1982). *Spreading the American Dream: American Economic and Cultural Expansion, 1890–1942.* New York: Hill and Wang.

Said, Edward W. (2002). *Reflections on Exile and Other Essays.* Cambridge, MA: Harvard University Press.

Takagi, Dona Y. (1994). "Maiden Voyage: Excursion into Sexuality and Identity Politics in Asian America." *Amerasia Journal* 21.1: 1.

Takaki, Ronald (1993). *A Different Mirror: A History of Multicultural America.* Boston: Little, Brown.

Troeltsch, Ernst (1923). *Christian Thought: Its History and Application*, trans. Baron F. von Hügel. London: University of London Press.

Uchida, Yoshiko (1987). *Picture Bride.* Flagstaff, AZ: Northland.

7 Out of Places: *Asian Feminist Theology of Dislocation*

Namsoon Kang

> One is always on the run, and it seems I haven't really had a home base – and this may have been good for me. I think it's important for people not to feel rooted in one place.
>
> – Gayatri C. Spivak

> Theory is a product of displacement, comparison, a certain distance. To theorize, one leaves home.
>
> – James Clifford

> Space is all one space and thought is all one thought, but my mind divides its spaces into spaces into spaces and thoughts into thoughts into thoughts. Like a large condominium. Occasionally I think about the one Space and the one Thought, but usually I don't. Usually I think about my condominium.
>
> – Andy Warhol

Planting a Sign in a Deterritorialized Space

Questions of one's dis/location are becoming more and more elusive today, geopolitically, historically and discursively. Trying to find an answer to this question of one's dis/location is becoming a more and more serious ontological endeavour of finding one's way of be-ing as an ever-moving verb, not a never-moving noun.[1] One's dis/location is ever-becoming and ever-moving. "Politics of location," first coined by Adrienne Rich, has emerged as a discourse of difference, especially in the US academic feminist discourse, as a method of scrutinizing and dismantling the fixed position, identity and privilege of whiteness in the early 1980s (cf. Rich 1986). This discourse of a "political location" is an outcome of more than a decade of struggles over the defining

and positioning of feminism as theory and practice and can be regarded as eruptions of "difference" after the painful splits especially
among women of different race.

Nowadays one must also confront what one is thinking, saying
and writing from one's dis/location by positioning oneself along the
axes of religion, race, ethnicity, class, gender, physical ability and/or
sexual orientation. Furthermore, the pressure and internal demand
to mark and locate oneself is far greater on scholars of *colour* than
on those who are *non-colour*, white. Here I want to make myself
clear that personally I am not content with using the term *woman of
colour*, in spite of its well-intended meaning by some people. The
term, *people of colour*, underlies a very ambivalent meaning. One
can use it as one of the positive achievements of multiculturalism's
celebration of diverse racial and ethnic people, and as a positive
claim of self-identity and self-politicization by those of "colour." But
at the same time, it could continue to perpetuate a racial distinction
made by the "non-colour," the whites who were never a part of the
people of "colour," as if "white" were not a colour. In doing so, the
whites, the people of non-colour, become the normative human-
hood. In using the phrase, "women of colour," in my essay, I would
like to underscore the fact that "without adequately analyzing power
differentials among groups positioned by racial categorizations and
inequalities, the phrase 'people of color' still implies that white culture is the *hidden norm* against which all other racially subordinate
groups' so-called 'differences' are measured" (Roman 1993: 71;
original emphasis).

Positioning oneself along analytical axes such as race, class, gender
or sexual orientation should not be, however, "static positions" because one's life is in itself fluid, complex and multiple in many ways.
Such a mode of *strategic self-location* can be, however, one way to
make a connection between the private and the public, between the
personal and the academic. This self-positioning is a political or historical choice and becomes one's site of enunciation and discursive
space. When I identify myself as a woman or heterosexual, this self-
positioning is not just a biological statement but denotes a political,
cultural, societal and historical standpoint. In the same vein, positioning myself as a feminist, postmodern or postcolonial theologian,
I am making a firm political statement which clearly indicates what I

am committed to. Identifying myself as an *Asian* feminist theologian is not a geographically/culturally essentialist statement, as is true for some theologians, but a political/historical statement. I am very critical about blind dichotomies between men and women, people of colour and white people, heterosexual and homosexual, or the West and the East.

The separation of the personal and the academic has been a general practice in academia. But feminist theorists have argued that this binarism of the personal and the academic is not just insufficient or inappropriate but damaging by seriously lacking the very materiality of knowledge that one produces. It took me so long time to realize this newly emerging "mandate" in academic thinking. My initial realization of the strong need/urge of connecting the personal and the academic began during the time when I left Korea in the middle of 1980s, for Germany, to do my postgraduate work. I felt a huge discrepancy between "the world in front of my desk" and "the world behind it." I did not know what language I should employ to analyse why I felt what I felt. I didn't even know what to do with this discrepancy and my losing an academic passion that I used to have. I grew very gloomy during my time in Germany. I felt that I lost not just external language but also my internal language that I used to use in order to "organize" both my internal and external life experience. In recent years, cross-cultural movement has become the norm rather than the exception and leaving one's native country is simply not as dramatic as it used to be. But at that time, detachment of my identity from a specific geographic place was a very shocking experience for me. Through my first geopolitical dislocation in my life journey, I began to feel the deep-seated ontological dislocation in my reality as one positioned in the intersection of patriarchy, racism, sexism and classism as a married, female, foreign student with no economic "faculty" in such an affluent western country as Germany.

The great first lessons of my uprooting from my physical homeland, though by my choice, were in the tremendous importance of language and of culture. In other words, I realized that language and culture constitute us in a way of which we perhaps remain unconscious if we stay safely ensconced within one culture and the same geographic place. I felt the departure from my homeland for Germany was somehow irrevocable, even when I would have returned to my homeland later because I felt that I could not be the same person as the one before the departure. Even though the point of departure and arrival could be spatially the same, I knew that I could never be the same inside. Those academic books that I used to read on my desk did not deal with such pressing issues that I had to wrestle with in my physical reality behind the desk.

The feminist theology seminar I took as a doctoral student in the United States, after I left Germany, became the epistemological space where I began to learn the internal languages with which I could organize my experience, analyse why I feel what I feel, negotiate the gap between the two contradicting worlds – in front of and behind the desk, and eventually affirm the fact that it is possible and even necessary to connect the personal to the academic. This exposure to feminist discourse became my "epistemological/ontological conversion" experience that made me realize that the reality was not the reality that it appeared to be nand that we should "materialize" theology by interlinking the academic/theological and the personal in a specific time and space. Otherwise theology can be just an instrument for a certain group of people to seize a discursive hegemony by "universalizing" their abstract speculation on the world, in the name of objectivity, universality and value-neutrality of academism, both wittingly and unwittingly. In this regard, the personal is not just political, as feminists have argued: The personal is not only political but cultural, sociological and theological as well.

Since feminism touched my life, I have begun to have mixed feelings: feeling myself standing on the wrong corner wherever I am in my reality but, at the same time, feeling that I have found a new space in which I can finally be who I really am. I realized however that the more I became intrigued by feminist discourse, the more I felt "out of place" in my materialized reality. Living simultaneously in two spaces – the actual space of patriarchy and the discursive space of feminism – means living in an in-between space. So I have become an ongoing "traveller," travelling back and forth between these two worlds. At the same time, entering this "feminist space" means I experience a constant "ontological displacement" in my physical reality where patriarchy permeates every sector of society. I begin to feel "out of place" as if there were no places to which I belong. This is a feeling of being uprooted from every sector of reality and not "at home" in any. Since then, the question of "home" has been lingering deep in my mind. What would one mean by being "out of place," being dislocated from the point of departure?

Ever since I left my "home" in Asia, where the physical address of my personal place used to be, the most frequent question that I receive from people is "where are you from?" It did not take a long time for me to realize the harsh reality of deep-seated racism, even in people with good will. And it becomes clearer that "who" is asking this question "to whom" has a totally different political connotation.[2] This question often entails the underlying presupposition that "you do not belong here" and that "you have a 'home' to go back to." It did not matter whether I was a student, full-time pastor, or a full-time professor. Neither did it matter whether I had lived for a month or for seven years, nor had a permanent resident card or student visa. This where-are-you-from question is also a question of one's identity, and tends to force one to formulate her/his identity grounded on where s/he "belongs," binding one to the past. So how I would interpret this question, seemingly simple but politically very complicated, depends on "who" is asking this question and what kind of discursive consequences it would bring.

I often answer this where-are-you-from question as, "I am from where I am," especially when it is asked by folks, who, I wish to believe, would eventually understand the political and discursive implication of the question. This periodic "where-are-you-from" question has made me aware how one's life is located in the intersection of sexism, racism, classism and *linguicism*, which Robert Phillipson defines as "ideologies, structures, and practices which are used to legitimate, effectuate, and reproduce an unequal division of power and resources (both material and immaterial) between groups which are defined on the basis of language" (Phillipson 1992: 47). Certainly this "home-question" does not just simply convey a geographical concern. It very often carries, wittingly or unwittingly, a racist implication, especially when asked by racially privileged people, those who are thought as "normative." It is very clear to me that how one understands "home" is not just a question of geographical, historical or any sort of physical space. Instead, the home-question, the where-are-you-from question, is indeed a very complex political question that reveals one's geopolitical, epistemological and ontological location.

What interests me is the fact that the question of home is tied to the multiple questions of one's ontological, geopolitical and theological awareness. And how and who defines "home" is not just a personal matter but also a societal matter which is always related to the *glocal* reality today. Furthermore, one's being out-of-place reveals the discrepancy between "home" and "un-home" and furthermore the disparity of power between those who have home by being rooted in a certain territory and who have not by being deterritorialized, either by internal choice or by external force. I come to believe that theology cannot be acquiescence in the status quo. Theology of dislocation that I propose here starts with straddling the "home" and "un-home" to state and elaborate the conditions of "imaginary geography" of home, with one foot in and one foot out being both in a world of "already" and of "not-yet."

Out-of-Places as Transformative Relocation

The discourse of dislocation in Christianity begins with the dislocation of Adam and Eve from the Garden of Eden, after eating the fruit of the Tree of Knowledge, and continues in God's command to Abraham to leave home. It is interesting to see how Eve's "epistemological" awakening to the good and the bad, after having eaten the forbidden fruit of the Tree of Knowledge, has the consequence of her "ontological" dislocation from Garden of Eden – the home. Exodus experience in the wilderness for forty years is also a collective experience of dislocation. In this sense, it is not wrong to say that Judeo-Christianity starts with the *theology of dislocation* from the outset and that the discourse of dislocation is in fact not new. But we live in a historical and geopolitical juncture when the discourse of dislocation has captured the imagination of many people. The new interest in the "home discourse" stems from the awareness that "our contemporary world has seen migrations of people on a scale as never before in human history" and that "[f]or colonized peoples, migrations by 'choice' and/or by economic necessity are rooted within a colonial and postcolonial history and within continuing imperialist dominations today" (Katrak 1991: 649). Therefore, the politics of home and of de/territorialization of the empire continues to influence current ideas of identity – both individual and national. A displaced person draws attention to the precariousness of home as materialized location and to the experience of the "unhomely" (cf. Bhabha 1992) in a contemporary geopolitical reality. The contemporary experience of transnational migration and exile have also been accompanied by the discourse of dislocation. Considering the current situation in global context, articulating how one understands the experience of uprootedness, of dislocation, of deterritorialization or of homelessness is an urgent and significant theological task today.

Dislocation, whether geopolitical or ontological, entails in a way the loss of all familiar external and internal parameters, and could be therefore very painful. However, there is also gain, not just all pain. This dislocation could make a different understanding possible and it gives a perspective, a vantage point. This experience of dislocation as an experience of "not-being-at-home" can also be a crucial liberating step in self-discovery. Becoming out-of-place makes one distance oneself from who one used to be and makes one rewrite oneself from a totally new point of view. Furthermore, being a feminist, for instance, also means being in exile even in one's own homeland. Although being in exile is "compelling to think about but terrible to experience" (Said 1990: 357)[3] this experience of out-of-place can develop into a way of thinking about home. This situation creates a kind of paradox between loss and recovery. An experience of dislocation can be an experience of radical, transformative re-location. And the displaced person becomes a permanent homeless traveller who is looking for home by being displaced from home. The daily experience of "homeless traveller" as a metaphor is complex and paradoxical, whose life is constantly on the margins.

One of the few benefits of the condition of exile is an "originality of vision," which is the product of seeing "the entire world as a foreign land" (Said 1990: 366). Being unattached to or detached from an existing world, those who are discursively or geopolitically dislocated can be in the best position to demystify the transparence of social relations and the self-evidence of religious or sociopolitical ideologies. It also seems that "dislocation" can be the instigator of new vision.

But I wish neither to romanticize being out-of-place nor to underestimate the sheer human cost of actual exile/dislocation as well as of its psychic implications. I am also fully aware of the different kinds of status of being out-of-place, of not-being-at-home, some chosen, some not. I am also interested less in the epistemological/cognitive advantages of being dislocated and more in its other productive consequences, especially in terms of transformative theological construction. I believe, however, in "being-out-of-place" – whether it be geopolitical, ontological or epistemological – and believe in its capacity for deterritorialization, transgression, and radical openness to the new that one can channel into the fight against sexism, classism, racism, ageism, linguicism, xenophobia or homophobia that draw a rigid boundary between people on various grounds. The experience of marginality by those who have "escaped" from home or are forced to leave home can be an experience of developing who they are and what they are capable of. They become sensitive to the issue of who is "in" and who is "out" of the mainstream of a given society and concern for those who are out of the dominant circle – those dislocated and deterritorialized.

Nomadism or pilgrimage entails a constant state of "in-process" or "becoming," which Rosi Braidotti refers to as "the philosophy of 'as-if.'" Her figuration of the nomad is a political definition as well as a critical consciousness, an attempt to "explore and legitimate political agency, while taking as historical evidence the decline of metaphysically fixed, steady identities" (Braidotti 1994: 5). The practice of "as-if" is a "technique of strategic re-location in order to rescue what we need of the past in order to trace paths of transformation of our lives here and now" (Braidotti 1994: 6). She also understands "as-if" "as the affirmation of fluid boundaries, a practice of the intervals, of the interfaces, and the interstices." While grounded in postmodernist theory of repetition, parody, pastiche, etc., she is insistent that for "as-if" to be useful, it must be grounded in deliberate agency and lived experience. Postmodern subversions and parody in the "as-if" mode "can be politically empowering on the condition of being sustained by a critical consciousness that aims at engendering transformations and changes," and opens up "in-between spaces where new forms of political subjectivity can be explored" (Braidotti 1994: 7).

Although I do find empowerment in the discourse of nomadic subjects, I would like to employ the term *the dislocated*, rather than nomad, as a metaphor for an articulation of my theologizing. Nomadism seems to me to have a danger of being ageopolitical and ahistorical by tending to celebrate a constant travelling, even without having to physically move from one's habitat to another, due to the absence of critical engagement of the subject in the specific context for transformation. The point of departure and the point of arrival for a nomad do not have to be different, while for a dislocated person the difference between the two places is crucial. Unlike a nomad, when the dislocated travels, s/he looks for a home. Here, "travel," as a metaphor, provides a possibility for an intellectual/cognitive uprooting and contains the potential for transformation. For me, identifying oneself as a "dislocated traveller" is making a political statement that reveals what is lacking in the existing reality that makes oneself uprooted and dislocated, and therefore demands a need to establish an authentic Home where one is able to feel truly "homely," and to be truly the whole self, not a fragmented self. Looking for *Home* from *homes* requires a radical transformation of one's relationship with self, community, and the Divine. It also requires a radical openness to those who are dislocated on various grounds because they are the ones with whom the "homeless, dislocated traveller" could share what they are yearning for and what they need to do to actualize the home in a geopolitical reality. Here there is a possibility of passionate solidarity among/for those out-of-places.

I also believe in being detached from everything familiar, either by choice or force, because it would make for a certain creative de-familiarization which often gives one new ways of observing and seeing the world. In this context, leaving home for Home or being displaced can be a liberating step in self-discovery. By being defamiliarized, one can see in reality what one has not seen due to the sociopolitical or religious convention and practice that constrain one's view of the world. In this regard, one can join in the "gatherings of exiles and émigrés and refugees, gatherings on the edge of 'foreign' cultures … gathering in the half life, half-light of foreign tongues … gathering the past in a ritual of revival; gathering the present," as Homi Bhabha points out (cited in Woodhull 1993: 9). When God commands Abraham, "leave your country, your people and your father's household"(Genesis 12:1), Abraham's leaving home is a journey of "defamiliarization" which gives him new eyes through which he is able to see the self, the world, and the Divine from a totally different perspective, seeing everything afresh. The Bible does not clearly give the reason why God commands Abraham to leave his home. It seems to me, however, very clear that Abraham must have experienced total dislocation – loss of familiar space and life, fear and frustration for the unknown future, yearning and longing for Home away from home, ongoing daily survival, and hope and vision for the future Home. Through this experience of being out-of-place, Abraham becomes who he is. In this case, dislocation turns out to be a transformative relocation, which offers a powerful mode of interpretative in-between space as a form of accountability to more than one location.

Asian Feminist Theology as Deep Minority Discourse

> *The likeness will meet and make merry, but they won't know you. They*
> *won't know the you that's hidden somewhere in the castle of your skin.*
> – George Lamming, *In the Castle of My Skin*

Gilles Deleuze and Felix Guattari distinguish "minority discourse" from great literature by citing three characteristics, which are deterritorialization, an emphasis on politics, and a collective value. In discussing the deterritorialization of a major language through minor literature written in a major language from a marginalized or minoritarian position, Deleuze and Guattari explain that it does not arise from literature written in a "minor" language, or in a formerly colonized language. Rather it is written in a major language which is "affected with a high coefficient of deterritorialization" (Deleuze and Guattari 1986: 16). The second feature of minor literature is its emphasis on politics. Everything in the "minor literature" is political, in terms that the individual subject is linked to the political. Therefore, "its cramped space forces each individual intrigue to connect immediately to politics" and the "individual concern thus becomes all the more necessary, indispensable, magnified, because a whole other story is vibrating in it" (Deleuze and Guattari 1986: 17).

The third characteristic of "minor literature" is its collective value. The collective value refers to the writer's terrain, where utterances reflect a community's usage, which is inseparable from the political nature of a "minor literature." Deleuze and Guattari argue the inextricability of the political and the collective, which seems to me very much coinciding with feminist argument for the motto, "the personal is political." Deleuze and Guattari rightly point out that what each author says individually already constitutes a common action, and what he or she says or does is necessarily political, even if others aren't in agreement. The political domain has contaminated every statement. But above all else, because collective or national consciousness is "often inactive in external life and always in the process of break-down," minor literature finds itself positively charged with the role and function of the collective and even revolutionary enunciation. Its enunciative value is both political and collective, and therefore even what an author says individually is necessarily political and revolutionary. The evolutionary potential of "minor literature" is written from the margins, deterritorializing the "fragile community" from the border from where it is possible "to express another possible community and to forge the means for another consciousness and another sensibility." In this sense, "minor literature" is political and subversive because it creates "the opposite dream" (Deleuze and Guattari 1986: 27).

It is very clear, according to the articulation of "minor literature" by Deleuze and Guattari, that feminist theological discourse is certainly a minority discourse. But are all feminist theological discourses the same in the degree of their being "minor"? The answer for me is definitely no. I would argue that *Asian* feminist theological discourse is on the margins of the margin in a global "discursive" world. Those Asian feminist theologians are the ones who are doing theology in the intersection of not only racism, sexism and classism, but also *linguicism*. I would argue that in an era of so-called globalization, we have to add "language" to those discursive axes of race, gender, class, and sexual orientation, because of the influential power of *linguicism* in every sector of our reality today, especially in the form of *English linguistic imperialism*, which Robert Phillipson defines as "the dominance of English is asserted and maintained by the establishment and continuous reconstitution of structural and cultural inequalities between English and other languages" (Phillipson 1992: 47). When English is considered a "normative" language, those whose first language is not English are considered "sub-social," especially in the English-speaking countries of the global North. That all knowledge production and reproduction in the world is bound up with the hegemony of English today, which is called *English linguistic imperialism*, means the politics of hegemonic language is strongly tied to "linguistic terrorism." It is also becoming so problematic, especially in an era of globalization, that all "international" meetings are always dominated by those who speak English as their first language, which often end up being "English-national," instead of "inter-national." In this sense, English-holder becomes power-holder. Needless to mention, language has been a powerful means of imperialistic domination. Gloria Anzaldua shows how the hegemony of English terrifies people of other language than English which she calls "linguistic terrorism": "Because we speak with tongues of fire we are culturally *crucified*. Racially, culturally and linguistically ... – we speak an *orphan tongue* ... as long as I have to accommodate the English speakers rather than having them accommodate me, my tongue will be illegitimate" (Anzaldua 1987: 58–59; italics mine).

In this regard, Asians are doomed to be considered "sub-social" in the global context because they are the ones who permanently speak in "orphan tongues" in today's world where English has become an exclusively "global language," and where only former colonial languages are officially translated and considered "normative" languages. English-centrism justifies an ideology of superiority of the English-speaking people and their culture, and English has become also as determinant of whether one is intelligent and accountable enough. *It would be interesting to see the difference between feminist theologians from the West and those from the non-West in terms of their global status, along the lines of an analysis of the difference between anti-Semitism and racism against "Negroes."* Analysing the difference between Jews and Negroes, Oliver C. Cox points out:

> The dominant group is intolerant of those whom it can define as *anti-social*, while it holds race prejudice against those whom it can define as *subsocial*... Thus we are ordinarily intolerant of Jews but prejudiced

against Negroes. In other words, the dominant group or ruling class does not like the Jew at all, but likes the Negro in his place. To put it still another way, the condition of its liking the Jew is that he cease being a Jew and voluntarily become like the generality of society, while the condition of liking the Negro is that he cease trying to become like the generality of society and remain contentedly a Negro… We want to assimilate the Jews, but they, on the whole, refuse with probable justification to be assimilated; the Negroes want to be assimilated, but we refuse to let them assimilate (Cox 1959: 400–401; italics mine).

Although this analysis does not show the sophisticated nature of the power disparity between feminists from the global South and those from the global North, it shows how racism or racial prejudice can work in the intersection of sexism and other forms of discrimination. While people would consider feminist theologians of the global North as "anti-social" due to their "violation" and "transgression" of sociocultural code, they would regard feminist theologians from the global South as "sub-social" due to their second-class status on a global context. It is misleading therefore if we reduce racism/ethnocentrism and classism to sexism and search for a "general" theory of oppression incorporating race, gender, class and ethnicity with various linguistic dis/ability. In this regard, Asian feminist theological discourse is not just minority discourse, but *deep* minority discourse which is more repressed or marginalized than those feminists whose "heart language" is a dominant language, due to the "hegemony of English," which entails the neo-imperialistic reality that the women from the global South experience. Linguicism in the construction of theological discourse on a global level is not just the struggle between hegemonic culture and minorities. It is also a struggle with the homogenizing power that exoticizes or stereotypes Asian as "Orientals" in Said's notion of Orientalism. Considering the complexity and diversity of minority discourse, the political concerns of Asian feminist theological discourse, as **deep** minority discourse, has its unique tasks in a global context.

Toward an Asian Feminist Theology of Dislocation in Global Context

I have often met Asian theologians, both women and men, who reject "feminist" theology as a western construct and instead claim that "Asian" theology defends the uniqueness and rights of Asians. Such a nativist stand is "a real denial of history" because the concept of human rights, including women's rights and the rights of the ethnically/racially marginalized, has "a deep complicity with the culture of imperialism" (Spivak 1991: 232). I am clearly aware of the problems of the feminists in the global North in often denying the otherness of women in the global South and judging them according to the "high feminist norm" of the global North or patronizing them by participating in an "information retrieval" approach, grounded in a "what can I do *for* them" attitude (Spivak 1988: 135). However, overlooking the ideological intersection of sexism and ethnocentrism in such nativist claim for Asian culture and tradition by Asians is as dangerous as the uncritical absorption of the "western" feminist claims.

Theologizing in an *Acquired Language* in Global Context

Articulating feminist theology in an internationally accepted "vehicular" language, which is English, is doing theology with an *acquired language*, not with a *heart language*. Vernacular language is, according to Deleuze and Guattari in their adoption of the linguistic theories of tetralinguistic model, a *language of territorialization*, in which the vehicular language is "a language of the first sort of deterritorialization." They go on to explain that the four languages in the tetralinguistic model differ according to spatiotemporal location: "vernacular is here; vehicular language is everywhere; referential language is over there; mythic language is beyond" (Deleuze and Guattari 1986: 23). The distribution of these language functions is also determined by historical, cultural and national location, as Deleuze and Guattari illustrate through the shifting functions of Latin – vehicular in the classical Roman era; referential in the mediaeval period; mythic during the Renaissance and after. According to Deleuze and Guattari, these language functions "can have ambiguous edges, changing borders that differ from this or that material... Each function of language divides up in turn and carries with it multiple centers of power. A blur of languages, and not at all a system of languages" (Deleuze and Guattari 1986: 24).

I have experienced that articulating theology in this "global" vehicular language, English, is a process of "becoming minor" and that I feel "a sort of stranger within" (Deleuze and Guattari 1986: 26) the language that I am using: a stranger within the allegedly "vehicular" language, language of everywhere. But will there be any time in human history when the hegemony of English will give away its power of being a global vehicular language to other language, as is the case in Latin, especially in this era of neo-imperialism? My observation does not give a positive answer to this question yet. In this current geopolitical context, as long as my first language, Korean, remains only a "referential" language, constructing theological discourse in a global context will remain a *deep* minority discourse. This "fate" of *the dislocated*, Asian feminist theologians in a global context, who become the writers of theology in an acquired language, shall have to offer a vision of a transformative theologizing with their persistent attention to the complicated intersection of sexism, racism, classism, ethnocentrism, homophobism, linguicism and neo-imperialism in our geopolitical reality. The space of their theologizing should be a space of deterritorialization that resists "microfascisms" which homogenize, exoticize, stereotype, totalize, and subjugate people on any ground. For we need to make a "qualitative shift away from hegemony, whatever its size and however 'local' it may be" (Braidotti 1994: 5).

Dismantling *Naturalization* of Asian Women

Ecofeminism analyses Western tradition's naturalization of women and feminization of nature, drawing the conclusion that the domination of women and the domination of nature are inextricably connected and mutually reinforcing. This connection of the oppression of women and nature as "twin oppressions" gives rise to a common formative structure of *othering*. This epistemological framework of the naturalization of women and nature in the Western tradition can also apply to the naturalization and feminization of the Orient. As Edward Said rightly points out, the creation of the Orient is an outgrowth of a will to power of the West, and therefore Orientalism "is a Western style for dominating, restructuring, and having authority over the Orient" (Said 1978: 3). In this construction of the Orient, Asia is very often feminized and Asian women are more naturalized, mystified and exoticized both by the West and Asia. Albert Memmi articulates this process of naturalization of the colonized as follows (Memmi 1967: 85):

> The colonialist removes the factor from history, time and therefore possible evolution. What is actually a sociological point becomes labeled as being biological, or preferably, metaphysical. It is attached to the colonized's basic nature. Immediately the colonial relationship between colonized and colonizer, founded on the essential outlook of the two protagonists, becomes a definitive category. It is what it is because they are what they are, and neither one nor the other will ever change.

The danger of any naturalization of analytic categories such as "woman" or "the orient" is the fact that it ends in a de-historicization and mystification of difference between women and men, between the West and Asia, between Asian women and Western women. In the name of formulating "cultural difference" between Asia and the West, ethnic markers such as "Asian" easily become a method of differentiation and naturalization that blocks criticism from the critical task of theology and Asian theological discourses tend to be easily geographically deterministic and hence culturally essentialist.[4] Some may say that Edward Said's theory does not apply to East Asia because many East Asian countries such as Korea, Japan, Singapore or China, were not, territorially, Western colonial possessions. But this kind of positivistic approach is to overlook the colonial situation today, where the fate of Asia is entirely interlinked with the foreign policy of the US, the neo-Empire, with its major military bases in Asian countries such as Japan, Korea, Taiwan, the Philippines and Vietnam. As an Asian woman scholar teaching in the "first" world academia, I often find myself being located in the scene between Orientalism and nativism. When I do not play the role of a "native informant," people, both Asians and non-Asians, would suspect my "authentic" Asianness. Asian feminist theology in the global context has to thoroughly dismantle the *naturalization* of *Asian women* by moving beyond *Asian women's* identity politics which privileges the "authenticity" of Asian women. People too easily regard Asian women as "piece of exotica" and "manageable other" (Spivak 1990: 94, 114). This scene of postcoloniality is a site of Asian feminist theology of *dislocation*, which is to be a persistent critique of totalization.

Asian as *Postethnic*

What does make Asian theology *Asian*? This question is not as easy to answer as it sounds. It is obvious that what we call "Asian theology" does not simply mean theology done by the ethnically Asian. I do not agree with the idea that Asian theology is theology that "primarily" deals with Asian *unique* resources that the West does not have. "Asian" as uniqueness or specialness has both positive and negative connotations: positive when interpreted geopolitically as a subversive of the Westcentredness of theological discourse, and negative when understood in an essentialist way, which is misleading and confining. I do not have any problems with starting from the position that Asians are suffering from poverty and their context is religiously very plural (cf. Pieris 1980). I think that in order to start one's theological construction and practice, one has to have some kind of provisional starting point. But when such a claim becomes monolithic and essentialist and tends to define what constitutes Asian theology as such, that is when I begin to have trouble. It is true, simplistically speaking, that Asia, as the global South, is poorer than those countries in the global North. But it is also true that one cannot shift economic conditions at will, so that western people of a poorer class are not immediate oppressors of Asians of a much richer class. If one is aware of the tremendous complexity and diversity of the context of people in every continent of the globe, that awareness cleanses that kind of monolithic and essentialist claim that one is speaking for all Asian's suffering and oppression.

When academics or religious leaders in Asia involved in power struggle in a regional context, which is quite often the only really "political" activity they are fully engaged in, use the excuse of Asian's "universal" suffering and oppression, they are certainly not think-ing about their institutional hegemonic power that oppresses other people in their own academia and denominations, or of the urban sub-proletariat in New York, or about women's issues in Uganda or India. Using "Asian" in an essentialist way oversimplifies the dif-ferences between and among Asian countries and overlooks the ironical contrast between the rich in "poor" Asia and the poor in the "rich" West. I use the word, *Asian*, with full awareness of its problems, when interpreted in a geo-culturally essentialist way. It is a general principle of feminist inquiry to be sceptical about any ac-count of human relations that fails to mention gender or consider the possible effects of gender differences: for in a world in which there is sexism, obscuring the workings of gender is likely to involve – whether wittingly or unwittingly – obscuring the workings of sexism. We thus ought to be sceptical about any account of race/ethnicity relations that fails to mention gender. Asian theologies often fall into a trap of *genderlessness*.

One's identity is defined in terms of one's gender, race, class, sexual orientation, religion, educational background or family back-ground, etc. It is thus evident that thinking about a person's identity as made up of only neatly distinguishable parts may be very mis-leading. It can be misleading to talk about only *Asian* as a generic working category, as if race or ethnicity exists in isolation from other variables of human identity such as gender, class or religion. In this sense, we need to go beyond the cultural essentialist perception of *Asian*, and perceive Asian as "postethnic," which denotes "a radical and necessary extension of the 'ethnic'" (Radhakrishnan 1996: 65). The situation of the sociopolitical and historicoeconomic specificity of Asia cannot be a ground of essentializing Asia. *Asian* feminist *the-ology of dislocation* requires, I would argue, a discursive move from "politics of homogeneity" to "politics of heterogeneity," the hetero-geneity not as a political indifference but a political affirmation of the diversity among, between, and in us, *Asian*-women.

Theology from Liminal Consciousness and Consciousness of Dislocation

Asian feminist theology is more and more lacking a sense of adventure and risk-taking. I would say that one of the reasons is an internalized intellectual defeatism among Asian feminist theologians; it is the case, at least, in my context where patriarchy is still extremely prevalent and the backlash against feminism is very strong. So the technique of survival is a very serious issue for Asian feminist theologians. After all these several decades of feminist movement in Christianity and society, many feminist theologians realize that little fundamental change has occurred in the *malestream* of Christianity. So survival, for feminist theologians, is a serious issue to which we need to pay serious attention. How to survive in an extremely patriarchal society and religion is becoming more and more difficult to find an answer. Unless they survive, to challenge and transform Christianity and society is very hard to achieve. I strongly feel that the early intellectual/ theological excitement about feminist theology has become routinized and, in a way, institutionalized. It becomes just a theoretical production without having a sense of passion for transformation. The absence of passion for change is, I believe, a consequence of internalized defeatism of those women who have hardly been in charge in the *malestream* religion, and who are ongoingly threatened by the *malestream*. I have seen how vulnerable feminist theologians both in academia and in the church are to tenure and to ordination, for example. In particular those in theological schools and seminaries are totally vulnerable to dismissal at any time.

Doing feminist theology means to imagine a religion and world in a totally different way and to envision an alternative way of practising religion – religion and world without any kind of hierarchy or exclusion of the poor, of women, or of sexual minorities. The criterion for measuring whether a religion is egalitarian and liberating consists in the practical test of whether it allows for the full participation and leadership of women. Since the control of public discourse is a principal element of maintaining authority and power, the absence of central feminist questions from public theological discourse is an important form of women's ecclesial exclusion. Broadly speaking, a primary goal of the construction of feminist theological discourse is to promote humanization by transforming self, community and the world with the spirit of radical equality and inclusivity.

Here we need to wrestle with the following issues: What is the goal of Asian feminist theology? How far is it possible for feminist theologians to make *Exodus* from the existing traditional religion and institution as their survival itself is ongoingly threatened even by their act of raising voices against patriarchalism in religion? If we understand *Exodus* not just as a metaphoric meaning but as a physical and materialized act, how far can we expect the feminist theologians take an action for *Exodus-making*? What has to be done to broaden and radicalize feminist theology?

Doing Asian feminist theology requires creating ways of thinking without home, and carrying a perspective of interstice, which goes beyond the trap of fixed identity of as-*Asian*-women. Taking *dislocation* as a metaphor becomes an element in the very staging of "the feminist" in an extreme patriarchal culture, and being a Christian theologian in a multi-religious society, in which people still regard Christianity as *foreign* religion and disregard feminism due to its "foreign" origin, means to be constantly out-of-places. These three components of hyphenated-identity – Asian, feminist, Christian theologian – lead Asian feminist theologians to a peculiar space of uprootedness and dislocatedness: They are constantly in exile even in their own home country. Due to "gender illiteracy" in their homeland, Asian feminists leave home for Home either by choice or by institutional force. This being dislocated gives rise to a new consciousness – a consciousness of dislocation.

The feminist consciousness of dislocation here refers to a kind of critical consciousness that resists settling into socially coded modes of thought and behaviour, and to the subversion of conventions that define Asian women as exoticized and idealized both by Asia and the West. Asian feminist identity of dislocation is the starting point through which s/he connects with the rest of humanity, not the end point used to distance oneself from it. S/he would feel a true "homecoming" in a space of resistance, solidarity and compassion. Being an Asian feminist theologian, one is often required to reside simultaneously in more than two worlds. Feminists are those who are homesick. Being homesick is a desire of becoming other than what one is. "Becoming other than what one is" involves not only philosophical work but also work on the self. The strategic work of self-transformation requires not only the genealogical practice of defamiliarizing the present, but also the invention of new forms of discipline. Many feminist theologians are constantly exposed to condemnation as "heretics" and exclusion from patriarchal religion and society. Such exposure to condemnation creates the need and the capacity for spiritual exercises, for self-mastery and transformation. Feminist theologians are those who *counter* to "common" sense, who swim against the tide, who shake the fundamental epistemological framework of theological institution, church and society, and who have "in-between" consciousness standing in in-between-space of the world of *already* and of *not-yet*.

Those who have a history of being marginalized on the basis of their skin colour, gender, class, sexual orientation, or any other axis of categorization, are reading, writing and theologizing in the interstices of dominant culture, moving between the language of the centre and that of marginality, which is rightly depicted in a writing by an Argentinean philosopher, Maria Lugones (1991: 35):

> I wrote this paper from a dark place: a place where I see white/anglo women as "on the other side," on "the light side." From a dark place where I see myself dark but do not focus on or dwell inside the darkness but rather focus on "the other side." To me it makes a deep difference where I am writing from.

Similarly those who have an experience of crossing the borderline between the cultures, languages, and the various configurations of power and meaning in complex "hegemonic" situations, possess what I would call "liminal consciousness." This consciousness is an "in-between consciousness" or "consciousness of interstice." This liminal consciousness could give one the ability to see things from "multiple perspectives." Being and living the multiple interstices may have the potential to lock oneself away in isolation and hopelessness as well as the potential for critical consciousness and particular creativity in thinking, observing, and being engaged with reality. Rather than being trapped in anger, pain or isolation, developing this liminal consciousness in a creative way in the experience of dislocation has the potentiality for resistance against hegemonization and

homogenization of the marginalized and the possibility of forming solidarity with the racialized, genderized or sexualized "other."
    Radhakrishnan rightly argues (1994: 232):

> [T]he diaspora is an excellent opportunity to think through some of these vexed questions: solidarity and criticism, belonging and distance, insider spaces and outsider spaces, identity as invention and identity as natural, location-subject positionality and the politics of representation, rootedness and rootlessness.

Asian feminist theology today in a global context is relevant only when we *Asian* feminist theologians utilize our being "dislocated" from multiple "places" to destabilize unexamined or stereotypical images of certain groups of people that are vestiges of colonial discourse and other manifestations of neo-imperialist structural inequalities among people of different race, gender, class, ethnicity or sexual orientation. I believe that feminist theologians today need to consciously develop a "geopolitical sensitivity" in their theologizing by embarking a "world-travelling," a process of simultaneous displacement and placement that acknowledges multiple locations. This "world-travelling" as a theological/discursive "travel" would offer us alternatives to theological/cultural/geopolitical imperialism and appropriation because:

> [t]hrough travelling to other people's "worlds" we discover that there are "worlds" in which those who are the victims of arrogant perception are really subjects, lively beings, resistors, constructors of vision even though in the mainstream construction they are animated only by the arrogant perceiver and are pliable, foldable, file-awayable, classifiable (Lugones 1990: 402).

The rhetoric of Asian feminist *theology of dislocation* indicates a kind of theological progression that is constantly marking out new thresholds, and keeps crossing and transcending these thresholds in this very marking. It also represents a discovery of a "temporality" that relativizes and dismantles the absolutized authority and discourse that have justified domination of one group of people over the other. This experience and its theological construction of dislocation would offer a critical and passionate energy to work for justice, peace and equality of all living beings. Asian feminist theology of dislocation is, in its true sense, an ongoing theological "world-travelling" for discovering the others as really, lively subject beings who cannot be "classifiable."

Works Cited

Anzaldua, Gloria (1987). *Borderlands/La Frontera: The New Mestiza*. San Francisco: Spinsters/Aunt Lute.

Bhabha, Homi (1992). "The World and the Home." *Social Text* 10.2-3: 141–53.

Braidotti, Rosi (1994). *Nomadic Subjects: Embodiment and Sexual Difference in Contemporary Feminist Theory*. New York: Columbia University Press.

Cox, Oliver C. (1959). *Caste, Class and Race*. New York: Monthly Review.

Daly, Mary (1985). *Beyond God the Father: Toward a Philosophy of Women's Liberation*. Boston: Beacon.

Deleuze, Gilles and Felix Guattari (1986). *Kafka: Towards a Minor Literature*. Minneapolis: University of Minnesota Press.

Katrak, Ketu H. (1991). "Colonialism, Imperialism, and Imagined Homes." In *The Columbia History of the American Novel*, ed. Emory Elliott. New York: Columbia University Press.

Lamming, George (1991). *In the Castle of my Skin*. Ann Arbor, MI: University of Michigan.

Lorde, Audre (1995). "A Litany for Survival." In idem, *The Black Unicorn: Poems*. New York and London: W.W. Norton.

Lugones, Maria (1990). "Playfulness, 'World'-Traveling, and Loving Perception." In *Haciendo Caras/Making Face, Making Soul*, ed. Gloria Anzaldua. San Francisco: Aunt Lute.

Lugones, Maria (1991). "On the Logic of Pluralist Feminism." In *Feminist Ethics*, ed. Claudia Card. Lawrence: University Press of Kansas.

Memmi, Albert (1967). *The Colonizer and the Colonized*. Boston, MA: Beacon.

Phillipson, Robert (1992). *Linguistic Imperialism*. Oxford: Oxford University Press.

Pieris, Aloysius (1980). "Towards an Asian Theology of Liberation: Some Religio-Cultural Guidelines." In *Asia's Struggle for Full Humanity*, ed. Virginia Fabella. Maryknoll, NY: Orbis.

Radhakrishnan, R. (1994). "Is the Ethnic 'Authentic' in the Diaspora?" In *The State of Asian America: Activism and Resistance in the 1990s*, ed. Karin Aguilar-San Juan. Boston: South End.

Radhakrishnan, R. (1996). *Diasporic Mediations: Between Home and Location*. Minneapolis: University of Minnesota Press.

Rich, Adrienne (1986). *Blood, Bread and Poetry: Selected Prose, 1979–1985*. New York: Norton.

Roman, Leslie G. (1993). "White is a Color!: White Defensiveness, Postmodernism, and Anti-racist Pedagogy." In *Race, Identity and Representation in Education*, ed. Cameron McCarthy and Warren Crichlow. New York and London: Routledge.

Said, Edward (1978). *Orientalism*. New York: Vintage.

Said, Edward (1990). "Reflection on Exile." In *Out There: Marginalization and Contemporary Cultures*, ed. Russell Ferguson, et al. Cambridge, MA: MIT Press.

Song, C. S. (1986). *Theology from the Womb of Asia*. Maryknoll, NY: Orbis.

Spivak, Gayatri C. (1988). "French Feminism in an International Frame." In idem, *In Other Worlds: Essays in Cultural Politics*. New York: Routledge.

Spivak, Gayatri C. (1990). *The Post-Colonial Critic: Interviews, Strategies, Dialogues*. New York and London: Routledge.

Spivak, Gayatri C. (1991). "Neocolonialism and the Secret Agent of Knowledge." *Oxford Literary Review* 13: 220–51.

Woodhull, Winifred (1993). "Exile." *Yale French Studies* 82.1: 7–24.

8 Re-covering, Re-membering and Re-conciling the History of "Comfort Women"

Hisako Kinukawa

Creating Alternative History

1. Trial of Japanese Military Sexual Slavery

The Women's International War Crimes Tribunal 2000, the people's tribunal, finally opened in Tokyo on December 7, 2000, and lasted for only five days. It was the outcome of rigorous efforts by the members of Violence Against Women in War Network (VAWW-NET) Japan, the International Advisory Committee, and Asian women's groups and human rights organizations, supported by many non-government organizations (NGOs) throughout the world. Thousands of women and men of Japan, as well as people representing thirty different countries, packed the hall every day and watched the process of the court with great expectation and moral support.

The main purpose of the tribunal was to pass verdicts on the perpetrators of war crimes against women committed by the Japanese imperial government and military power during the Asia-Pacific War (1931–1945). The War, needless to say, accompanied colonizing Asian countries, which implied that women of the colonized countries were free to be used and thrown away as if they were commodities.

At the tribunal, aptly named the Trial of Japanese Military Sexual Slavery, were 64 "comfort women" survivors from nine countries: East Timor, Indonesia, Japan, Malaysia, the Netherlands, North and South Korea (jointly), the People's Republic of China, the Philippines, and Taiwan. Listening to their witnessing stories was the most important part of the tribunal.

Most of the "comfort women" were 16–20 years old at the time of their abduction. They were forced to receive 10 to 50 soldiers per day. Under tight military surveillance, they rarely succeeded in escaping from the "comfort stations" to which they were drafted without their knowledge. If they tried to escape or resist against what was expected of them, they were tortured and even killed. Physical abuse and harassment were daily routines.

Barely ten years ago several Asian women begun to break almost five decades of painful silence, daring to speak out about their heinous experiences in the unrecoverable time of their youth which had been kept hidden deep in the bottom of their hearts. At the end of the war, they were abandoned like dust by the military. Many committed suicide and many did not go back to their home towns as they were afraid they would be rejected by their own families and societies. Confucian teaching taught them that it was shameful to be physically polluted. Until recently, most of these women were consigned to a life of isolation, poverty and relentless suffering, both physically and mentally. There was no time for them to be free from the trauma of their horrendous experiences.

Their voices were gathered one by one with support from many women and men in Korea, Japan and throughout Asia. Finally, the action swelled into one big wave to demand a full apology and legal responsibilities including compensation for atrocities executed during the War. In the past, nine women from South Korea, forty-six women from the Philippines, one Korean woman resident in Japan and two women from the Netherlands filed their suits at the Tokyo District Court, and four women from South Korea filed theirs at the Shimonoseki Branch of Yamaguchi District Court. But the courts failed to fully acknowledge the legal responsibility of the government, and also, in some cases, rejected even to acknowledge that the women were victimized. It was another heart-breaking experience to see the Tokyo District Public Prosecutor's Office refuse to receive the letter of accusation brought by a group of Korean women survivors in 1994.

The Japanese government repeatedly maintained that reparations have already been paid through bilateral peace treaties between Japan and each country. Therefore no individual reparation to any non-Japanese national, including ones from colonized countries who had to become Japanese soldiers, was ever paid out (see Ogoshi and Shimizu 2000 and Barstow 2000 for steps leading up to the tribunal).

Here are some witnesses given at the tribunal, which cannot be heard without acute pain and tears (see McDonald et al. 2002: #2).

I was given a Japanese name, Masako, which was written on the name plate of the door. Japanese soldiers lined up in front of the door waiting for their turn. I want Japan to ask for forgiveness. I ask the Japanese government to apologize and redress us. – Yuan Zhulin, China

Justice abandoned us. I could only cry when I was coerced to follow Japanese soldiers. I seek for justice. – Maxim Ragala dela Cruz and others, Philippines

Most of the survivors are now in their 80s and are aware that their days on earth are numbered. This is one of the reasons they began raising their voices in public. The terms "comfort women" and "comfort stations," coined by the Japanese imperial military and popularly used, conceal the atrocity and the magnitude of what was done to the women. The phrases should be "sexual slaves" and "rape centers," rightly stated by Korean women (in the indictment).

Their courage inspired hundreds more survivors throughout the Asia-Pacific region to speak out. Together, they have awakened the world to the horror of the Japanese military's institutionalization of rape, sexual slavery, trafficking, torture and other forms of sexual violence inflicted upon an estimated minimum of 200,000 girls and women (McDonald et al. 2002: #1).

The tribunal had several objectives:

1. To prosecute Emperor Hirohito, high-ranking officers in the military, and the government of Japan so that the vicious cycle of impunity would end, though all the individuals, including Emperor Hirohito, who were prosecuted are now dead.
2. The process is necessary so that these women's dignity and human rights might be restored.
3. That the government of Japan might realize its responsibility to apologize and compensate the victims.
4. The ultimate aim was to prevent war itself and violence against women.

2. Being Touched and Disturbed

The first time I had the shocking opportunity to listen to first-hand testimonies by survivors was at the International Public Hearing held in Tokyo in 1992. Since then, I have been working as a member of the NCC Women's Committee, YWCA and Japan Woman's Christian Temperance Union, which are the main Christian bodies seeking a solution to the issue. It is always suffocating to sit in the hall listening to their experiences. It was even more so for the survivors who dared to re-member, re-tell and re-experience the atrocities done to their bodies and minds. Some survivors passed out after or during their testimonies. Jan Ruff-O'Herne, a Dutch woman, gave her testimony amid other Asian women; this was her first time to come out and tell the story. She was born in Indonesia, a colony of her mother country, Holland, and she was taken to a slavery centre for two months. The only way she could keep her dignity was by clinging to the Christian faith her mother had taught her. Because of her faith, she dared to tell the soldiers who raped her that it was against her will to be there. She said in the witness box,

> But there was one thing that they could never take away from me. This was my faith and my love for God. It was my most precious possession and nobody, nobody could take that away from me. It was my deep faith in God that helped me survive all that I suffered at the brutal, savage hands of the Japanese. I have forgiven the Japanese for what they did to me, but I can never forget.

I was deeply touched by her testimony and was obliged to participate in activities that demand our government to acknowledge its guilt, apologize, and compensate these women. Her story was distinctive in the way she expressed her Christian faith which sustained her during moments of despair. As far as I heard, there was no reference to faith in other women's stories.

These women were the victims of the imperial military power under the colonizing policy of Japan, but it must be carefully noted that they were sexually enslaved because they were women. We must not overlook that the crime was gender specific and it was legitimized and systematized by the state.

3. Seeking Justice

None of those accused by Tribunal 2000 faced charges at the International Military Tribunal for the Far East (the original Tokyo Tribunal), which was held between April 1946 and November 1948. Very little attention was paid then to cases of sexual slavery and other crimes involving sexual violence against women, despite the fact that there was clear evidence of such crimes.

The Tokyo Tribunal 2000 chose to apply the then applicable law, adjudge the accused, and accept as established the relevant legal and factual findings of the original Tokyo Tribunal. Its power lay in its capacity to examine the evidence and develop an enduring historical record, with the hope and expectation that such atrocities will never happen again, especially the historic tendency to trivialize, excuse, marginalize and obfuscate crimes against women, particularly sexual crimes (McDonald et al. 2002: ## 4–6).

4. Gender Bias and Impunity

After the Second World War, Japan signed a number of treaties, but women, either as individuals or as a group, did not have an equal voice or status to men at the time of the conclusion of the Peace Treaties. As a result, the issues of military sexual slavery and rape were not addressed. Gender negligence or indifference in international peace processes may have contributed to the continuing culture of impunity for crimes perpetrated against women in armed conflicts in Asia and other parts of the world (McDonald et al. 2002: ##29–30).

At the end of the Tribunal 2000, the four judges – Gabrielle Kirk McDonald (USA, presiding), Carmen Argibay (UK), Christine Chinkin (Argentina) and Willy Mutunga (Kenya) – produced a hefty document entitled *Summary of Findings of Women's International War Crimes Tribunal 2000 for the Trial of Japanese Military Sexual Slavery in the matter of the Prosecutors and the Peoples of the Asia-Pacific Region v. Emperor Hirohito et al. and the Government of Japan*. Number 33 in the document states:

> Successive governments of Japan have continually violated their duty to acknowledge Japan's wrong doing, even until this day. The prosecutors and many of the survivor witnesses underscored the demand for a

meaningful apology – that is, an apology based on full acknowledgement of the wrongdoing and clear acceptance of legal responsibility. We find, however, that the official Japanese position has moved first from the destruction of incriminating documents, to silence, to blatantly false denials of military involvement, to a partial "apology" which does not comport with international obligation. The state of Japan's deliberate resistance to fully acknowledge its wrongdoing has perpetuated the shame and silence, inflicting indescribable pain upon the survivors and depriving them of the possibility of living in peace (McDonald et al. 2002: #33).

The final judgment by the above four judges was announced nearly a year later on December 4, 2001, in Hague. Emperor Hirohito and nine individuals were sentenced as guilty. As for the Japanese government, it says Japan has violated treaty obligations, including the 1907 Hague Convention Respecting the Laws and Customs of War on Land, the 1921 International Convention for the Suppression of the Traffic in Women and Children, and the 1930 ILO Convention Concerning Forced Labor. It has also violated norms of customary international law, including those prescribed in the 1907 Hague Convention and 1926 Slavery Convention. Upon these, the government is sentenced responsible for its continual failure of the obligation to impeach the criminals and redress the damage caused by Japanese military sexual slavery practices (VAWW-NET-Japan News 2001, 20 December, p. 3).

The representative of VAWW-NET-Japan, Yayori Matsui, said at the Hague meeting, "The Women's International War Crimes Tribunal 2000 showed that women have power not only to re-write history but also to create a new history" (VAWW-NET-Japan News 2000, 20 December, p. 4). I believe the miraculous success of the court could not happen without the earnest desire of women of the victimizing country to respond to the voices of the victimized women and to be responsible for their guilt. It must also be highlighted that this was possible because there were powerful and tenacious efforts and work by women of the victimized countries as well as by women engaged in pursuing this gender-specific issue of the war.

The atrocity that women experience because "we are women" is inseparable from the subordinate relationships women are forced to have with men in our daily life. Such a mind-set is commonly found in the worldwide pattern of gender stereotyping that continues to be pervasive today. The extreme forms of depersonalization of soldiers seen in their behaviours of sexual atrocity are a consequence of gender discrimination, elevated by the abnormal circumstances of wars and conflicts. The question, then, is what will lead us towards transformation?

When the sentence was announced at the end of the Tokyo Tribunal 2000 by the chief judge McDonald, all the survivors burst into an emotional explosion, expressing their joy and relief with tears and cries, which was followed by stepping up to the stage and sharing their happiness with the judges. Seeing their faces and actions, the whole audience gave an extended standing ovation. We could see from their expressions that the survivors felt their dignity as human beings regained and assured.

Our present task is to keep pressing the government to carry out its obligation to the victims: disclose the truth, acknowledge it, record it, express full apology, compensate the victims, teach children the history, and so forth.

Towards our Next Generation

One of the main obligations of the Japanese government in response to the Tribunal 2000 is to teach the history of the "comfort women's" issue to the next generation. References to the issue appeared in school textbooks in 1996, but since then, a backlash reaction has been gaining more power. There are currently several textbooks that devote only a few words to the issue.

In relation to this concern, one of the leading thinkers on the issue, Tetsuya Takahashi, raised a significant question. He argues that re-membering the "shameful history" and continually feeling ashamed of having such history as ours is very important. The re-membering may lead us to a new horizon that shows us a possibility of new ethical and political commitments. Having heard the voices raised by the women, we need to realize how serious our obligation is and how shameful it is that we know too little about the incident. Then we may begin to ask why it is that we feel so ashamed (Iwasaki 1997: 86–90).

His suggestion is especially significant in the sense that the voices we have heard are from the women who were completely ignored as "other" in the history and whose voices have been so long suppressed. The voices are witness to another history which relates experiences that should never have happened. In order to let their history become the true history, we are called to listen intently to and accept what they tell us. Facing up to the reality with them implies our acceptance of their call for sharing their pain and the loss of human dignity.

I agree with Takahashi when he says the call is an invitation to us to create new relationships with them (Sukimoto 1997: 28–32). The invitation implies our wilful commitment to struggle with them for their liberation and recovery of wholeness as human beings. Only then may we go beyond the question of whether their stories are true or not. The question of veracity has often been asked by scholars, as memories of the "comfort women" are old and from a time when they were young. We may conclude that listening and re-membering has in its core the energy to engender our critical attitude towards the officially acknowledged history. We see then in the officially acknowledged history the residue of imperial and colonial mind-set, from which we want to be liberated.

The stories of these women prove how the reality made invisible by the hegemony of historians may become visible if we change perspectives and if we shift the paradigm in recording history. They also ask us critically to see the "official" history that has been written by those on the side of power. They awaken our blinded minds towards more stories told by the invisible, yet hidden, participants in those stories.

As if responding to this, a new joint women's project of re-writing a history book for the next generation has emerged. Two international groups in Japan and South Korea (*Association for Research on the Impact of War and Military Bases on Women's Rights in Japan* and the *Korean Council for Women Drafted for Sexual Slavery by Japan*) agreed to cooperate on writing a new history book to be used in schools. The project began in 2002 and completed in October 2005 with the publication of a textbook in both Korean and Japanese (Japan/Korea working committee 2005). Acknowledging that the history books we inherit have been interpreted and written with male-centred, power-oriented and patriarchal mind-sets, the project intends to re-discover the past through the eyes of women, the victimized and marginalized in society. The colonial dominion of Japan in Korea, the subordination of women, war crimes and Japan's responsibility, the Emperor system, the problems in the teaching of history at school, and so forth, were re-searched from a gender perspective. The two teams searched documents and stories which had been hidden and forgotten so that we may bring the unknown to light. The history book is mainly concerned with the modern age and written in relation to the rest of the world. Scholars in history, sociology, philosophy, cultural anthropology, religion, as well as civil activists, participated in the project. The diverse perspectives of both countries reconstructed and reinterpreted the history. The results of the research were shared with the research done by partners in other countries to keep perspectives relational and interactive. The guidelines leading the research and writing are (1) peacemaking, (2) seeking human rights, and (3) advocating justice for those with less power. The first symposium was held in Seoul on October 4–6, 2001, and the second in Seoul in March 2002 and a third in Japan in June 2002 (Shimizu 2001; Okoshi 2001). More than sixty women from Korea and Japan participated in writing parts of the book.

What Edward Said remarked after the incident of September 11, 2001 is true if he agrees that education means to reveal reality from diverse phases of history: "In the long run, education is the most important. Through education, we can teach children not accusation or hostility, but co-living, curiosity, concern, multi-identity, etc., though it is a long process of continuous struggles" (Said 2001). Without struggling, we will again lose our sight.

Theological Reflection

1. Prosecution of Crimes against Humanity

We may easily say from what we have observed and analysed so far that

> In times of wars and conflicts, women's bodies become part of the territory of the battle. Women are seen as the property of the men of the

opposing side and thus, physical and especially sexual abuse is a way of both intimidating women as citizens and insulting the "manhood" of the men of their nation or community (*Public Hearing on Crimes Against Women* 2000: 2).

Ruth Seifert describes such a situation as "the ultimate symbolic humiliation of the male enemy" (Seifert 1993: 21). However, atrocities experienced only by women are inseparably connected with the subordinate relationships women are made to have with men. Women are considered to be one of the weapons, a part of the spoils of war, or a way for soldiers to take out their frustrations. Therefore, the women in Asian countries were doubly colonized, first by the invasive power, the Japanese Imperial Army in this case, and by the male power of men from their own countries.

Regrettably, this is still a commonly found and worldwide pattern of gender stereotyping that continues to be pervasive even today. From a feminist point of view, the extreme forms of depersonalization evidenced in the soldiers' behaviours of sexual atrocity are a consequence of sexism, racism and nationalism. We should never give credit to such a claim that those behaviours are inevitable in the abnormal circumstances of war and conflict. The fact that the world did not condemn such violence as a crime for so long implies that the vicious cycle of impunity is alive and well.

We can therefore see why the "comfort women's" issues have never been on the agenda of any court related to the Asia-Pacific War. Women have never been involved in decision-making about when to begin wars and when to end them. It is ironic to see soldiers who were commissioned to destroy the lives of their enemy, and who were themselves ready to sacrifice their lives for the sake of their Emperor, at the same time seek comfort for themselves and apparently did not feel any contradiction in doing so thus killing any emotion which would make their actions seem wrong.

This explains why the Women's Tribunal adopted the principle of *jus cogens*: some cases were excused from immunity or the statute of limitations. Neither the Japanese government nor the allied powers of the war thought the sexually related violence and crimes were worthy or significant matters to be judged before the courts.

We need to dig up more voices and stories of marginalized women and men that have been hidden behind the "official" history, since the history we have was written by a few elite men and governmental officials. As Geneviève Jacques says, "It is a burning question within nearly every country where impunity has been granted to people whose hold on power has made them virtually untouchable under the law" (Jacques 2000: 10). All the more if the crimes relate to sexual abuse and rape. Nevertheless, we need to exercise our right to know the truth and engage in listening to the forgotten voices so that we may take a step forward in restoring true reconciliation as well as a more truthful history.

In another geographic context, it is important to note that some significant progress has been made in the last decade towards recognizing and prosecuting crimes of sexual violence in the International Criminal Tribunals for the former Yugoslavia (1993) and Rwanda (1994). There, rape was recognized as an independent charge and as a crime against humanity for the first time in history. In this respect, the Tokyo Tribunal 2000 is another step towards ending the vicious cycle of impunity and reversing the total disregard of bodily integrity and personal dignity, and the very humanity of women.

As another remarkable event of history, we should keep our eyes on the International Criminal Court, whose statute was finally adopted in Rome in 1998. It is to be a permanent tribunal for justice on war crimes, crimes against humanity, and genocide. The statute makes it clear that crimes committed in the past will not be covered by its jurisdiction, but there is great hope that the vicious cycle of impunity will be cut down when the Court is fully established. Furthermore, it is great news that the members of the International Women's Caucus worked very hard and succeeded in making the statute the first international legally binding document specifying rape, sexual slavery, forced prostitution, forced pregnancy, forced sterilization and other forms of sexual violations as crimes against humanity.

This new wave proves that the prosecution of individuals, including Emperor Hirohito, is what we cannot avoid if we want to seek justice and peace with the "comfort women" and their countries. At the same time, we should re-member that the court is not enough to achieve peace or guarantee justice, even though it is inseparable from seeking justice and peace.

In order for the "comfort women" to recover their dignity as human beings, a healing process must be carefully provided. Since it is impossible for them to return to their pre-violated state, whatever help they might need must be given. It is necessary to acknowledge them as victimized survivors of crime and to liberate them from putting blame on themselves and from the trauma they have carried for so long. Not only they, but the whole world, needs to acknowledge that what happened to them should never have happened, and further to assure them that such atrocities will never happen again. The tribunal can be the fundamental witness to the symbolic break with the past. The healing process must be given to them through supplying safe space and time.

Unfortunately, the Japanese government has constantly denied its responsibility. If it is to seek reconciliation in this issue, it needs to formally express an apology for the crime and redress each individual. Such action will be a minimal symbolic reparation to compensate what was lost since it is impossible to restore to the victims what they wish to retrieve: their youth, their lost life, and their happy family life. The political and legal measures are the least that might be done as a part of the healing process of social relationships between human beings (cf. Kimura 2000: 25–33). Only after these measures are executed will Japan as a nation at last be allowed to implore reconciliation from the women and Asian countries because reconciliation is granted only when the victimized are able to forgive the victimizer.

2. Reconciliation

For Christian churches, justice, as long as it is sought only in legal terms, does not mean reconciliation. Legal and political measures are the basis from which new steps towards reconciliation can be initiated, and reconciliation is our final aim. Reconciliation has more to do with spirituality than a particular strategy, according to Robert J. Schreiter (Schreiter 1998: 16; cf. Jacques 2000: 43).

Mercy Amba Oduyoye writes, "Reconciliation happens when we come to a common mind after a period of alienation and hostility" (Oduyoye 1999: 18–21) quoting Jesus' advice in Matthew 5:21-24.

> You have heard that it was said to those of ancient times, "You shall not murder"; and "whoever murders shall be liable to judgment." But I say to you... So when you are offering your gift at the altar, if you remember that your brother or sister has something against you, leave your gift there before the altar and go; first be reconciled to your brother or sister, and then come and offer your gift.

These words teach us that any violence, whose most extreme expression is "war," is defined as murder or a rebellion against the integrity of God's creation. God creates each individual as equal (Gen. 1:27; Gal. 3:28) in the image and likeness of God, and therefore there is no right for anyone to ignore, alienate, discriminate, subjugate, violate, victimize, assault, colonize or kill others. Jesus puts reconciliation as the highest priority. The most important and urgent question to be asked is how we can come to the place where we can say we have a common mind.

The biased concept of sexuality, which we have seen in the case of the "comfort women," is interrelated with an irresponsible understanding of human rights. When human rights are neglected, a society shows its immaturity in its understanding of justice. Even justice sought judicially and legally must be linked with individual rights and dignity that make it possible for one to live as a human subject. Justice is lost when the life of a person is despised and made worthless. Justice is lost when a person is abused, raped or enslaved (cf. Kinukawa 2001). Then we have difficulty in having a common state of mind.

There is no war that can be executed under the name of "just" cause. It is the most extreme form of murder committed by human arrogance. When we ignore the dignity of life as divinely given, we may easily fall into the vicious cycle of violence.

Oduyoye further says, "reconciliation is about positive change, a change for the better, a change that enhances shalom, alafia, fullness of life" (Oduyoye 1999: 19). In order to gain positive change, we need to seek for forgiveness that may only be granted by the victimized. Geneviève Jacques defines reconciliation as "a movement, a process of restoring broken relationships and beyond that, of re-creating right relationships between individuals and peoples" (Jacques 2000: 43). As long as the Japanese government refuses to acknowledge its guilt and stays away from fulfilling its responsibility, any proposal of reconciliation will be unacceptable to the victimized in Asian countries. Where is our hope of getting reconciliation then?

> It is the cry of victims for the restoration of their humanity that restores the humanity of the victimizer, calls the wrong doer to repent and the wronged to forgive. In this human act of recognition of sin, repentance, confession, and call for forgiveness, we see the Divine initiative (Oduyoye 1999: 20).

If we understand history to be the reality in which the life of human beings is affirmed and sustained by God, then that history is not ours, but God's and of God's whole creation. Therefore, history is ideally to be the grounds or foundation on which human beings can rely as God's safe space of reign and interaction with us. In such circumstances, what should we choose to devote ourselves to, other than seeking justice, valuing human rights, and making our highest efforts to keep peace with each other? This task is an urgent matter for churches to bear because the administration of the laws does not bring reconciliation automatically. It may be there that we see God's initiative and thus the churches are called to act as the instruments of God (so Oduyoye). By committing ourselves to the task, and in the process of struggling together for that purpose, we may experience God's reign as present and real.

So that we may become close to this theological reality, we need to re-member the past, embrace it, and seek ways of reconciliation. Repentance is also a religious concept, though it is said that "repentance has become an essential component of the spirit of the age" (Moreau Defarges, cited in Jacques 2000: 48). Repentance is not easy because it opens up the most inner part of the mind, dismantles what was done and expresses the wrongness. Repentance is not easy because it cannot happen without transformation.

Churches are invited to be the spiritual and moral accompaniment of the transformation and push the process so that all are re-integrated into humane relationships in true reconciliation.

As long as we devote ourselves to standing firm against the government, until it admits its injustice, we are not far from true liberation. When we see legal justice effected, we may see our apocalyptic hope coming closer to its realization. There is still a long way to go, but we cannot quit working, asking and creating alternative history with a vision of reconciled human community that centres around the wholeness of its members. The vision is derived from the concept of God's shalom as well as the hope that God is working with us.

> Maturity is, in the last analysis, the capacity to transform, and to bring forth new life. Transformation is the continuous process by which human beings exercise choice, change reality, and find meaning (Readon 1996: 97).

Works Cited

Barstow, Anne Llewellyn (2000). "The United Nations' Role in Defining War Crimes." In *War's Dirty Secret: Rape, Prostitution, and Other Crimes Against Women*, ed. Anne Llewellyn Barstow, 234–43. Cleveland, OH: Pilgrim.

Iwasaki, Minoru (1997). "Basis to Criticize the Desire to Dig 'Stories of the People'." *Sekai* 640 (October): 86–90 [in Japanese].

Jacques, Geneviève (2000). *Beyond Impunity: An Ecumenical Approach to Truth, Justice and Reconciliation.* Geneva: WCC.

Japan/Korea working committee (2005). *Japan/Korea Modern History from Gender Perspectives.* Tokyo: Nashinoki-Sha.

Kimura, Kouichi (2000). "Toward Theology of War-Crime Prosecution beyond War-Crime Confession." *Fukuin to Sekai* (December): 25–33 [in Japanese].

Kinukawa, Hisako (2001). "Justice, Gender, and Human Rights." Keynote speech at the annual meeting of the International Association of Methodist-Related Schools, Colleges and Universities held at Belfast, Northern Ireland on July 17, 2001.

McDonald, Gabrielle Kirk, Carmen Argibay, Christine Chinkin and Willy Mutunga (2002). *Summary of Findings of Women's International War Crimes Tribunal 2000 for the Trial of Japanese Military Sexual Slavery in the matter of the Prosecutors and the Peoples of the Asia-Pacific Region v. Emperor Hirohito et al. and the Government of Japan.*

Oduyoye, Mercy Amba (1999). "Costly Reconciliation: Reconciliation is Costly." *World Day of Prayer International Committee Meeting Report: In Christ, Global Partners in Reconciliation*, 18–21. New York: World Day of Prayer International Committee.

Ogoshi, Aiko and Kiyoko Shimizu (2000). "Japanese Women who Stand with Comfort Women." In *War's Dirty Secret: Rape, Prostitution, and*

Other Crimes Against Women, ed. Anne Llewellyn Barstow, 26–37. Cleveland, OH: Pilgrim.

Okoshi, Aiko (2001). "Report on the First Japan-Korea Symposium on the Collaborative Project of Re-writing History Book." *Newsletter of Association for Research on the Impacts of War and Military Bases on Women's Human Rights* 10 (November): 1–4 [in Japanese].

Public Hearing on Crimes Against Women in Recent Wars and Conflicts: Compilation of Testimonies. New York: Women's Caucus for Gender Justice, 2000.

Readon, Betty A. (1996). *Sexism and the War System.* New York: Syracuse University Press.

Said, Edward (2001). "Interview." *Asahi News Paper* (December 31, 2001) [in Japanese].

Schreiter, Robert J. (1998). *The Ministry of Reconciliation: Spirituality and Strategies.* Maryknoll, NY: Orbis.

Seifert, Ruth (1993). "War and Rape." In *Women in the Peace Process: The Difference Women Make. Case Postale 28.* Geneva: The Women's International League for Peace and Freedom International Secretariat.

Shimizu, Kiyoko (2001). "Responding to the Success and the Spirit of 'Women's International War Crimes Tribunal 2000'." *Newsletter of Association for Research on the Impacts of War and Military Bases on Women's Human Rights* 10 (November): 1–4 [in Japanese].

Sukimoto, Yumiko (1997). "Nationalism and the 'Comfort Women's' Issue." *The Report on Japan's War Responsibility* 18 (Winter 1997): 28–32 [in Japanese].

9   Integration and Disintegration of Tamils in London Diaspora

Albert W. Jebanesan

It is estimated that over 35,000 Sri Lankan Tamils have settled in London since 1983 as a consequence of the prolonged armed conflict between the government military forces and the Tamil militants in the North and East Provinces of Sri Lanka (see Grenier 1997). Tamil-speaking Sri Lankans entered the UK as asylum seekers and live in Greater London in small groups. In my first visits to the Tamil clusters of London, I spent many hours wandering around, reliving the familiar in Sri Lanka and becoming familiar with the unfamiliar in London. I visited temples, grocery shops, restaurants, and many other enterprises run by Sri Lankan Tamils in London.

Tamil refugees try to replicate, as far as possible, the pattern of life in their original villages; being far from home, I felt at home, but not quite at home: "Even Tamil food in London does not taste the same as in Sri Lanka, does it?" a friend once exclaimed. "No, it doesn't," I replied. An old man complained to me: "Back in Sri Lanka I was a village leader, people respected me and my relatives even venerated me in my own house; but here they find me a nuisance." A middle-aged man complained that children and women here enjoy more freedom than is becoming to them. University students stated that they abandoned their Hindu religious practices as soon as they arrived in London, and that "Hinduism has lost its impact here." I realized that Tamils were adopting new sets of values and mores, and that even the most sacrosanct "blood solidarity" had lost its compelling force. By the end of my stay among Tamil refugees I felt that I was a Tamil among my own people, and the refugees considered me as one of them. And then I felt the painful necessity of leaving London in order to write about "them" as if they were strangers to me.

It seems easier to define "cultural disintegration" than the positive "cultural integration": we discover the meaning and value of health when we are sick; we discover the meaning and value of integration of a culture when that culture crumbles and is on its way to disintegration. Scholars of culture have attempted hundreds of ways to describe complete configurations of cultures as integral units composed of multiple traits. If there was disagreement about the concept of culture, one can expect as much disagreement in the concept of "cultural integration." Sri Lankan Tamil life has been open to alien influences for over two millennia now, yet it preserves its observable stability and identity. It enjoys a high degree of elasticity, so typical of Hinduism. Tamils are certainly a people with a culture, but they are also a people without a nation and without a State. If the State is the most formidable creation of a culture (the peculiar mode of distributing and administering the power that comes from and reposes on the people), then Tamils have not been the organizers and administrators of their own power for at least the last five hundred years. Sri Lankan Tamils sometimes do not seem to be sure whether they are a prolongation of India's Tamil Nadu or the periphery of a Sinhala nation. So in this respect we cannot claim that Sri Lankan Tamil culture is "tightly integrated"; it is too complex for that. Now, Tamils violently uprooted from their village soil and transplanted into an alien soil find it difficult to accommodate, to survive and live meaningfully in London.

With their exodus to London, Tamil culture collapsed in the minds of the refugees and gave place to British culture, which Tamil refugees did not understand. Many Tamil refugees saw themselves as respected and civilized members in Sri Lanka, but not so in London. For example, Ganesh was a teacher and people saw him as a leader in Sri Lankan society. But in London, he works, like so many others, in a grocery store. Ganesh said that he was "lost" in London.

The Tamil refugees are not ignorant. Yet they expressed their inability to cope with the demands of a different lifestyle and culture that has been forced upon them. The entire concept of lifestyle has changed very quickly, even before they realized that they needed to change themselves. The contrast between the "out here" and the "back there" is dramatized by the case of Ratnam, the practising solicitor in London who felt that "Peace of mind is not here." "Peace of mind" or "inner peace" summarizes the feeling of happiness resulting from a good relationship with house, temple, and community of family, relatives and acquaintances who "mingled with us like one family." The opposite of this kind of peace is not war, but restlessness and insecurity.

Most of the interviewees said that leaving their homeland created new unexpected problems in their daily lives. All of them were explicit and concordant when they spoke of their integrated life in Sri Lanka. However, their explanations and viewpoints grew in drama till they reached peaks of intensity in their words and gestures and silences, when they referred to "problems" that forced them to leave Sri Lanka. They were willing to give lengthy explanations about their past life and present life in London, but they said very few things about their transition from Sri Lanka to London. The explanation about their diaspora occurred when the interviewees discussed specific news from Sri Lanka in their get-togethers, not so much in our individual interviews.

Tamil refugees bring with them the memories of horror, and they know that it was precisely because of the horrors of the war that they were accepted in this new society and given temporary shelter, protection and acceptance. However, is London a shelter for them? They are protected against racial riots in Sri Lanka, but are they equally protected against the racial prejudice of the white population in London? Are they truly accepted, as they are, in their new motherland? They feel that they have no safe shelter, no sure protection and no full acceptance in London. This feeling provokes in them a reaction of frustration, anger and self-estrangement in different degrees; often the interviewees told me that they are aware that their presence is not wanted, that they do not belong, that they feel despised and rejected, and that at any moment they can be deported.

The hostile graffiti found on walls, public toilets, elevators and so forth ordering them "Pakis go home!" plus remarks in the most offensive abusive language often thrown against the Tamil presence in London are like spit on their faces. There is little they can do, because "even the police look elsewhere when Tamil refugees are being victimized."[1] Besides, the British government's continually changing asylum policies, introducing tighter measures against accepting any more refugees and deporting a good number of them are frequent discussions in newspapers and television channels. For the British population, the refugees are a problem to them, not just people who came with a problem. If they accept the mass media alarmist programmes uncritically, British people will come to the conclusion that their government tried to solve the problems of the refugees and, by doing so, introduced a new problem to the white British population. Ratnam, a solicitor, reflected with sadness: "Now they want a united Europe; perhaps they mean a united white Europe." Tamil refugees just do not understand. After the horror and trauma of disintegration of their houses and families and villages and their corresponding exile, now they need permission from the authorities to live, to exist, and to be. If they do not have that permanent or temporary permission, they are no longer refugees and have become transients and even fugitives from the law of the country that offered them "refuge." Mere survival has become their main goal in life. To achieve this goal, all means are legitimate in their view, but even so they live a "dog's life," without meaning or purpose.

I met Hanna at a Tamil Church. I introduced myself and asked: "How's life in London?" Her abrupt reply opened for me a new avenue of exploration on the life of Sri Lankan refugees in Western countries:

> **Albert**: How is your life in London?
> **Hanna**: What is this life? This life is a dog's life!

That is not the answer one expects to a greeting. I could detect bitterness, anger and frustration in her words and in her eyes. Her reply made me feel that she had some grievances about her life in London; later I realized that she has only a small circle to move among. So I persisted:

> **Albert**: Why do you say that your life here is a dog's life?
> **Hanna**: There is no peace in my mind here ... No peace, happiness, culture, climate or language available for me in this country... As a Hindu I spent time in temples, and wanted to do the same here; but that was denied to me.... I was busy in Sri Lanka, and had friends and relatives; even that has been refused to me here.

In this verbal outburst (which I have shortened), we immediately identify several "generative words"[2] often repeated with equal emotion by other interviewees: peace, happiness, culture, climate, language, family, friends, relatives, etc. Her life in Sri Lanka was filled with life; in London her life seems filled with a void, an empty life, the life of a dog.[3] It is true that, comparatively speaking, her standard of living in London was higher than in Sri Lanka, but her quality of life was at the lowest ebb. According to her, standard of living has to do with material things; the quality of her life has to do with things spiritual; they may not be in opposition, but they must not be confused, either.

For some time I wondered whether I could find a single term or expression that could encompass the many terms Tamil refugees use to express the disillusion and misery they found in London, after their dreams and initial sense of relief and elation at reaching their intended destination subsided. Finally I thought that the striking Tamil expression "a dog's life," repeated often in conversations, and with the utmost intensity by two women, Hanna and Saro, was a graphic and accurate expression. In my search for an equally appropriate and more respectable term for translating dog's life I came across the word *anomie* (see Orru 1987; Passas 1989; Clinard 1964; Passas and Agnew 1997). They live a dog's life, a life in a prolonged state of *anomie*.

In a flash thousands of Sri Lankan Tamils have made the transition from a pre-industrial society to a post-industrial mass culture, from a pre-modern environment of rural landscapes to a post-modern environment of skyscrapers. This transition shattered their ancestral family life. They feel suffocated and dizzy in the trepidating rhythm of the modern Western city. The word *anomie* was introduced into the vocabulary of the social sciences by the French sociologist Emile Durkheim in his study on suicide (Durkheim 1951: 241–76; see also Durkheim 1984), precisely to explain what happened to the peasant masses that had to abandon their ancestral rural villages and settle in the newly grown industrial cities during the industrial revolution in Europe. The term comes from the Greek *nomos*[4] with a negative prefix: *a-nomos*, "absence of nomos." The *nomos* of a society is the ordering principle that gives the network of relations among its members a commonly accepted meaning and purpose for living together. This *nomos* can be shattered by catastrophic events that severely unbalance the coherence of the social whole; when this happens, that society falls into a state of *anomie* or *anomic* state (Levin 1988: 300). One of the most dissolving forces that destroy the *nomos* of a society is the state of war, and very specially the state of prolonged civil war of one segment of society against the other. We could safely say that the general state of civil strife of a society is equivalent to a general state of *anomie* in that society. In a general context, the American sociologist Levin expressed this very clearly:

> Suddenly the rules that regulated daily life are thrown into turmoil, and the resulting confusion about how to act is called *anomie*, or the state of normlessness (Levin 1988: 300).

The values and norms by which people had ruled their lives are no longer viable for life, and people have to devise schemes to cope with the new unexpected reality. One instance of this dramatic and sudden transition from a normal state (state with norms) to an abnormal state (state without norms) was the industrial revolution in the West, which is the background of Durkheim's study. Another instance was the conquest, subjugation and domination of the South (Africa), the East (Asia and the Pacific) and the Far-West (America) by Western powers (Spain, Portugal, England, Holland). Another instance of destruction of the familiar ordered universe and the fall into a state of no-norms is the present prolonged ethnic war in Sri Lanka (see Horowitz 1985 concerning ethnic conflict).

The destruction of the cosmos and descent into chaos in societies has some effects on individuals and groups; they fall into a state of shock, numbness and utter confusion, which Durkheim calls *anomie*. According to him, one of the possible consequences of the state of *anomie* is the suicide of many, a refusal to cope with the new reality in desperation. This fact, discovered by Durkheim in the nineteenth century, is now widely recognized as one acute problem of planetary dimensions. The total transformation and even destruction of traditional cultural patterns may be the result of the sudden introduction of modern technology, with the corresponding destructive results of a state of *anomie* in entire cultures.[5] Levin gave a most comprehensive definition of *anomie* in these terms:

> A condition of social ambiguity in which an individual does not know how to act because the rules of behaviour (norms) are either unclear, entirely absent, or in some way unsatisfactory (Levin 1988: 299; see also Merton 1968).

In this definition the ambiguity of not knowing the norms for relating with others is not only a transitory state of *anomie*, but also a prolonged state, or even a permanent condition. Levin applies his definition to "individuals"; in this study, we extend it also to groups. This prolonged state of confusion prevalent among Sri Lankan refugees is understandable only when we let the refugees express their own living conditions in exile. Let me explore this with the stories of Sathivel.

A Wandering Tamil

The case of Sathivel, though not typical of all, is symptomatic of the restlessness and insecurity of life in exile, a life not worth living, "a dog's life." I offer here an abridged narrative in Sathivel's own words.

From Sri Lanka to Sweden

Soon after the Elephant Pass battle in 1992, I left Sri Lanka and went to Sweden. The Swedish authorities rejected my asylum application in June 1993. There were several cases of Sri Lankans rejected along with mine. They kept us in a detention camp till the deportation orders were completed. We were terribly frightened and sad about the decision. We knew that once we got back, we would end up in one of the Colombo prisons. The Sri Lankan government was arresting all the Tamils, deported from other countries, for interrogation. I had heard that many of them have ended up in indefinite imprisonment… So all the inmates in the detention camp got together and made a big protest to the Swedish authorities. One held in custody poured petrol on his body and set fire to himself… That did not solve the problem…

From Sweden to Norway

I managed to escape to Norway in April 1994. I changed my name because I was afraid that the Norwegian authorities would discover my identity. If they found out that I had lived in Sweden for some time, they would immediately send me back to Sweden… My new life in Norway did not last long. The Norwegian authorities too rejected my case.

The Stigma of Criminality

I was arrested and taken to the police station. I was told that they were going to deport me to Sri Lanka. They also informed me that changing one's name is a criminal offence. Also I was informed that they had found out my previous stay in Sweden as a refugee... They also said that I would be locked in the remand prison until a decision was made on my case. They took photographs of me and ordered me to wear the prisoners' uniform.

"From the depths I cry out to you, Lord" (Ps. 130:1)

I was wearing a small cross in my neck chain. I had to remove that as well. I was not a Christian at that time, but I had the feeling that the cross was a protective symbol, and I had been wearing it for a long time. Though I was a Hindu, belief in Jesus was not a problem. The Hindu religion is like an ocean that can absorb different religions in its fold. I have seen this practice [of cross wearing] among many Hindus... Even the LTTE cadres wear crosses in their neck chain. They may not be Christians, but they believe that the cross is a protective symbol. While in Norway, I had also been to a few Christian churches to pray, and the cross in my neck chain was a meaningful symbol to me... Just before removing the chain, I held the cross and said, *Jesus! If you are a living God, save me from this trouble. I do not want to go back to Sri Lanka!* I just prayed without knowing any implications about Christian prayer.

Utter Degradation

I was kept in a prison cell without light. Every hour someone would come and, with the help of torchlight, looked at what I was doing. The prison cell looked like an animal cage in the zoo. I started crying and prayed throughout the night. At about 3 o'clock in the morning a policeman came, opened the prison cell, and told me: "We have decided not to deport you to Sri Lanka. We have received a message from the Swedish authorities saying that they are willing to accept you." It was a shock to me! Several others who had been arrested along with me had been deported or were still in prison; but I was taken out of the prison cell. I could not believe my eyes! ... The Norwegian police took me and handed me to the Swedish police. The Swedish police asked me why I had left the country. I told them that I did not want to go back to Sri Lanka. They said that they could not make decisions about me now, and that I had to wait until a decision was made. Just imagine my situation! I thought that I was going to be accepted by the Swedish government [as I had been told in Norway] but now they were telling me that I had to wait for a decision. Later I was sent to the refugee camp where I had stayed earlier... I lived in Sweden for six months, but in Sweden refugees are not allowed to work.

Escape to Denmark and Deportation Back to Sweden

Again I left Sweden and this time went to Denmark to find employment. I was arrested by the Danish police and handed over to the Swedish authorities...

Dislodged to Sri Lanka

In the meantime in Sri Lanka there was a peace accord between the government and the LTTE in the later part of 1994. At this point the Swedish government deported many of us to Sri Lanka. I reached Sri Lanka in June 1995...

From Sri Lanka to London

I started again on my carpentry work in Jaffna... At that time the security forces killed my sister-in-law's husband... My brother-in-law, who was living in the United Kingdom, was willing to pay money to a travel agent and sponsor my sister-in-law's eldest son to travel to the UK. They wrote to me asking for my assistance to bring him to Colombo, because of the security risks involved for a young person to travel alone. So the two of us travelled to Colombo and, while we were there, my brother-in-law told me over the phone that he was willing to give me a loan to pay the travel agent... Although I had no plans to go abroad again, I decided to give it another try. I agreed to the proposal, paid the money and landed in the UK on the 22nd of November 1996...

The life of Sathivel started once again in a new country, the UK. Sathivel testified: "I felt that I was hounded down like an animal." The condition of being a fugitive rather than refugee forced him to separate from the whole of reality; the supreme value of his life was just to keep alive, a refugee from Sri Lanka and a fugitive from three Scandinavian countries. The experience of restlessness, fear and rejection developed in him an acute anomic condition. Yet he is trying to break this situation by taking the new emerging reality courageously upon himself and enter the new social order to save what was left of his human dignity. Sathivel's Tamil culture and religion did not provide any meaning or purpose to his life; and the present British culture in which he found himself immersed also could not give any meaningful content to his life. He was tossed by invisible and incomprehensible political powers from one country to another, from one location to another, with nothing to look forward to, except the preservation of his life; and even this preservation was in the hands of others. Sathivel is one of many who were forced to exist with new ideas and values, but his social points of reference were elsewhere. Once you have been uprooted from the soil, any location is good enough if it provides a shelter for survival in the storm. Yet the traumatic fact is that many refugees experience a mere biological existence, not a social or culturally meaningful existence. They do not know where they are heading until they reach a specific Western country and precariously settle in it. I found many stories of Tamil refugees stranded in remote countries, in Eastern Europe and in Africa, without even knowing the name of the country of their arrival, in their attempt to reach the Western European countries. Satha told the following story, with jovial humour:

> About five years ago, one day I received a telephone call from a shop owner in my village. Someone from Heathrow Airport telephoned, asking me to come to identify this man and release him from the immigration authorities. I went there immediately and helped him. As soon as we came out of the airport he said, "Brother! Your father told me that you were living in London; how come that you are in Germany?" I said, "This is London." Then the fellow said, "My agent told me that they were taking me to Germany. I do not know what happened; it looks like they have put me on a London flight."

This experience of living an unstable and transient existence impels them to improvise norms and rules that are valid "for the time being." This experience reveals and reinforces an acute anomic condition that, among other ill effects, separates the refugee from the whole surrounding reality. Durkheim very appropriately said (Durkheim 1951: 248):

> All man's pleasure in acting, moving and exerting himself implies the sense that his efforts are not in vain and that by walking he has advanced. However, one does not advance when one walks toward no goal, or – which is the same thing – when his goal is infinity.

In Sri Lanka, Tamils lived in community and had communion and communication with each other. They lose all of that in London. Their exodus and diaspora are so recent and have come so suddenly. In order to live in a community, the refugees have to create it; and to create their own community they have to devise certain methods of socialization in London. They seek and find shelter and security, and the possibility of intimacy with friends and acquaintances, in the creation of their own ghettos to replicate the social atmosphere of the village as far as it is possible, with necessary adaptations. They create their own community, and from the bosom of their newly created (not newly found) community they look at their surroundings with a sense of self-affirmation. The transition to a metropolitan environment has shattered the ancestral family life. They wanted to experience an extended family system, but that was not available to them.

The need to belong (see Trawick 1990: 89–116) is, no doubt, a universal biological, social and spiritual requirement for us if we are going to be fully human; without belonging somewhere we are spiritually, socially and even biologically dead. Erich Fromm, a psychoanalyst and philosopher, expressed the need to be related and to belong in these vigorous terms (Fromm 1969: 36):

> Unless he belonged somewhere, unless his life had some meaning and direction, he would feel like a particle of dust and overcome by his individual insignificance. He would not be able to relate himself to any system which would give meaning and direction to his life, he would be filled with doubt, and this doubt eventually would paralyse his ability to act – that is, to live.

For many Sri Lankans, their entire worldview was shattered in London. When they came to London they had grandiose dreams about their future. They thought that all their problems could be solved once they reached their dreamland. But they soon found that they were not accepted and that they belonged nowhere, neither here nor there; without belonging they felt cut off, amputated from reality.

Erich Fromm stressed that humans have a compelling need to belong to a community, "to avoid aloneness" (Fromm 1969: 34). This is indeed the universal human predicament, because humans are by nature social animals. This is more acutely felt by pre-industrial cultures, such as Tamil village culture. Without adequate companionship, Tamils feel that they do not exist, or if they exist, their existence is empty. The emotional feelings Tamil refugees shared about their lonely life in London corresponds closely to Fromm's analysis on solitude and belonging. Erich Fromm concludes his analysis:

> To feel completely alone and isolated leads to mental disintegration just as physical starvation leads to death. This relatedness to others is not identical with physical contact. An individual can be physically alone for many years and yet he may be related to ideas, values, or at least social patterns that give him a feeling of communion and "belonging." On the other hand, he may live among people and yet be overcome by an utter feeling of isolation, the outcome of which, if it transcends a certain limit, is the state of insanity, which schizophrenic disturbances represent. This lack of relatedness to values, symbols, patterns, we may call moral aloneness and state that moral aloneness is as intolerable as the physical aloneness, or rather that physical aloneness becomes unbearable only if it implies also moral aloneness (Fromm 1969: 34).

We do not need to expand on the disintegrating effect of suddenly being thrown out into the unfamiliar and unknown, and the consequent feeling of solitude and void. It is no surprise to hear the expression "I feel lonely" even from the lips of people who have managed to bring their families or have formed a family in their new location.[6] Aimless wandering is a life without a destination and a goal, without a "Promised Land." If there is no goal, there is no direction; if there is no direction, there is no purpose; and if there is no purpose, then life has no meaning. Tamils often lament the lack of meaning and purpose of life. In extreme cases, as in the case of Singam, there is serious consideration of and attempt at suicide.

We are comfortable and feel happy when we are able to interpret our reality within and without ourselves. In order to interpret reality, and find meaning in life, we need an interpretative key adequate to open the doors of perception to that reality. Sri Lankan refugees have a different key. Social reality is a system of strange signs and symbols (Ganesh). In order to understand reality we have to "signify" it, to enclose it within a code or system of signs, thus giving it "meaning" or "signification." But Tamil refugees come with a different constellation of symbolic meanings and meaningful symbols (Satha). They cannot understand one culture in terms of the other; social reality is strange to them, and also they are strangers to it; they may learn and discover the meaning of reality, but they can impose meanings on the symbolic reality that they see. For example, a pub in Britain may be a symbol of conviviality. But for Suriya, it may be a symbol and source of "drunkenness," the beginning of "vandalism," "sex without commitment" and other evils. Instead of decoding that particular symbol, Suriya imposes his own meaning on the symbol.

When the conventional inherited symbols are no longer bearers of meaning, as Levin points out, when there are no clear guidelines in the social system to control people and give their lives meaning and purpose, people will fall into confusion (anomic confusion). They will tend to reduce their world, and escape from the larger world they no longer understand or accept. Social interaction and inter-personal communication require a commonly accepted system of signs and symbols with their respective meanings. The lack of correspondence between signs and reality results in the sense of meaninglessness (Blauner 1964: 22). When the old familiar signs have lost their significance and no new signs have developed to explain the new reality, we have the phenomenon of *anomie*; one of its most common expressions is meaning-less-ness.

Meaninglessness produces an acute sense of anxiety or anguish which Paul Tillich understands as "due to the loss of a spiritual centre" (Tillich 1952: 48). In describing the nature of humans Paul Tillich analyses three types of anxieties as responses to the threat of non-being, namely (Tillich 1952: 65):

a.   Anxiety of fate and death (ontological anxiety);
b.   Anxiety of emptiness and meaninglessness (spiritual anxiety);
c.   Anxiety of guilt and condemnation (moral anxiety).

Durkheim's sociological concept of *anomie* and Tillich's theological and philosophical concept of anxiety are closely related. When we turn to the oral testimonies of the Tamil refugees in London, we obtain interesting data in this respect. First, in the interviews there is no single mention of sin, forgiveness, reconciliation or other terms associated with guilt and salvation. An important corollary is that Tillich's "anxiety of guilt and condemnation" seems to play a shadowy secondary role in the Tamil perception of their human condition in exile. Second, it is surprising, in interviewing people familiar with death and dying, to find no explicit mention of fear of death; consequently, Tillich's "anxiety of fate and death" also plays a secondary role in the lives of Tamil refugees. Third, the frequent mention of "lack of meaning" accompanied with "no-peace of mind" and with "no-purpose" is so overwhelming that Tillich's "anxiety of emptiness and meaninglessness" acquires an importance of high proportions. Tillich writes (Tillich 1952: 47):

> We use the term meaninglessness for the absolute threat of non-being to spiritual self-affirmation, and the term emptiness for the relative threat to it. They are no more identical than are the threat of death and fate. But in the background of emptiness lies meaninglessness as death lies in the background of the vicissitudes of fate.

Tillich then proceeds with his characteristic theological terminology of "ultimate concern" (Tillich 1952: 47):

> The anxiety of meaninglessness is anxiety about the loss of an ultimate concern, of a meaning, which gives meaning to all meanings. This anxiety is aroused by the loss of a spiritual centre, of an answer, however symbolic or indirect, to the question of the meaning of existence.

Then Tillich continues with the definition of "anxiety of emptiness" which resembles our concept of self-alienation so characteristic of Tamil refugees in London (Tillich 1952: 47–48):

> The anxiety of emptiness is aroused by the threat of non-being to the special contents of the spiritual life. A belief breaks down through external events or inner processes: one is cut off from creative participation in a sphere of culture, one feels frustrated about something which one had passionately affirmed, or is driven from devotion to one object of devotion to another and again to another, because the meaning of each of them vanishes and the creative Eros is transformed into indifference or aversion. Everything is tried and nothing satisfies.

The contents of tradition, however excellent, however loved once, lost their power to give content today. And present culture is even less able to provide the content.

I can find no more accurate description of the human predicament of Tamil refugees in London, especially among teachers, students and professionals, who constitute the majority. Tillich continues with relentless clarity and accuracy (Tillich 1952: 48):

> Anxiously one turns away from all concrete contents and looks for an ultimate meaning, only to discover that it was precisely the loss of a spiritual centre, which took away the meaning from the special contents of the spiritual life. But a spiritual centre cannot be produced intentionally, and the attempt to produce it only produces deeper anxiety. The anxiety of emptiness drives us to the abyss of meaninglessness.

Tamil refugees in London feel acutely that they have lost that centre to which they can turn to orient their lives at all moments, and which irradiates meaning to life in all situations. The family is lost, the village is lost, the temple is lost; can they recreate these three pillars in London? That would be a goal to achieve that could give direction, purpose and meaning to their lives. At least many of them have attempted the task.

We may safely conclude that Sri Lankan Tamil refugees are not only the children of war, but they also carry a war within themselves in their lives in exile. They find no inner peace; only turmoil and conflict between opposing cultures, interests, values and codes of conduct. There is also a conflict between their expectations of the new reality on the one hand, and the expectations of the new social reality around them on the other: a conflict between promise and fulfilment, between expectations and achievements. In a situation of war, all norms and values are denied or temporarily suspended. After overcoming the shock of disintegration of their families and villages, they find themselves in London in a state of "culture shock." When prolonged without a satisfactory solution, this state has led to their anomic state. In London, the centre of their lives has been shifted or totally removed (see Durkheim 1951: 252). They have tried to create that centre but it is impossible to do so individually, hence the longing and quest for community. In their new social and cultural environment they feel lonely, confused, living aimless lives, under the spell of "anomic terror."

Works Cited

Blauner, Robert (1964). *Alienation and Freedom: The Factory Worker and his Industry*. Chicago: University of Chicago Press.

Clinard, Marshall Barron (ed.) (1964). *Anomie and Deviant Behaviour: A Discussion and Critique*. New York: Free Press of Glencoe.

Durkheim, Emile (1951). *Suicide: A Study in Sociology*. Trans. J. A. Spaulding. New York: Free Press.

Durkheim, Emile (1984). *The Division of Labour in Society*. Trans. W. D. Halls. Basingstoke: Macmillan.

Edwards, Paul (eds.) (1967). *The Encyclopedia of Philosophy (Vol. Six)*. London: Macmillan and Free Press.

Freire, Paulo (1968). *Pedagogy of the Oppressed*. New York: Seabury.

Freire, Paulo and Macedo, Donaldo (1987). *Literacy: Reading the Word and the World*. South Hadly, MA: Bergin & Garvey.

Fromm, Erich (1969 [1941]). *Escape from Freedom*. New York: Avon.

Grenier, Matthew (1997). *Protection Denied: Sri Lankan Tamils, the Home Office and the Forgotten Civil War*. London: The Refugee Council.

Holmes, W. Robert. (1980). *Jaffna (Sri Lanka)*. The Christian Institute for the Study of Religion and Society of Jaffna College.

Horowitz, Donald L. (1985). *Ethnic Groups in Conflict*. London: University of California Press.

Levin, William C. (1988 [1984]). *Sociological Ideas – Concepts and Applications*. Belmont, CA: Wadsworth.

Mead, Margaret (ed.) (1961). *Cultural Patterns and Technical Change*. New York: New American Library of World Literature.

Merton, Robert K. (1968 [1949]). *Social Theory and Social Structure*. 2nd ed. New York: Free Press.

Orru, Marco (1987). *Anomie: History and Meanings*. Boston and London: Allen & Unwin.

Passas, Nikos (1989). *Merton's Theory of Anomie and Deviance: An Elaboration*. Unpublished PhD thesis, University of Edinburgh.

Passas, Nikos and Rogert Agnew (eds.) (1997). *The Future of Anomie Theory*. Boston: Northwestern University Press.

Tillich, Paul (1952). *The Courage to be*. New Haven and London: Yale University Press.

Tournier, Paul (1962). *Escape from Loneliness*. Philadelphia: Westminster.

Trawick, Margaret (1990). *Notes on Love in a Tamil Family*. California: University of California Press.

Winger, Michael (1992). *By What Law?: The Meaning of Nomos in the Letters of Paul*. Georgia: Scholars.

10 Newsprint Theology: Bible in the Context of HIV and AIDS

Gerald O. West

Introduction

At the end of the Contextual Bible Study workshops we are surrounded by newsprints. The walls of our meeting place are full of sheets of newsprint. Almost everything said in the workshop has been written on newsprint, and the newsprint has been stuck onto every available surface. We are surrounded by our words.

Even those who cannot read can point to what they said on the newsprint. They have watched in amazement what they have said being recorded. They know exactly where on which sheet of newsprint it has been written, for they are not used to having their words listened to, let alone being written down. This is why our Bible studies begin with a general question, like "What is the text about?" This question indicates the intention of the Bible study to include everyone and, indeed, to begin with the participants. Responses are slow initially, for the participants cannot quite believe that we really do want to know what they think the text is about. But when one or two of the bolder participants offer up a tentative comment, and we warmly receive it and write it down in front of them on the flip-chart, there is an almost ceaseless rush to contribute. Nothing is rejected, everything said is acknowledged by the facilitator, who affirms the contribution and encourages the speaker to elaborate. The "scribe" who records the process struggles to keep up as more hands shoot up, waiting their turn to speak, telling what they think the text is about.

The Bible study continues with other questions, which are discussed in small groups and reported back to the plenary. What we as the facilitators of the Bible study workshop say – the vast majority of which is in the form of questions – is written, for example, in black.

What the participants say is written, for example, in red. At the end of the workshop the predominant colour, by far, on the newsprint is red. The red on the newsprint is an articulation of the local, embodied theologies of the participants. It is not fully fledged theology; it is inchoate and incipient. It is the raw material of theology, what might be called "newsprint theology."

Human dignity, even the most damaged and denigrated of humanity, is a powerful force for the formation of discourses of resistance, survival and life. Those who are used to inhabiting the underside of our world may not articulate these discourses, even to themselves, but they do embody them. And such is the drive for human dignity that its embodied forms will find ways to express themselves in the public realm, albeit in disguised forms. In contexts such as South Africa the discourses of the marginalized have an explicitly theological dimension, for all of our reality remains intensely religious. Their embodied discourses might reasonably be expected to take on theological forms.

This essay reflects on three components of these discourses, namely, the human demand for dignity, the embodied forms that discourses of dignity construct, and the role of the socially engaged biblical scholar and theologian in collaborating with the marginalized to articulate and own their embodied discourses.

The Reality of Dignity

In his insightful study of domination and resistance, James Scott allocates an important role to human dignity. Indeed, Scott privileges "the issues of dignity and autonomy, which have typically been seen as secondary to material exploitation" (Scott 1990: xi). All forms of asymmetrical power, but particularly systems like slavery, serfdom, the caste system, colonialism, racism, global capitalism, and patriarchy "routinely generate ... practices and rituals of denigration, insult, and assaults on the body" (Scott 1990: xi–xii). While systemic exploitation may appear to be impersonal, Scott makes the point that domination always tends to take on an individualized form: "one pays homage as a person, is punished as a person, is slighted as a person." Domination, Scott continues, without which no systematic exploitative appropriation takes place, "particularly leaves its mark on personal dignity – if not on the physical person" (Scott 1990: 112–13).

There are, of course, many conditions of domination and subordination, and we must be careful not to generalize and conflate them. Indeed, to identify a particular form of domination and subordination is to learn the particular shape of a particular person's indignity (Scott 1990: 113). For it is these experienced indignities that form the bridge between a person's condition and his or her consciousness (Scott 1990: 113). Scott goes on to argue, "Dignity is at once a very private and very public attribute. One can experience an indignity at the hands of another despite the fact that no one else sees or hears about it." "What is reasonably clear, however," says Scott, "is that any indignity is compounded greatly when it is inflicted in public" (Scott 1990: 113), especially if it is inflicted in front of those "before whom one's dignity, one's standing as a person, is most important because it forms the social source for one's sense of self-esteem" (Scott 1990: 114). Significantly, this is also the social circle in which such a one can at least partially re-establish his or her dignity, for those in this social sector usually "have a shared interest in jointly creating a discourse of dignity, of negation, and of justice." "They have, in addition," Scott continues, "a shared interest in concealing a social site apart from domination where such a hidden transcript can be elaborated in comparative safety" (Scott 1990: 114).

The damage that domination does to human dignity stems from the suppression of part of the self that dominating power requires of its subordinates. "Discretion in the face of power requires that a part of the 'self' that would reply or strike back must lie low." Fortunately, it is this self "that finds expression in the safer realm of the hidden transcript," where it is a form of "self-disclosure that power relations normally exclude from the official transcript" (Scott 1990: 115).

This assertion of dignity, however, "involves far more than the creation of a social realm in which the missing part of the subordinate's replies and assertions may be safely spoken." For, "Inasmuch as the major historical forms of domination have presented themselves in the form of a metaphysics, a religion, a worldview, they have provoked the development of more or less equally elaborate replies in the hidden transcript" (Scott 1990: 115). The Christianity practised by African slaves in America when they were not under the surveillance of their masters and madams is a good example. As Scott argues, African-American slave Christianity negated the style and content of white American Christianity (Scott 1990: 116–17; see also Hopkins 2000). Similarly, among untouchables in India "there is persuasive evidence that the Hindu doctrines that would legitimize caste-domination are negated, reinterpreted, or ignored" (Scott 1990: 117; see also Staal 1963). While particular practices of resistance "may mitigate the daily patterns of material appropriation, and the gestures of negation in the hidden transcript may answer daily insults to dignity," "at the level of systematic social doctrine, subordinate groups confront elaborate ideologies that justify inequality, bondage, monarchy, caste, and so on" (Scott 1990: 117–18). Resistance at this level, Scott argues, "requires a more elaborate riposte, one that goes beyond fragmentary practices of resistance." Resistance to ideological domination "requires a counterideology" (Scott 1990: 118) or, in religious terms, a counter theology.

The Body as a Site

In analysing the kind of social sites which marginalized sectors have constructed and in which the hidden transcript develops, Scott makes an important point, for my purposes, when he says that "the hidden transcript has no reality as pure thought; it exists only to the extent it is practiced, articulated, enacted, and disseminated within these offstage sites" (Scott 1990: 119). It therefore follows that the hidden transcript – an assertion of human dignity – will be least inhibited when two conditions are fulfilled:

> first, when it is voiced in a sequestered social site where the control, surveillance, and repression of the dominant are least able to reach, and second, when this sequestered social milieu is composed entirely of close confidants who share similar experiences of domination. The initial condition is what allows subordinates to talk freely at all, while the second ensures that they have, in their common subordination, something to talk about (Scott 1990: 120).

With respect to the first condition, the development of "a thick and resilient hidden transcript is favored by the existence of social and cultural barriers between dominant elites and subordinates" (Scott 1990: 132). With respect to the second condition, the social cohesion of a particular hidden transcript "would seem to rest on both the homogeneity of the domination and the social cohesion of the victims themselves" (Scott 1990: 134). But what if, as Scott notes in passing, subordinates are entirely "atomized," isolated? In such cases, Scott goes on to acknowledge, "there is no lens through which a critical, collective account can be focussed" (Scott 1990: 134). This does not mean, however, that dignity does not demand a response in the case of these severely alienated sectors; it does. But instead of participating in the practices of others like them in safe sequestered sites, they have little option but to embody their response to power.

It is here that I must leave Scott's analysis, focusing as it does on the hidden transcript as "a political dialogue with power in the public transcript" (Scott 1990: 138). His focus requires a level of elaboration of the hidden transcript among close confidants in particular subaltern controlled and patrolled sites that is not always apparent among those marginalized with whom I work (see West 2003a), though they remain, fortunately, a minority.

Though not the focus of his analysis, Scott does offer some reflection on the conditions that mitigate against the formation of a thick and resilient hidden transcript. The first of these conditions is when "there is a strong probability that a good many subordinates will eventually come to occupy positions of power" (Scott 1990: 82). In such cases there is "a strong incentive ... to legitimate patterns of domination." "It encourages," Scott continues, "patience and emulation, and, not least, it promises revenge of a kind, even if it must be exercised on someone other than the original target of resentment." Indeed, if this supposition is correct, "it would help to explain why so many ... systems of domination seem to have such durability" (Scott 1990: 82). The solidarity necessary for the formation and articulation of the hidden transcript is seriously diminished in such situations.

As I will argue more fully below, the post-liberation context of South Africa since 1994 may in both general and specific terms be a factor in the exacerbation and destabilization of subordinate solidarity. In general, our liberation has certainly offered many historical subordinates the prospect of social, economic and/or political power. Many previously oppressed individuals and sectors now have a stake in the system. South Africa's economic system has shifted, Sampie Terreblanche argues, "over the past 30 years from one of colonial and racial capitalism to a neo-liberal, first-world, capitalist enclave that is disengaging itself from a large part of the black labour force" (Terreblanche 2002: 422). This transformation, though it has "coincided with the introduction of a system of representative democracy which is effectively controlled by a black, predominantly African, elite," still exhibits "an ominous systemic character":

> In the new politico-economic system, individual members of the upper classes (comprising one third of the population) profit handsomely from mainstream economic activity, while the mainly black lumpenproletariat (comprising 50 per cent of the population) is increasingly pauperised. Ironically, individual members of the black and white upper class in the new system seem as unconcerned about its dysfunctionality as individual members of the white elite were about that of the old. The common denominator between the old and the new systems is that part of society was/is systemically and undeservedly enriched, while the majority of the population were/are systemically and undeservedly impoverished – in the old system through *systemic exploitation*, and in the new system through *systemic neglect* (Terreblanche 2002: 423; original emphasis).

More specifically, and this is my focus, fractures in the solidarity forged in resistance to apartheid have arisen not only around our macro-economic policies, but also around how much emphasis to place on gender justice and the HIV/AIDS pandemic. Our liberation, the last on the African continent, has ushered in calls for an African renaissance and the proclamation of the African millennium, and rightly so. But such discourse makes it difficult to foreground the ambiguity of African culture for women and difficult to admit to a disease that is decimating African peoples. Some have a stake in retaining the dominant systems of patriarchy and HIV/AIDS denial. This is also complicated by a prevalent discourse which links HIV/AIDS to witchcraft (Ashforth 2005: 9–10, 18, 89, 108), for it is extremely difficult to forge a counter-discourse which is perceived to align itself to malign forces.

The second, related (in my analysis), condition Scott identifies that mitigates against the formation of a thick and resilient hidden

transcript is when "subordinates are more or less completely atomized and kept under close observation" (Scott 1990: 83). In such
situations "the social conditions under which a hidden transcript
might be generated among subordinates are eliminated," so that
there is "the total abolition of any social realm of relative discursive
freedom" (Scott 1990: 83). In South Africa the era of HIV/AIDS has
ushered in sustained surveillance, particularly in rural communities,
for those who have declared their HIV-positive status or whose status
has become known through the symptoms of the disease or through
their regular visits to the local clinic for antiretroviral treatment.

In analysing these related conditions the analysis of domination
and resistance by Jean and John Comaroff is particularly helpful.
Adopting a similar position to that of Scott, the Comaroffs also
affirm that the ideology of the dominant is always contested; it
"is always threatened by the vitality that remains in the forms of
life it thwarts" (Comaroff and Comaroff 1991: 25); consequently it
"is always intrinsically unstable, always vulnerable" (Comaroff and
Comaroff 1991: 27). In their analysis, the Comaroffs pay particular
attention to how social knowledge and experience might shift along
the unconscious–conscious continuum. Consciousness, according
to them, is a continuum "whose two extremes are the unseen and
the seen, the submerged and the apprehended, the unrecognized
and the cognized" (Comaroff and Comaroff 1991: 29). So, "the
submerged, the unseen, the unrecognized may under certain conditions be called to awareness," and "things once perceived and
explicitly marked may slip below the level of discourse into the unremarked recesses of the [individual and] collective unconscious"
(Comaroff and Comaroff 1991: 29). Though they may not approve
my addition (in the square bracket above), their analysis of consciousness is, in my view, relevant to both the community and the
individual. Of special relevance to my essay is their identification
of "the most critical domain of all" along the continuum between
the conscious and the unconscious for the analysis of domination
and resistance.

> It is the realm of partial recognition, of inchoate awareness, of ambigu-
> ous perception, and, sometimes, of creative tension; that liminal space
> of human experience in which people discern acts and facts but cannot
> or do not order them into narrative descriptions or even into articulate

conceptions of the world; in which signs and events are observed, but in a hazy, translucent light; in which individuals or groups know that something is happening to them but find it difficult to put their fingers on quite what it is (Comaroff and Comaroff 1991: 29).

It is from this realm, the Comaroffs suggest, "that silent signifiers and unmarked practices may rise to the level of consciousness, of ideological assertion, and become the subject of overt political and social contestation – or from which they may recede into the hegemonic, to languish there unremarked for the time being" (Comaroff and Comaroff 1991: 29). It is also the realm, they continue, "from which emanate the poetics of history, the innovative impulses of the bricoleur and the organic intellectual, the novel imagery called upon to bear the content of symbolic struggles" (Comaroff and Comaroff 1991: 29). This is this "middle ground" that "human beings often seek new ways to test out and give voice to their evolving perceptions of, and dispositions toward, the world" (Comaroff and Comaroff 1991: 30).

This is the realm of embodied theologies. There is something inchoate and incipient (to use James Cochrane's [1999] pregnant phrase) in this realm, in this middle ground; a construct which dignity demands and forges in the deepest recesses of the human being. In conditions where there is a safe sequestered site and considerable social cohesion the experience of domination generates a hidden transcript which is practised, articulated, enacted and disseminated. Under conditions of vigilant surveillance and atomization of the individual or conditions of considerable sectoral dissonance and the collapse of solidarity, the incipient hidden transcript cannot be practised, articulated, enacted and disseminated; but it remains embodied.

At this point in my analysis, as I search for a vocabulary with which to understand our Contextual Bible Study experiences, I turn to the work of Pierre Bourdieu. "The world is comprehensible, immediately endowed with meaning, because," says Pierre Bourdieu, "the body ... has the capacity to be present to what is outside itself, in the world, and to be impressed and durably modified by it," and because the body "has been protractedly (from the beginning) exposed to its regularities" (Bourdieu 2000: 135). Bourdieu goes on immediately to argue that the body,

[h]aving acquired from this exposure a system of dispositions attuned to these regularities, ... is inclined and able to anticipate them practically in behaviours which engage a *corporeal knowledge* that provides a practical comprehension of the world quite different from the intentional act of conscious decoding that is normally designated by the idea of comprehension (Bourdieu 2000: 135; original emphasis).

This is what Bourdieu calls the *habitus* of an embodied social group (Fowler 2000: 4). In brief, the *habitus* is "society written into the body" (Bourdieu 1990: 63):

By *habitus* Bourdieu understands ways of doing and being which social subjects acquire during their socialization. Their *habitus* is not a matter of conscious learning, or of ideological imposition, but is acquired through practice. Bourdieu's sociology rests on an account of lived "practice," and what he terms "the practical sense" – the ability to function effectively within a given social field, an ability which cannot necessarily be articulated as conscious knowledge: "knowing how" rather than "knowing that." *Habitus* names the characteristic dispositions of the social subject. It is indicated in the bearing of the body ("hexis"), and in deeply ingrained habits of behaviour, feeling, thought (Lovell 2000: 27).

As Terry Lovell notes, however, while contemporary feminisms of difference share with Bourdieu's sociology of practice "a common focus upon 'the body'," Bourdieu's embodied social actor lacks the agency which feminists posit for their subjects (Lovell 2000: 27–28). Poststructuralist and postmodernist discourses, says Lovell, "celebrate flexible selves, permeable or semi-permeable boundaries, the journey travesed rather than origins or lasting determinations" (Lovell 2000: 30). However, argues Lovell, "Boudieu's theory, although resolutely non-essentialist and insistent that we are always dealing with 'cultural arbitraries,' nevertheless makes it difficult to understand how one might ever appear, convincingly, to be what one is not," for, she goes on to say, "his account of the acquisition of social identity through practice, *habitus*, emphasizes its corporeal sedimentation" (Lovell 2000: 30). Lovell's question is an important one, for Bourdieu's sociology seems to fly in the face of Scott's.

Lovell acknowledges, as do I, that what is compelling about Bourdieu's position is that it offers "a way of understanding *both* the arbitrary, and therefore contestable, nature of the social, *and* its compelling presence and effectiveness" (Lovell 2000: 31). "Social reality" is both socially constructed and real. But while "Bourdieu's strength lies in his insistence upon the well-nigh permanent sediments and traces which constitute embodied culture, ... he draws attention away from those other areas of social space where the constructedness of social reality may be tacitly acknowledged or exposed" (Lovell 2000: 32). As Lovell notes, for Boudieu the "scope of human freedom ... is not large" (citing Bourdieu and Wacquant 1992: 199; Lovell 2000: 34), and while he recognizes that "there exist dispositions to resist" (citing Bourdieu and Wacquant 1992: 81; Lovell 2000: 34), he insists on the necessity "to examine under what conditions these dispositions are socially constituted, effectively triggered, and rendered politically efficient" (citing Bourdieu and Wacquant 1992: 81; Lovell 2000: 34). This is precisely what I am attempting to do in this essay, and Bourdieu offers a reasonably adequate language with which to make the attempt.

Society writes the dominant (and dominating) theology into the body of believers. It is acquired through their socialization and particular bodies have been protractedly exposed to its regularities. It even compels a set of practices. But, I would argue, social reality does not always (or ever?) produce a unified *habitus*. Bourdieu admits as much in his analysis of the "contradictions and suffering" occasioned by "fathers and mothers who project their desires and compensatory projects on their son, asking the impossible of him." Indeed, he says, "A great many people are *long-term* sufferers from the gap between their accomplishments and the parental expectations they can neither satisfy nor repudiate" (Bourdieu 1999: 508; original emphasis). And it is just "such experiences," Bourdieu goes on to argue, which "tend to produce a habitus divided against itself, in constant negotiation with itself and with its ambivalence, and therefore doomed to a kind of duplication, to a double perception of self, to successive allegiances and multiple identities" (Bourdieu 1999: 511). "This explains," continues Bourdieu (and here he echoes Scott, the Comaroffs, and Cochrane),

> the way that narratives about the most "personal" difficulties, the apparently most strictly subjective tensions and contradictions, frequently articulate the deepest structures of the social world and their contradictions. This is never so obvious as it is for occupants of precarious positions who turn out to be extraordinary "practical analysts": situated at points

where social structures "work," and therefore worked over by the contradictions of these structures, these individuals are constrained, in order
to live or to survive, to practice a kind of self-analysis, which often gives
them access to the objective contradictions which have them in their
grasp, and to the objective structures expressed in and by these contradictions (Bourdieu 1999: 511).

So while most of Bourdieu's work does "not adequately equip practical agents with reflective and critical abilities which would make it
possible to describe how they might initiate … transformative processes, or to understand how they might succeed in enlisting the
cooperation of other agents in transforming social identities and
conditions" (Bohman 1999: 143), the above case shows Bourdieu
in a more nuanced light. Here we have what James Bohman finds
generally lacking in Bourdieu's sociology, namely, "reflective agency, the capacities of socially and culturally situated agents to reflect
upon their social conditions, criticize them, and articulate new
interpretations of them" (Bohman 1999: 145).

Bohman critiques Bourdieu's emphasis on cultural misrecognition, "the sort of mechanism which inhibits deliberation, criticism,
and revision" of one's social reality, for he argues that "there is no
reason to believe that practical and public reasoning cannot detect
at least some of these cultural biases and constraints, and that at
least some reflective agents may be able to convince others that
suppressed forms of expression and alternatives absent from deliberation ought to be seriously considered on their merits" (Bohman
1999: 147). In taking this stance he is close to the kind of position
advocated above by the Comaroffs, where silent signifiers and unmarked practices may rise to the level of reflectiveness and become
the subject of overt political and social contestation. But in making
this argument, Bohman recognizes that "misrecognition and biases
can be built into … public institutions and their practices, especially
if groups do not have free and equal access to epistemic authority
or effective modes of public expression" (Bohman 1999: 147). This
brings us back to those sectors of society I am concentrating on,
namely, those who are severely socially constrained, under sustained
surveillance, and unable to access sites and resources in and with
which to reflect among others like them. This is the situation for
many of those struggling to live with HIV and AIDS.

In the absence of a safe sequestered site and considerable social cohesion, in Scott's terms, or in the absence of access to epistemic authority or effective modes of public expression, in Bohman's terms, Bourdieu, somewhat surprisingly, reminds us of the body/*habitus* divided against itself. But whereas Bourdieu sees such individuals as doomed, I do not, for our experience in Contextual Bible Study is that when such an individual comes together with other such individuals in a safe and sacred site, they are able to negotiate their multiple allegiances, identities and theologies, and to reconstruct them into something transformative.

Delving into this body of contradictions and suffering is to enter that middle ground referred to above, which is characterized by the inchoate and incipient. But this realm, the Comaroffs tell us, "is also the realm from which emanate the poetics of history, the innovative impulses of the bricoleur and the organic intellectual, the novel imagery called upon to bear the content of symbolic struggles" (Comaroff and Comaroff 1991: 29). It is also the realm, Bourdieu admits above, from which practical analysts are able to articulate the deepest structures of the social world and their contradictions. These references to cultural agents, whether bricoleurs and organic intellectuals (Comaroffs), reflective agents (Bohman) or practical analysts (Bourdieu), point to the role that facilitators or animators might play in accessing and articulating the inchoate embodied theologies of ordinary people.

The Role of the Facilitator

The varied yet related analysis put forward by James Scott, Jean and John Comaroff, James Bohman, and Pierre Bourdieu allows for a role for the socially engaged (organic) intellectual, but the role is not as prominent as that assigned to the intellectual by classical Marxism, where the intellectual is much more of an interventionist, who steps in to break "the culture of silence" and free the people from their false-consciousness (Frostin 1988: 10). South African Black Theology recognized this difference with classical Marxism in its work during the 1980s. Both Takatso Mofokeng and Itumeleng Mosala argued that sectors of the black South African oppressed, black youth (Mofokeng 1988: 40) and "the largely illiterate black working class and poor peasantry" (Mosala 1986: 184; 1989: 24), had broken with the dominant biblical hermeneutics of "an ahistorical, interclassist" faith "that transcends social, political, racial, sexual, and economic divisions" (Mosala 1989: 18). They were, in the African American Cornel West's terms, cultural agents, for "[t]hough Marxists have sometimes viewed oppressed people as political or economic agents, they have rarely viewed them as *cultural* agents." "Yet," continues West, "without such a view there can be no adequate conception of the capacity of oppressed people – the capacity to change the world and sustain the change in an emancipatory manner. And without a conception of such capacity, it is impossible to envision, let alone create, a socialist society of freedom and democracy." Somewhat ironically, "It is, in part, the European Enlightenment legacy – the inability to believe in the capacities of oppressed people to create cultural products of value and oppositional groups of value – which stands between contemporary Marxism and oppressed people" (cited in Frostin 1988: 183; West 1984: 17).

South African Black Theology, while indebted to Marxist forms of analysis, particularly in Mosala's work (Mosala 1989), has nevertheless not entirely bought into its claim that religion is the opiate of the people (cited in Frostin 1988: 42; see the comments by Julius Nyerere of Tanzania, Nyerere, 1969: 14). As Frostin shows, while there are a number of similarities between South African Black Theology and classical Marxism (see Frostin 1988: 181–82), there are also significant differences. Central to my argument in this essay is that "the circumstances that condition human thought are defined differently in classical Marxism than in [South African Black] liberation theology, even though both represent a socio-logy of knowledge perspective." Classical Marxism, Frostin argues, is clear that "material production conditions human thought," whereas South African Black Theology emphasizes "the creativity of the oppressed in a way that differs fundamentally from classical Marxism (Frostin 1988: 182–83).

In my analysis, the *organized* poor, working class, and marginal-ized already have their safe sequestered sites in which their dignity is given voice and where a thick and resilient hidden transcript is constructed. As Cochrane adds, incipient theology "is not absent from this base insofar as ordinary Christians reflect upon their faith in the light of their daily experiences, their suffering, their struggle for existence, and their hopes for healing and comprehensive well-being" (Cochrane 1999: 63). "Their reflection may be," Cochrane continues, "and usually is, that of the theologically untrained mind. It may be naive and precritical; it may be unsystematic and scattered; it may draw incongruently on a range of symbols, rituals, narratives, and ideas that express the encounter with the sacred." It may be all these things, but it is there! It does have a voice! And while "the theology present in communities of ordinary Christians may be seen as incipient rather than overtly articulated ... it remains," Cochrane insists, "theology" (Cochrane 1999: 63).

The role of cultural agents in such *organized* contexts is that of the facilitator or animator, one who comes alongside those who are struggling to assert their dignity and its concomitant ideology/theology. Among *unorganized* individuals, the role of the intellectual may appear to be more interventionist, though it remains, I would argue, fundamentally facilitatory. Similarly, among those who have been atomized or kept under constant surveillance, it may appear that their human dignity has been so damaged that a false-consciousness has enveloped them. But, I would argue, this apparent silence is not the silence of consent to hegemony, but the silence of an embodied but yet to be articulated ideology.

I realize that in making this argument I may simply be exhibiting my own identity dilemmas as a white, male South African. For whom am I to intervene in breaking the culture of silence of blacks or women? So instead of naming false-consciousness for what it is, I call it something else, so assigning myself a less problematic role. I am sure there is something to this, and identity politics may play an important role in how we describe what it is we do as socially engaged (organic) intellectuals (Haddad 2000; Maluleke and Nadar 2004; Nadar 2003; West 2003a). Given my analysis, however, I can only accept, as some of my colleagues cited above have argued, that our (or their) role is to "conscientize" those who (appear to) have "internalized" their oppression and who may even (appear to) actively resist emancipatory forms of knowledge (see Giroux 1985, talking about the work of Paulo Freire), if by "conscientize" we mean something like "to move along the continuum towards the conscious," as seems to be advocated by the analysis of the Comaroffs. For I would read the analysis of the Comaroffs as saying that what is unconscious is not absent (or distorted) ideology; it is merely unconscious, but present, ideology. Dignity demands a response to power, even if the *habitus*/body does not quite know what to say or how to say it.

I can accept too that those of us who are not organic intellectuals in socio-economic terms envisaged by Antonio Gramsci (to whom the term is most often attributed) may not have the same role as those who are organic intellectuals in working with the poor, working class, and marginalized. However, with Antonio Gramsci I find the notion of an "organic intellectual" both useful and problematic. It is useful in that it can be used to designate those intellectuals who a particular social group "creates together with itself," who "give it homogeneity and an awareness of its own function," economically, socially and politically (Forgacs 1988: 301). What makes them "organic" intellectuals is precisely what Gramsci asserts, namely, that they *are produced* by a particular social group. A loose use of the term, therefore, in which those who are organic intellectuals within one social group imagine themselves to be organic in another, even similar, social group is deeply problematic (as in Maluleke and Nadar 2004), as Gramsci points out. Intellectuals who have become separated from the social group who created them are in danger of becoming intellectuals who have become autonomous and unconnected to particular political and social forms (Forgacs 1988: 302–303). Indeed, the modern "democratic-bureaucratic system," says Gramsci, has given rise to a host of this kind of unconnected-intellectuals (Forgacs 1988: 307–308).

The African-American womanist biblical scholar, Renita Weems, captures both the danger and the appropriate response when she says that the difference between "reading *on behalf of* previously unheard from communities of readers" and reading "*with* previously unheard from communities of readers ... is all the difference in the world" (Weems 1996: 259). Speaking from her realities as an African-American woman, Weems goes on to offer profound insights into what it means for those who are from among poor and marginalized sectors to read with "one's own" – a commitment "fraught with ambivalence" (Weems 1996: 260). For, in reading with one's own,

> We see how much we remain indebted to members of our commu-
> nities for our insights, our creativity, our subversive strategies, and for
> our passion for our work. More importantly, however, reading *with* them
> means for us who are both scholars and products of these communi-
> ties to confront the ways in which we have been permanently changed
> by our academic training and new class privileges. Returning home and
> reading *with* our ancestors forces us to observe on a personal level the
> way education has altered our relationship to power in the society. We
> are forced to consider then that reading *with* poor and marginalized
> readers, or with any other ordinary reader for that matter, is potentially
> dangerous work. It is dangerous because it exposes scholars – and it ex-
> poses scholarship – to those elements of human interpretation that defy
> scholasticism and forces us to examine the concrete ways in which our
> scholarship and our privileges as scholars rely on the status quo (Weems
> 1996: 260; original emphasis).

For those like me who have not been formed by the social sectors in which I have chosen to work, the dangers are even greater. We have no organic link with or even the memory of the social formations with which we work, and so conscientizing or reading on behalf of "others" is profoundly inappropriate. We need to be invited into these social sites by those who inhabit them and we need to work with them and their organic intellectuals, being partially re-constituted by this work (see West 1995, 2003a).

For those who have survived the sustained theoretical analysis above, I turn now to a less theoretical and more practical account of our role as socially engaged intellectuals in facilitating Bible studies which establish lines of connection between embodied theologies and the Bible.

Contextual Bible Study

Using a Contextual Bible Study method that has developed in the ongoing praxis cycle of action/reflection, my organic intellectual col-
leagues and I in the Ujamaa Centre for Community Development and Research (formerly the Institute for the Study of the Bible & Worker Ministry Project) work with the Bible in a way which

facilitates community and individual transformation (for a summary see West 2000). The Bible study form we follow uses community consciousness questions (which draw directly on the resources and experiences of the community) to frame the Bible study, beginning and ending with these kinds of questions. In between, we use critical consciousness questions (which draw directly on the resources of biblical scholarship) to engage with the biblical text. This middle set of questions attempts to give the biblical text a voice by offering additional resources to ordinary "readers" (whether literate or illiterate) to engage with the biblical text in, first, its literary context, and then, second, in its socio-historical context, before shifting back into community consciousness questions which facilitate an appropriation of the text to the theme the community has identified. In our view, the resources of biblical scholarship, together with the resources a community already has, enable lines of connection to be established between embodied theologies and the Bible (for a fuller discussion see West 2006).

As socially engaged biblical scholars we allow ourselves to be made use of. As South African theologian and activist Albert Nolan has so carefully argued in the context of constructing a workers' theology, the appropriate partnership in constructing local embodied theologies is not that the biblical scholar or theologian "*makes use of* the insights of workers, but that workers *make use of* the expertise and technical knowledge of academics, so that it is, and remains, in fact, a worker's theology" (Nolan 1996: 217; original emphasis). What this means in practice, Nolan continues, is that "we, the trained theologians and clergy, have to learn the skill of being used, of putting our expertise into the hands of the working class as service to them, what Jesus called 'learning to serve rather than to be served'" (Nolan 1996: 217). What the Contextual Bible Study offers is resources to assist in the construction of a safe site, facilitation resources, and the critical resources of biblical scholarship.

If the Bible study site does become a safe one, embodied theologies may be articulated by the community participants and, if what is articulated resonates with the group, owned. Often what is embodied is difficult to articulate, both because it has been suppressed and because it is inchoate. In this way, embodied theologies find their way into the safe Contextual Bible Study site in fragments and in disguised form, waiting for a resonance with and the recognition of others in the group. When this is found, the collective energy in the group becomes focused, as do their collective resources, often leading to a preliminary articulation and ownership of an embodied theology.

This is why we use newsprint to record what is said in the contextual Bible study process, for it provides a record of the emergence of inchoate and incipient embodied theologies. The words and/or pictures on the newsprint (and the dramatizations which are sometimes used in group report-backs) are the raw materials produced by the Contextual Bible Study process.

An HIV/AIDS Bible Study

The Bible study described below was constructed in collaboration with Siyaphila, a community-based organization established as a support group for people who had tested positive for HIV. It was formed in 1997, as a project of the Ujamaa Centre in Pietermaritzburg, South Africa, in response to a vacuum in our South African healthcare system. Bongi Zengele, a staff member of the Ujamaa Centre and a Graduate Assistant doing her Masters degree at the time, led the initiative, working together with another two Ujamaa Centre staff, Mzwandile Nunes and Chris Mbude. Siyaphila is now independent of the Ujamaa Centre, having established its own institutional structures, but we continue to work closely with them, particularly in the area of Contextual Bible Study (for a fuller discussion see West and Zengele 2006).

In our early Contextual Bible Study work with Siyaphila we noted a sustained interest in gospel texts in which Jesus took sides with marginalized sectors against the dominant socio-religious sectors (West 2003b). These texts tapped into their embodied theologies, assisting them to articulate their deep sense that God/Jesus was "on their side," even though their families, the church, and society at large proclaimed otherwise. God and/or the ancestors, they were uniformly told, were punishing them, either for something they had done or that their (deceased) parents or grandparents had done. (A variation, which I will not pursue any further in this essay, for it has not been given any prominence in our work with Siyaphila or other groups with whom we have done HIV/AIDS-related Contextual Bible Study, is that they have been bewitched.)

In discussing this embodied resilience to a positive image of God/Jesus with a colleague in the Ujamaa Centre, Phumzile Zondi-Mabizela, we wondered whether the resolutely positive image of God that black South Africans have, despite the theological depravities of colonialism and apartheid, would endure the constant theological battering that those living with HIV and AIDS received from their families, the church, and society in general. Our discussion prompted me to recall the work of Bob Ekblad and the People's Seminary. In the People's Seminary, a project which works among peasant immigrants from southern Mexico who are drawn to Skagit County (Washington State, USA) by the abundance of seasonal labour harvesting strawberries, raspberries, blueberries, cucumbers, apples and other fruits and vegetables, a similar Bible reading methodology has evolved. Facilitated by Bob Ekblad, a biblical scholar and social activist, Bible study takes place in the local jail, in immigration detention centres, in the crowded apartments and migrant labour camps in which the workers live, and on the premises of the People's Seminary in Burlington. The basic interpretive methodology is similar to that of the Contextual Bible Study process of the Ujamaa Centre, but there is a notable difference with respect to the embodied theologies of our respective constituencies. The migrant workers with whom the People's Seminary mainly works have a negative image of God: "God is seen as a strict, easily angered, punishing judge best kept at a distance to avoid more trouble" (Ekblad 2005: 25). What compounds this view of God is their view of the Bible. "The Bible is viewed as containing the laws by which God and his law-enforcement agents judge the world. The Scriptures are often feared and avoided for the 'bad news' they are expected to contain rather than welcomed as words of comfort" (Ekblad 2001: 3–4). And yet Ekblad's experiences of reading the Bible with those who believe they are damned demonstrate that through a facilitated rereading of the detail of particular texts they too have profound moments of recognition of another Bible and another God (Ekblad 2005).

While the inherent image of God of most South Africans, including those who are members of Siyaphila and the other groups with whom we work around HIV and AIDS, is a positive one, we have begun to wonder if this can be sustained amid the relentless stigmatization and discrimination that those living with HIV and AIDS experience from their families, their churches, and their society. In recent work with one of the Siyaphila support groups which meets in our Ujamaa Centre offices in downtown Pietermaritzburg, Bongi Zengele and I asked the group to reflect on their experience of the Bible prior to joining Siyaphila and since. The dominant metaphor used to describe the experience of most members of the Bible prior to their joining the Siyaphila Bible studies was one of distance. The Bible was there, but far off. Not one of the members portrayed the Bible in a negative manner. *Distance* was the issue, not negativity. Related to this image of distance was the image of place. The Bible was located in particular places, mostly in the church, but also on the shelf at home. In only one instance did the Bible have a place in the life of a participant prior to their membership of Siyaphila. As one person expressed it, the Bible "was opened and closed in church." A related image used was that of *belonging*; the Bible belonged to others. For most, the Bible belonged to the minister/pastor/priest. For some the Bible had some sense of belonging in their homes, usually with a parent or grandparent. But even in these few cases, the Bible belonged predominantly in the hands of the professionals.

Another related image used of the Bible prior to their participation in the Siyaphila support group was that of its relative *silence*. As one member put it, the Bible required a preacher to make it speak. What she wanted to convey in saying this, when probed, was that the Bible was a holy book and could therefore only be made to speak by those whose task it was to do so. As one person put it, it was a book "handled" by others. In fact, this person reported, she had been expressly forbidden to touch the Bible, given that she was HIV-positive! Only holy people should "handle" the Bible. When the Bible did speak to them personally, it was used negatively. As we have already said, there was no sense that the Bible itself was negative, but there was general agreement that the Bible was used in a negative way to speak about people like them, namely, those living with HIV and AIDS.

All of these images had been reversed by their membership of the Siyaphila support group. What was far off had become close; what had no place now had a place; what belonged to others now belonged to them; what had nothing relevant to say now spoke directly to their condition; what could not be touched or made to speak by them was now in their hands and they could make it speak; what had brought judgement, stigma and discrimination now brought healing, hope and life. The Bible was no longer far off. It affected them personally, dealt with daily issues and challenged them. As one person said, it affirmed to her that she was made in the image of God and supported her in her inner struggles. The Bible also belonged in a new way. As one person put it, now that she actually owned a Bible, she was aware of how much the Bible was used selectively in church by the church leadership. She now understood the wider context of the Bible. One of the most startling changes was that the members had come to see that the Bible dealt with real-life issues. The Tamar Bible study (on 2 Sam. 13:1-22) more than any other had contributed to this new perception (West and Zondi-Mabizela 2004; West et al. 2004). They were amazed to discover that things that were happening in their contexts are "in the Bible."

But what of their image of God? Had the generally positive image of God which had sustained millions of black South Africans during colonization and apartheid (Mofokeng 1988: 38) begun to be tarnished by the relentless proclamation that God was punishing them with HIV and AIDS? As I have already mentioned, when given the opportunity in Siyaphila Bible studies to choose their own texts, they tended to choose those texts in which Jesus took a stand with the stigmatized and discriminated against in his society. Such choices seemed to suggest that they were consciously nurturing this image of Jesus (and God?). But what of others who are not as organized or as conscious of the effects of stigma and discrimination on their theological *habitus*?

Learning from their choice of texts, we began to construct Contextual Bible Studies around the image of Jesus/God when we were invited by other communities to do Bible studies on the theme of HIV and AIDS. Drawing on what we had learned from Siyaphila and from my visits to the People's Seminary, we developed a Contextual Bible Study which might have the potential to create

a safe and sacred space to talk about HIV and AIDS and our images
of God.

What follows is the Contextual Bible Study we have used quite
extensively in the past two years:

Plenary
1. Read Mark 3:1-8 together. What do you think the text is
    about?

Plenary report-back and newsprint recording

Small groups
2. What is the Pharisees' image of God?
3. What is the Pharisees' view of synagogue tradition?
4. What is Jesus's image of God?
5. What is Jesus's view of synagogue tradition?

Report-back to plenary, summarized on newsprint

Small groups
6. What image of God does the disabled man have?
7. What view of synagogue tradition does the disabled man
    have?

Report-back to plenary, summarized on newsprint

Small groups
8. What image of God do people living with HIV and AIDS
    have; responses which reside on the many pages of news-
    print piled up in our Ujamaa offices?
9. What view of church tradition do people living with HIV and
    AIDS have?
10. Why was Jesus angry?
11. How should the church respond to people living with HIV
    and AIDS?
12. What will you now do to assist your church to work more
    "positively" with people living with HIV/AIDS?

Report-back to plenary, including newsprint action plan

Here I will not analyse this Contextual Bible Study in any detail
with respect to its process or products (but for another example see

West 2006). I will simply focus briefly on responses over the past two years to question 8. Though not conclusive, there are indications that the image of God is becoming more ambiguous, perhaps even negative. When we first used this Bible study there were hardly any expressions of ambiguous or negative images of God, even in Contextual Bible Studies in which the prevailing discourse was that of lament (West and Zengele 2004). But ambiguous and negative images have become increasingly apparent during the past two years. How we are to understand this development is not clear, but it does seem to indicate that the deeply embedded and resilient embodied image of a God who enables at least survival (Haddad 2000, 2004), and the hope of fullness of life, is being eroded by the church and society's proclamation of a God who punishes with HIV and AIDS.

Conclusion

Our Contextual Bible Studies continue, using this text and others as resources to talk about and plan actions in response to HIV and AIDS. The newsprint piles up, testimony to the impulses of dignity to talk back to power and its dominating discourses. That these incipient newsprint theologies will be incorporated into the public theology of our churches appears to be a distant hope (West 2005), but one which we in the Ujamaa Centre will not give up on. While we wait, there is plenty of work to be done alongside those who are struggling to live positively in the context of HIV and AIDS.

Works Cited

Ashforth, A. (2005). *Witchcraft, Violence, and Democracy in South Africa.* Chicago: University of Chicago Press.

Bohman, J. (1999). "Practical Reason and Cultural Constraint: Agency in Bourdieu's Theory of Practice." In *Bourdieu: A Critical Reader*, ed. R. Shustermann, 129–52. Oxford: Blackwell.

Bourdieu, P. (1990). *In Other Words: Essays Towards a Reflexive Sociology.* Cambridge: Cambridge University Press.

Bourdieu, P. (1999). "The Contradictions of Inheritance." In *The Weight of the World: Social Suffering in Contemporary Society*, ed. P. Bourdieu et al., 507–13. Cambridge: Polity Press.

Bourdieu, P. (2000). *Pascalian Meditations*. Cambridge: Polity Press.

Bourdieu, P., and L. Wacquant (1992). *An Invitation to Reflexive Sociology*. Cambridge: Polity Press.

Cochrane, J. R. (1999). *Circles of Diginity: Community Wisdom and Theological Reflection*. Minneapolis: Fortress.

Comaroff, J., and J. L. Comaroff (1991). *Of Revelation and Revolution: Christianity, Colonialism and Consciousness in South Africa*, vol. 1. Chicago: University of Chicago Press.

Ekblad, B. (2001). *Reading for Good News among Mexican Immigrants and Inmates Submerged in the Bad News*. http://www.peoplesseminary.org/english/publications/120301.html

Ekblad, B. (2005). *Reading the Bible with the Damned*. Louisville: Westminister John Knox Press.

Forgacs, D. (ed.) (1988). *An Antonio Gramsci Reader: Selected Writings 1916–1935*. New York: Schocken Books.

Fowler, B. (2000). "Introduction." In *Reading Bourdieu on Society and Culture*, ed. B. Fowler, 1–21. Oxford: Blackwell/The Sociological Review.

Frostin, P. (1988). *Liberation Theology in Tanzania and South Africa: A First World Interpretation*. Lund: Lund University Press.

Giroux, H. A. (1985). "Introduction." In *The Politics of Education*, ed. P. Freire, xi–xxv. London: Macmillan.

Haddad, B. G. (2000). "African Women's Theologies of Survival: Intersecting Faith, Feminisms, and Development." Unpublished PhD, University of Natal, Pietermaritzburg.

Haddad, B. G. (2004). "The Manyano Movement in South Africa: Site of Struggle, Survival, and Resistance." *Agenda* 61: 4–13.

Hopkins, D. N. (2000). *Down, Up, and Over: Slave Religion and Black Theology*. Minneapolis: Fortress Press.

Lovell, T. (2000). "Thinking Feminism with and against Bourdieu." In *Reading Bourdieu on Society and Culture*, ed. B. Fowler, 27–48. Oxford: Blackwell/The Sociological Review.

Maluleke, T. S., and S. Nadar (2004). "Alien Fraudsters in the White Academy: Agency in Gendered Colour." *Journal of Theology for Southern Africa* 120: 5–17.

Mofokeng, T. (1988). "Black Christians, the Bible and Liberation." *Journal of Black Theology* 2: 34–42.

Mosala, I. J. (1986). "The Use of the Bible in Black Theology." In *The Unquestionable Right to be Free: Essays in Black Theology*, ed. I. J. Mosala and B. Tlhagale, 175–99. Johannesburg: Skotaville.

Mosala, I. J. (1989). *Biblical Hermeneutics and Black Theology in South Africa*. Grand Rapids: Eerdmans.

Nadar, S. (2003). *Power, Ideology and Interpretation/s: Womanist and Literary Perspectives on the Book of Esther as Resources for Gender-Social Transformation*. Pietermaritzburg: University of Natal.

Nolan, A. (1996). "Work, the Bible, Workers, and Theologians: Elements of a Workers' Theology." *Semeia* 73: 213–20.

Nyerere, J. (1969). *Freedom and Socialism: A Selection from Writings and Speeches 1952–65*. Dar es Salaam: Oxford University Press.

Scott, J. C. (1990). *Domination and the Arts of Resistance: Hidden Transcripts*. New Haven and London: Yale University Press.

Staal, J. F. (1963). "Sanskrit and Sanskritization." *Journal of Asian Studies* 22.3: 261–75.

Terreblanche, S. (2002). *A History of Inequality in South Africa, 1652–2002*. Pietermaritzburg: University of Natal Press.

Weems, R. (1996). "Response to 'Reading with': An Exploration of the Interface between Critical and Ordinary Readings of the Bible." *Semeia* 73: 257–61.

West, C. (1984). "Religion and the Left: An Introduction." *Monthly Review* 36: 9–19.

West, G. O. (1995). *Biblical Hermeneutics of Liberation: Modes of Reading the Bible in the South African Context*, 2nd ed. Maryknoll, NY and Pietermaritzburg: Orbis Books and Cluster Publications.

West, G. O. (2000). "Contextual Bible Study in South Africa: A Resource for Reclaiming and Regaining Land, Dignity and Identity." In *The Bible in Africa: Transactions, Trends, and Trajectories*, ed. G. O. West and M. W. Dube, 595–610. Leiden: Brill.

West, G. O. (2003a). *The Academy of the Poor: Towards a Dialogical Reading of the Bible*. Pietermaritzburg: Cluster Publications.

West, G. O. (2003b). "Reading the Bible in the Light of HIV/AIDS in South Africa." *Ecumenical Review* 55.4: 335–44.

West, G. O. (2005). "Articulating, Owning and Mainstreaming Local Theologies: The Contribution of Contextual Bible Study." *Journal of Theology for Southern Africa* 122: 23–35.

West, G. O. (2006). "Contextual Bible Reading: A South African Case Study." *Analecta Bruxellensia* 10: 131–48.

West, G. O. and B. Zengele (2004). "Reading Job 'Positively' in the Context of HIV/AIDS in South Africa." *Concilium* 4: 112–24.

West, G. O. and B. Zengele (2006). "The Medicine of God's Word: What People Living with HIV and AIDS Want (and Get) from the Bible." *Journal of Theology for Southern Africa* 125: 51–63.

West, G. O. and P. Zondi-Mabizela (2004). "The Bible Story that Became a Campaign: The Tamar Campaign in South Africa (and Beyond)." *Ministerial Formation* 103: 4–12.

West, G. O., P. Zondi-Mabizela, M. Maluleke, H. Khumalo, P. S. Matsepe and M. Naidoo (2004). "Rape in the House of David: The Biblical Story of Tamar as a Resource for Transformation." *Agenda* 61: 36–41.

11 Isaiah 53 and the Suffering-less Servant in Australian Pentecostalism

Jacqueline Grey

Introduction

When the Pentecostal movement first emerged on the Australian landscape in the early nineteenth century, it faced marginalization and rejection from the "respectable" society and from some of the other established denominations. A movement led mainly by women[1] and an academically uneducated membership was "out of place" in conservative Australian societies, both religious and general.[2] This marginalization was considered by the fledgling movement as a reflection of the depravity of the "world" anticipated as a sign of the imminent return of the *parousia*. According to Wacker, Pentecostals were certain they were riding the crest of the wave of history that would involve them directly in the intervention of God in history marked by an intensification of the divine presence, and experience of the Holy Spirit for healing, global evangelism and spiritual warfare (Wacker 2001: 251–65).

In this apocalyptic-type worldview, the faithful must endure the present evil age in expectation of future glory. Their worldview and sense of persecution was reflected in the eschatological and apocalyptic emphasis of their writings and limited literature. As Hanson notes, the experience of alienation or times of crisis is the sociological context from which apocalypticism is generally understood to arise (Hanson 1987: 75). This feeling is reflected in a poem by H. S. Kilpatrick of Perth, published in the *Good News Journal* (18.1, August 1927), the most prominent publication from this emerging movement:

The Shout and The Trump!
Oh, Christ, my Saviour, Lord and King,
Thou art the Lamb that once wast slain,
That broke the bonds of death, to bring
A ransomed host with Thee to reign.
And through the earth, and air, and sky,
Signs potent and portentous tell
The coming of the Lord is nigh,
To bring His Bride with Him to dwell.

So, at the shout or trump of God,
At midnight or in noonday fair,
Up from the bursting, barren sod,
The dead in Christ shall cleave the air
To meet the Lord, oh! wondrous thought,
In splendor and in holiness,
With them, from 'mongst the living brought,
Who loved the Son of Righteousness.

Ring loud the bell, the bugles blow,
Haste, couriers, with the speed of fear,
Declare this truth to high and low:
"The coming of the Lord is near."
Changed in the twinkling of an eye,
To dwell forever by His side,
To see Him as He is! Oh, my
Rapt soul shall then be satisfied.

Yet for the early Pentecostals in the Australian context, this future glory was not just an eschatological dream, but a present reality as they experienced a foretaste of this glory in their immediate encounter with God. Not only were earthly events understood in the light of the supernatural world (as was common to apocalyptic orientated communities), but the supernatural world was experienced in divine encounter and the life of the Spirit. The impetus for public ministry in these formative years was the revival spirit in the last days the Holy Spirit would commission both men and women to service; ordination was not restricted to gender (Chant 1999: 428). This same Spirit that raised Jesus from the dead was active to continue the ministry of Christ through evangelism, healings and miracles. Christ's ministry of healing emphasized in Matthew became paradigmatic for the marginalized Pentecostal community, and Isaiah 53 functioned as a proof-text for the ministry of physical healing described in Matthew

8:14. This salvation and healing found in the atoning work of Jesus Christ was a preview of heaven in the midst of affliction and a soul-sick world for the Pentecostal movement in Australia.

These origins profoundly affected the worldview and theology of contemporary Pentecostalism in Australia. Because of this orientation towards the supernatural, Pentecostalism globally has flourished predominantly in the non-Western context, such as South America and parts of Africa. As Pentecostalism in Australia has increased numerically (more than 1,000 churches with over 160,000 constituents), it also began to increase in social stature. A corollary of this quest for wider societal approval was the marginalization of those formally at the forefront of the movement's growth, particularly women leaders and church planters, seen as too radical for conservative pre-World War II Australian society. This represents a sociological shift in the movement, rather than a theological one, as women constitutionally continued to be affirmed for leadership roles but not in practice. The process of institutionalization and adoption of wider cultural norms by a previously marginalized group in order to achieve social respectability has been the focus of various studies in Pentecostalism globally – a process from which the Pentecostal movement in Australia has not been immune (see Poloma 1989 concerning the AoG movement in USA).

The substantial numerical growth and subsequent process of institutionalization in the Australian Pentecostal movement has been a double-edged sword. While it has meant the introduction of stabilizing factors such as training institutions and the formulation of doctrine, there has also been a loss of the earlier revival spirit linked to the immediacy of the *parousia*. As Hutchinson notes, "Bigger congregations meant bigger churches meant, quite often, that we stopped looking for the millennium and started building for it" (Hutchinson 1998: 17). This growth and shift in ecclesiology have also impacted the wider mission of the Australian Pentecostal movement. Instead of identifying themselves as suffering servants awaiting deliverance from this evil age, Pentecostals in Australia began to see themselves as agents of change and transformation within the structures of society and government. No longer waiting for the *parousia*, the victorious life could be experienced here and now. While this has been a positive shift towards planning and development of institutional structures, it has come packaged in the wrapping of triumphalism. This feeling is reflected in the official statement outlining the values of the Assemblies of God in Australia (AoG) that includes this assertion:

> Life is meant to be lived as an increasing adventure in prosperity. God's intention is to prosper the righteous so that they can demonstrate the power of His Kingdom on earth. Prosperity is not an option but a mandate and responsibility given to all who believe in the authority of the name of Jesus. We are called to show forth the wonders of His increasing Kingdom, and this clearly requires an increasing measure of affluence so that we can have an increasing measure of influence.

The sense of expectation, triumph and focus on economic prosperity expressed in this text captures the feeling of contemporary Pentecostalism in Australia as it drives to make God's kingdom established here on earth, and not just in heaven!

This shift in Pentecostal mission has come with an enormous theological cost, from marginalization to mainstream, as contemporary Pentecostalism in Australia defines its mission through a triumphalist worldview. There is no longer a place for suffering, simplicity or elected poverty. The shift from simplicity towards triumphalism is particularly evident in readings by Pentecostals of the same biblical text, from early Pentecostalism to the contemporary context. In particular, a diachronic study of readings of Isaiah 52:13–53:12 (for convenience herein after referred to as Isaiah 53) from the spectrum of historical Pentecostal community from its origins to the present exemplify the theological shift and subsequent marginalization of a theology of suffering which now has little place or value within the present Pentecostal community. The passage, commonly described as Isaiah's "suffering servant," is a notoriously difficult passage for both the scholar and lay reader alike. The esoteric style, textual difficulties and elusive identities of the text add to the complexity.

Isaiah 53 in Biblical Scholarship

The "suffering servant" has captivated the interests of biblical scholars of both the Old and New Testaments (see Bellinger and Farmer 1998). The interest by New Testament scholars, particularly in the self-identification of Jesus Christ with this role, highlights the numerous difficulties of the text in its Old Testament context (see esp. Hooker 1998). The setting of Isaiah 53 is generally located within biblical scholarship during the Babylonian exile of Judah.[3] The exiled people were living amid the disease and corruption of a Gentile nation, separated from the only means by which they could be cleansed from this disease and corruption – the destroyed Temple in Jerusalem. In this context, the prophet offered the people a solution; they will be cleansed through suffering (Clements 1998: 51). In particular, the prophet offers them the hope that they will be cleansed by the suffering of an unidentified servant. While this servant is unidentified, they are described with vivid and esoteric poetic images that contribute to the mystery (see also Brueggemann 1998: 141–40; Childs 2001: 410–23; Goldingay 2001: 301–309).

The debate over the identity of the suffering servant is intensified by the ambiguity of the actions and role of this mysterious figure. Does the servant actually die, or is this simply vivid poetic imagery? Equally ambiguous is the nature of the servant's suffering: the servant is "crushed" (*dākā'*) for the "transgressions" (*pešaʿ*) of others. Yet, does this suggest for the Judean community that the role of the servant is to suffer vicariously for them? For scholars such as Clements, the suffering of the servant is on behalf of the people for their greater good. He writes, "God provided a new form of sin-offering through the sufferings of a righteous Servant, by which uncleanness could be removed" (Clements 1998: 53). However, according to Orlinsky, the concept of vicarious suffering fundamentally conflicts with the idea of covenant in which the guilty party bears the responsibility for their wrongdoing *quid pro quo* (in Childs 2001: 415). And yet, the "suffering" of a prophetic figure during their ministry, such as Moses or Jeremiah, is not uncommon to the Old Testament tradition. The lack of consensus among scholars concerning the actions of the servant highlights the speculation of his identity, as the two issues are essentially connected.

Yet, despite these difficulties in reading Isaiah 53 highlighted by biblical scholarship, it is a passage of enormous interest to the Christian church and the Pentecostal community, particularly in the development of the doctrine of salvation and the core Pentecostal doctrine of "healing in the atonement." The text has exerted a powerful influence on the Christian understanding of Jesus as the Messiah and fulfilment of the Old Testament through his passion, which is evident in Pentecostal readings of this text. However, what is equally insightful from a diachronic analysis of Pentecostal readings of Isaiah 53 is the developing shift in their theology away from an empathic acceptance of suffering as implicit in the life of a disciple of Jesus Christ, towards a triumphalism so that the concept of suffering is now "out of place."

Earlier Pentecostal Readings

These issues identified by biblical scholars are largely unknown or ignored by the majority of Pentecostal readers. Instead, their readings focus on Isaiah 53 as a prophetic announcement concerning the person, character and actions of Jesus Christ, fulfilled in the New Testament. While this view is consistent in both the early and contemporary Pentecostal readings, there is a definite shift in the attitude and expectation towards the personal suffering of disciples of Jesus Christ. The readings of the Pentecostal community analysed are drawn from an analysis of published writings produced from the constituency. Because their publishing activity is limited to a few journals and books (though this is not symptomatic of a disinterest in biblical texts, but rather a reflection of its predominantly oral culture), the Pentecostal community has primarily shared their interpretation of biblical texts through their liturgy. Therefore, this study will also include a study of a collection of sermons, songs, and interviews with contemporary readers to represent the diversity of the community.

Unlike biblical scholars, there was little dispute among early Pentecostal readers regarding the identity of the servant; almost all identified the servant exclusively as Jesus Christ. Reading through their christological lenses, Pentecostal readers unanimously identify the servant as a prophetic description of Christ, and Christ alone. In particular, they adopted New Testament readings to understand the nature and ministry of the "suffering servant." That this could refer to a figure contemporaneous with the writer (who suffered vicariously for the exiled nation) is generally not considered. Instead, the early Pentecostal readings emphasize the sacrifice of Christ to gain salvation and healing for all believers. In the April 1930 journal article entitled "Divine Healing" of the *Australian Evangel*, J. N. Hoover writes that:

> Healing is a part of the gospel of our Lord and Savior, Jesus Christ. According to the fifty-third chapter of Isaiah, healing is a part of the divine programme, for it is written, "He hath borne our griefs and carried our sorrows, and with His stripes we are healed." But some who have not come into the full light of this Scripture will say it refers to the sin-sick soul and not to the healing of the body. But is this true? Let us see. If you will turn to the book of Matthew, the eight chapter and the 16th and 17th verses, you will find an inspired and therefore a correct interpretation of Isaiah's prophecy. "When even was come they brought unto him many that were possessed with devils and He cast out the spirits with his word and healed all that were sick, that it might be fulfilled which was spoken by Esaias the prophet, saying, Himself took our infirmities and bare our sicknesses." To the reasonable mind this is final proof that provision was made in the divine atonement for every infirmity and sickness of man.

For the early Pentecostal community, Isaiah 53 tends to function as a proof-text for the ministry of physical healing by Jesus as described in Matthew 8. The biblical text is used to validate the ministry and experience of healing by the community and to offer a paradigm for their contemporary church. Yet, while the early Pentecostal community identified the sufferings of Jesus Christ for strategic purposes, was his suffering to be unique or paradigmatic for his disciples?

While Christ has achieved this salvation and healing for the early Pentecostal readers through his suffering, it does not exempt them, as disciples, from expecting to share in the suffering of Jesus Christ. According to Henry Proctor in the June 1930 issue of *Australian Evangel* that while the believer can claim by faith exemption from physical sickness and sin since through Jesus Christ there is forgiveness and healing, the believer is not exempt from joining in the sufferings of Christ. He writes,

> We do not necessarily share in the sufferings of Christ when we are sick, neither are we exhorted to glory in sickness, but only in the cross of our Lord Jesus Christ, and to rejoice when we are counted worthy to suffer shame for the Name, and to rejoice and exult and leap for joy, when all men speak evil of us, falsely for His sake, and that of the Gospel.

This is the kind of suffering that we are to glory in, knowing that our light affliction, which is but for a moment, is working out for us a far more exceeding and eternal weight of glory, and that tribulation is not worthy to be compared to the glory which shall be revealed in us. We are not to be surprised, if the fiery trial, the scorching flame of persecution, is raging among us, to put us to the test, as though some surprising thing were accidentally happening to us. On the contrary, in the degree that we share in the sufferings of Christ, we are to rejoice, so that, at the unveiling of His glory we may also rejoice with triumphant gladness. For we are to be envied if we are reproached for bearing the name of Christ, for in that case the spirit of glory, even the Spirit of God is resting upon us (1 Pet. 4:12-14).

From this article by Proctor, it is clear that the early Pentecostal movement anticipated some level of persecution at a societal level, and equated the sufferings of Christ with this rejection. The "suffering" Proctor anticipates is not due to internal physical sickness, but shame, slander, misunderstanding and rejection from an external source. The suffering in which Proctor rejoices is not personal bodily illness but the experience of marginalization – a direct result of their social location. While this expectation is reflective of the social status of the Pentecostal community in the 1930s as living on the fringes of mainstream Australian culture, it does indicate the integration of some understanding of suffering into their theological worldview, albeit compelled through their actual experience of marginalization. Rather than "triumphing" in social ascension, the early community "triumphed" in their persecution and rejection. This description of suffering marginalism is complete with apocalyptic-type imagery of "fiery trial" and the "scorching flame of persecution." For this outcast group, the dejected and rejected Jesus was a comforting image in which they could share.

The christological reading of Isaiah 53 is also the basis for the current theology of the Australian AoG that asserts the availability of healing through the atonement explicitly within its articles of faith: "We believe the redemptive work of Christ on the cross provides healing of the human body in answer to believing prayer (Isa 53:4-5; Matt 8:17)." The current statement also reflects the importance of faith by the believer and the traditional Pentecostal preference for Matthew's reading of Isaiah 53. Yet, while reading and "believing" healing in the atonement from Isaiah 53, these early Pentecostal readers did not suggest that everyone is healed automatically at their salvation or that every prayer for healing is actualized. The early Pentecostal community recognized that while not every believer was healed, this did not mean that God is incapable of hearing and healing every prayer request. Instead, they suggest that the reasons why prayers for healing may remain unresolved are potentially numerous, including issues such as unresolved sin in a believer or lack of faith.[4] For Bridges-Johns it is the God-centred nature of the Pentecostal worldview with its intrinsic mystery that allows the acknowledgement that not all are healed (Bridges-Johns 1996: 47).[5] Yet it is this recognition of an unanswered or delayed response to prayer along with social rejection that allows a place for suffering and pain within their conversation and public forum of theological reflection. However, with the gradual institutionalization and social acceptance of the Pentecostal community in Australia, as their social context began to change, so did their experience and expectation of suffering and marginalization.

Later Pentecostal Readings

While the earlier Pentecostal community in Australia was socially marginalized, there has been a shift in later Pentecostalism, particularly in the last decade, towards social engagement and acceptance. Rather than experiencing and expecting rejection from the broader Australian society, the Pentecostal community has changed to experience and expect reception and integration. All the suffering, pain and rejection they could and should experience were carried by Jesus on the cross. They are now free to live a victorious and flourishing life. As Bryn Barrett writes in the 1984 *Australian Evangel*:

> Isaiah had prophesied that "...as a sheep before her shearers is silent, so he did not open his mouth" (Chapter 53:7). Dumb He was before men! However, He poured out his soul to His Father. But He who had done His Father's will to the minutest detail is left alone, His prayer unanswered. It was terribly real, and thus it is told in prophecy and history.
> *"He hath spoken in the darkness,*
> *In the silence of the night."*
> (F. R. Havergal)

How eloquent his plea, that we might know not darkness, but light and have songs in the night season.

The exchange at the cross where Christ took on the sufferings of sinful humanity so that believers can know the freedom and light of light is emphasized in Pentecostal discussions.

The passage from Isaiah 53 is also seen as a promise to be appropriated by Pentecostal readers from the contemporary community. As the General Superintendent of the Australian AoG, Andrew Evans writes in the 1992 *Australian Evangel* concerning faith:

> God has already given us some 7,000 scripture promises to meet every need in our lives, therefore every need can be overcome by exercising faith in these promises. For example, if we are sick, we meditate on the healing promises of Ex 15:26; Ps 103:3; Isa 53:5; Mk 16:18 and the like. As revelation comes we can have faith and thus overcome sickness by the power of faith. So too when we need financial blessings, guidance or whatever.

To appropriate the promise, Evans suggests that the believer needs to exercise faith. He suggests meditating on appropriate Scripture passages relating to the issue until revelation (and, presumably, the awaited healing) comes. This leads to the suggestion that the reason for the lack of healing is the limited faith of the sick person. While this dilemma is also evident in earlier Pentecostal readings of Isaiah 53, it is an area vulnerable to the abuse of guilt and neglect of the long-term ill for those who are not healed instantaneously. For Evans, however, the expectation is that sickness, suffering and financial lack are all obstacles that can be overcome. The article by Evans suggests that the Bible promises victory over any negative event or experience through faith in these promises.

While not writing directly on Isaiah 53, the official statement of the values of the Assemblies of God in Australia (AoG) promotes the traditional Pentecostal expectation and experience of healing. Like Evans's article, it considered the healing found in Christ as part of a wider programme of blessing. The statement says:

> We believe that God wants to heal and transform us so that we can live healthy and prosperous lives in order to help others more effectively.

This statement represents a shift both culturally and theologically from the earlier Pentecostal writings. While the earlier Pentecostals promoted a doctrine of healing in the atonement, the contemporary community does not specify the basis of this theological statement other than an assumption of divine intentionality. However, it is not just a theological shift away from the doctrine of healing in the atonement, but also a cultural shift. Instead of expecting suffering and rejection from the wider Australian society, the contemporary community expects to prosper. The statement continues to associate this prosperity with success and happiness:

> The truth is God's plan for us is exciting. He plans for us to know happiness, prosperity, health and success. God's plan for us is a result of His love toward us – because he loves us He plans for our success. It was His love that caused Jesus to give His life for us and He wants us to know the best of God's purpose for our life. Finding and fulfilling God's plan for your life is the real purpose for your life.

> God's destiny is too valuable for us to live life outside of His plan for our blessing. It is extremely important for each of us to realise the blessing God plans for our life. That is why we respect the right of every individual to find and fulfil their God-given destiny. Only then can we be truly happy; and only then will we be successful.

Healing and salvation within the Pentecostal community is now seen to result in the transformation of the believer as a successful, healthy and happy individual. While it may be comforting to consider the plan of God directed towards the blessing of the individual, it appears that this blessing is defined as the individual's happiness and success. There is no room in this "plan" for pain, suffering, grief or loss. There is no expectation or attitude towards sharing in the sufferings of Christ.

The pastoral implications of this theological and cultural shift are enormous. It tends to alienate those within the community who are suffering outside the "plan of God." It perhaps suggests to those in distress that they lack faith or have unrepentant sin leading potentially to unnecessary guilt and condemnation. It has also disempowered the community to assist pastorally those dealing with these issues to whom they minister. When loss, grief or suffering is viewed as something to be "overcome," it is potentially ignored, suppressed or regarded as a character flaw. This does not allow the community to address issues raised by the suffering, reflect upon the theological implications or even be healed through the grieving process. Instead, the community should be prepared and equipped to deal, theologically and pastorally, with issues of theodicy and suffering to allow disciples to journey in the wholeness of relationship with God rather than the naïve utopianism of "happiness." While the theology and practice of the early Pentecostal movement was far from ideal and it is not the purpose of this essay to suggest a return to those "glory" days, there is something of the expectation of sharing in the sufferings of Christ (which has enormous theological and pastoral values) that has been lost by the community.

Yet there are signs that the limitations of this approach are being questioned by the grassroots community. During an interview of a cell group of Pentecostal young professionals reflecting on Isaiah 53, it was not the submissive attitude of Christ or his suffering that they noted but rather the nature of his appearance (Grey 2005: 108). Both women and men highlighted the offensive appearance of the servant. One participant commented on 53:2:

> He had no beauty or majesty to attract us to him, nothing that we should desire him. You know, despised, rejected … the whole; God's way is not the way of this world. It's just so different. It's hard to explain. God is just so much … I think God is more long-term, whereas this world is more short-term. You know – short-term preservation, but God is more lasting. Things just aren't what they seem to be in this world … He was Jewish, so he would have had a big nose … He was probably bald … Yeh, whatever, but he probably wasn't Brad Pitt, he was more Danny Devito. This whole thing about exterior, it's just not what it's about.

The group emphasized the counter-cultural nature of the servant's exterior (who they equated with Christ). Yet it was an understanding of culture based on their own experience. They equated being judged by their appearance and professionalism as being the opposite of what the servant-Christ represented. Their experience in the professional workforce meant that they felt an expectation to act, look and appear a certain way to be accepted within the wider culture. In the persona of the servant-Christ (as representative of the ways of God) they saw the opposite values to those that the "world" lived by. This reading emphasizes the uniqueness of Christ, who is considered counter-cultural to the experience of the Pentecostal readers.

The need for an emerging theology of suffering is identified among sections of the youth of the current Pentecostal community. A youth Bible study group interviewed regarding their reading of Isaiah 53 identified the work and person of Christ portrayed not only in the actions of the servant, but also through the various images presented in the text (Grey 2005: 107). In particular, the group resonated with the image of the sheep. One of the youth commented: "The lamb part is [that] he went gracefully, he didn't put up a fight. A lamb just goes, it knows it's going to be killed but just goes anyway. That's what I think Jesus did, he didn't put up a fight, he just went for us." Another continued the discussion: "Lambs are really cute, and why would you want to kill a lamb? – so it seems a bit stupid to kill a lamb, but then you do it and you can imagine how innocent the lamb would look up at you and you're sort of punishing it and the lamb won't do anything about it." While identifying Jesus' passion with the lamb, the young people saw the lamb as symbolic of his submissive attitude rather than a reference to the sacrificial system presented in the Old Testament. The lamb was perceived by the youth as innocent, submissive, silent, graceful, obedient and vicariously suffering; the same attitude they identified in Christ. This attitude of servant-Jesus perceived by the youth in Isaiah 53 is not just a theological truth, but an attitude which they, as Christians, should emulate:

> In Philippians (I think it's in Philippians) it says to have a Christ-like attitude and in Ephesians it says to be an imitator of God – they're really verses that I've been living off this year. Just to die daily on the cross is a lot like [our pastors] Marilyn and Nathan say in their sermons. And seeing "The Passion of the Christ" I just realize – yeah – that I have to, I have to die daily, I have to live every second of the day for Jesus because that's what my life is about basically.

The attitude and suffering of the servant-Jesus, according to the youth cell, is normative. The youth considered the vicarious suffering of the servant-Jesus not to be unique, but the exemplar for the Christian life. The passage is applicable to the youth as they also identify with the servant-Jesus; they must each symbolically die to themselves (their own will and desires) on their own cross. This reading is encouraging to the development of a theology of suffering within the Pentecostal community as it suggests that the reflection and need for further reflection on these issues has already (to some extent) begun, albeit at a grass-roots level.

Finding a "Place" for Suffering

So while the Pentecostal community in Australia had "found" a place for a possible theology of suffering among its early constituency but then "lost" that place, there is hope for future retrieval and adaptation. To develop a future role for suffering within the community it is appropriate to look again at the voice of the prophet in Isaiah 53 to "see" what this theology and attitude might look like. The "suffering servant" redefines the nature of success against the ancient Near Eastern (and contemporary) definitions of military victory and political accomplishment. Instead they present a figure of extraordinary self-sacrifice (perhaps even of their own happiness) to secure the stability, cleansing, healing and "greater good" of their community. While the result of their sacrifice is hope and joy for the community, they are not immune from the affliction experienced by the servant or the grief that issues from recognition of their loss. It is for their "transgressions" that the servant is "crushed."

This servant provides a model for the contemporary Pentecostal community of self-sacrificial living and commitment to their wider community that causes them to live beyond the naïve utopianism of individualistic "happiness." Yet the nature of suffering and sacrifice of this figure of Isaiah 53 is exemplified (and for the Pentecostal community "fulfilled") in the person and ministry of Jesus Christ. By reflection on the attitude and character of the "suffering servant" of Jesus Christ, in interaction with the social location and cultural context of the community, a model of discipleship is established that can pattern both the response and ministry to those suffering affliction, grief and loss. By reading Isaiah 53 as part of the wider narrative of the Bible it can provide the hopeful beginnings of a model and "place" for suffering within the Pentecostal community in Australia.

Works Cited

Bellinger, Jr, W. H. and W. R. Farmer (eds) (1998). *Jesus and the Suffering Servant: Isaiah 53 and Christian Origins*. Pennsylvania: Trinity.

Bridges-Johns, C. (1996). "Healing and Deliverance: A Pentecostal Perspective." In *Pentecostal Movements as an Ecumenical Challenge*, ed. J. Moltmann and K. J. Kuschel. Concilium. London: SCM.

Brueggemann, W. (1998). *Isaiah 40–66*. WBC. Kentucky: Westminster John Knox.

Chant, Barry (1999). "The Spirit of Pentecost: Origins and Development of the Pentecostal Movement in Australia, 1870–1939." PhD thesis, Macquarie University.

Childs, B. (2001). *Isaiah*. OTL. Louisville: Westminster/John Knox.

Clements, R. E. (1998). "Isaiah 53 and the Restoration of Israel." In *Jesus and the Suffering Servant: Isaiah 53 and Christian Origins*, ed. W. H. Bellinger, Jr and W. R. Farmer. Pennsylvania: Trinity.

Goldingay, J. (2001). *Isaiah*. NIBC. Massachusetts: Hendrickson, 2001.

Grey, Jacqui (2005). "Burning Tongues: Voicing a Pentecostal-Charismatic Hermeneutic of the Old Testament through Readings of Isaiah." PhD thesis, Charles Sturt University.

Hanson, Paul. (1987). *Old Testament Apocalyptic*. Nashville: Abingdon.

Hooker, M. D. (1998). "Did the Use of Isaiah 53 to Interpret His Mission Begin with Jesus?" In *Jesus and the Suffering Servant: Isaiah 53 and Christian Origins*, ed. W. H. Bellinger, Jr and W. R. Farmer, 88–103. Pennsylvania: Trinity.

Hutchinson, M. (1998). "The New Thing God is Doing: The Charismatic Renewal and Classical Pentecostalism." *Australasian Pentecostal Studies* 1 (March 1998): 5–21.

Poloma, M. (1989). *Assemblies of God at the Crossroads: Charisma and Institutional Dilemmas*. Knoxville: University of Tennessee Press.

Wacker, G. (2001). *Heaven Below: Early Pentecostals and American Culture*. London: Harvard University Press.

12 How can we Sing the Lord's Song in Africa?

Anastasia Boniface-Malle

Which Songs shall we Sing?

In exile, Israel faced many challenges to their faith and manner of worship. Without a temple, worship patterns needed to adapt. In Psalm 137, we hear that when the captors demanded that they sing "one of the Songs of Zion," Israel refused. They put their harps on the willows and cried, *How can we sing the Lord's Song in a foreign land?* (Ps. 137:4). Lament was the appropriate response in their *out-of-place* situation.

This is not how things are with African Christians. Most prayers in African churches are thanksgivings and praises. Charismatic and Pentecostal churches offer another type of prayer, exorcism, aimed to rebuke and cast out demons. This form of prayer overlooks how the "devil" may also manifest his activities in social evils. As such, confusion takes place and people fail to distinguish between evil spiritual forces and human-made evil practices. I would like to underline here that in the midst of oppression, suffering and pain, exorcism does not solve the situation. What is needed in such situations is the removal of the evil structures that cause and sustain suffering and oppression. In other words, the key issue needed is the rebuke of the evils that cause suffering and oppression in the lives of the people.

Absence of Lament

Lament psalms are among texts that do not have much impact on members of the Evangelical Lutheran Church in Tanzania (ELCT), the largest protestant church in Tanzania. The Bible is central, but the Old Testament is not given a proper place in ELCT teaching and worship services. For the most part, Tanzanian Christians understand Christianity to centre on New Testament teachings, summed up in Jesus' two great commandments: love for God and love for neighbour. Even when parts of the Old Testament are read, their theological and liturgical significance is not effectively explained. There is always a quick jump to the New Testament and its application to the practical life of Christians. These applications mostly consist of exhortations, warnings, and call to action.

Throughout my Christian life (formerly Roman Catholic), I have not heard the lament psalms read publicly in any of the churches I attended except for Psalms 51 and 22, read during Holy week, and Psalm 90:1-12, recited at burial services (omitting 90:13-17). The power of lament in the latter is played down as the focus falls on the hope of resurrection reinforced in the sermon, songs, and words of comfort and hope.

There are paradoxes in the overlooking of biblical lament traditions in the African context: (1) The African worldview relates closely to those of the Old Testament (OT) and as such one would presume that Africans would feel at home with the OT laments. (2) Psalms of lament give authentic expression to the existential pains of individual and communal life. The OT does not disguise or take pain for granted. Lament psalms give form and language to pain. "The prayers of lament in the Psalter give a form to the worst experience of life which follows the movement innate to human suffering and yet places it in the presence of the one who alone can be a decisive word to those who suffer" (Brueggemann 1977: 263). The lament tradition is necessary for faith, insofar as life of faith is not a life of denial but acceptance of reality. It is a life that sees the breadth, length, depth and heights of human life in relation to God and to society. It is a life that recognizes its heritage, and embraces the fullness of its theological heritage, as embraced by tradition.

Paradoxically, lament is part of the Tanzania heritage. People address life's adversities vocally, either to God, divinities or to ancestors. Pain was never silenced; it was made vocal. Similarly, the Bible indicates that pain and suffering were addressed to God, so that God can intervene and remedy the situation.

What Lies Behind the Absence of Lament

Early missionaries to Africa failed to integrate two of Christianity's religious heritages in prayer and worship. "The laments comprise more than one third of the Psalms, yet they are strikingly under-used in our worship" (Holladay 1993: 293). The lament tradition encompasses all three parts of the Hebrew Scriptures, from the Torah and prophetic literature (e.g. laments of Jeremiah) to writings such as Job and Lamentations. But much of this bulk of material is overlooked in the church in Tanzania. Whenever these Psalms are heard, negative emotional reactions emerge and overpower practical realities and logical reflection.

Western Culture in African Christianity

Western culture was equated to Christianity. Since Christianity came during the colonial period, even early missionaries shared most of the colonial perception about Africa and Africans. Colonialism was not interested in the African person or culture. Western missionaries preached the Gospel which at its deepest meaning focused on a person, but as Westerners their efforts were not free of prejudice. At the heart of missionary activity was also an attempt to "modernize" or "civilize" Africans. African belief, veneration, respect of gods, spirits and ancestors were discarded and condemned. Any African Christian who participated in one of the functions that is related to traditional religious practices was excommunicated. The missionary enterprise of the nineteenth century did not view African religion and culture as a dialogue partner the way it viewed Buddhism and philosophical Hinduism in Asia. The 1910 World Missionary Conference in Edinburgh concluded that African Traditional Religion, which it roundly described as Animism, probably contained no preparation for Christianity. When more positive appreciations gained currency, it was too late: the mission churches were already in place, marked generally by separateness from their cultures, rather than by their involvement in them. As a result, African Christians inherited a religion that was foreign to them, and that attempted to detach them from their Africanness. However, the detachment was practised externally. Deep inside, Africans continued to attach themselves to their culture and religion and whenever this becomes obvious, they were regarded as syncretistic.

On another level, Africans who were privileged in formal education developed a negative attitude to their own culture and religion. They felt embarrassed for their religion and culture. So they were ashamed to speak their mother tongue languages, participate in village rituals, and so forth. They viewed their religion as marginal and would not equate it to other world religions. Consequently, this attitude was reflected in the Bible translation, in theological articulation and in prayers. African cultural elements were removed from the Christian religion and from the expressions of faith. This included the way Western people read and treated the Bible.

This negative connotation of lamenting in Western culture (which was looked upon as superior and "Christian") intensified the rejection of African tradition of lament. The missionary analysis of the lament over death in northwestern Tanzania describes lament as fear, hopelessness and horror over the enemy of life. Otto Hagena (Bethel missionary in the northwestern part of Tanzania in Buhaya/ Kigarama between 1929–1939) narrates his observation of lamentations over the dead among the Haya of Tanzania as follows (translated by Wilhelm Richerbacher):

> In the middle of the night I woke up, frightened upon my bed. A long lamenting sound tears the silence, gets down in order to rise anew. And again, the same sound, the same voice, crying out of the darkness of the night ... Why all these days, yes, week-long lamentations, whereby the main lamentors sometimes carry on until their voices are gone? ... But anybody who has observed such lamenting more often from nearby knows: the basic tone of that is fear and the horror of the enemy of life with the creature (Hagena 1949: 3).

In the view of missionaries, such apparent desperation and hopelessness were brought about by the fact that people did not know the Lord of life. For them, the remedy is when the people see the light of Christ. The missionary era was also the time when lamenting was considered to be an embarrassment and a failure in the Western culture. The negative connotation of lamenting in the Western culture intensified the African tradition of lament.

The missionaries told the Africans what they needed to be saved from, but when Africans needed power to deal with the spiritual realm that was real to them, the missionary was baffled. The ancestors were to be ignored; infant mortality and premature deaths were purely medical matters. Failure of rains and harvest were acts of God. Childlessness had nothing to do with witchcraft, nor was there any spiritual aspect to any other physical disorder or infirmity (Oduyoye 1986: 41).

The missionary era was the time when lamenting was considered to be an embarrassment and a failure in the Western culture. The Western culture emphasized what can be known and proved rationally; problems were to be dealt with scientifically. It claimed to possess superior knowledge that could solve problems for Africans. By the time Christianity was brought to Africa, the missionary worldview had somehow detached distinctively from the worldview of the Bible. The Western worldview as critiqued by African scholars had by then become quasi-scientific. Abogunrin argues "Consequently, although the missionaries still talked about God, heaven, angels, Satan, Holy Spirit and evil forces, they were no more than cultural clutches that lacked the existential dynamism they once had before and during the medieval period" (Abogunrin 1986: 7).

Appropriating Lament Psalms

Effective application of the text in the lives of the reading community must first and foremost involve the process of self-realization and self-affirmation. This is what I would like to call "conscious reading." For effective reading and appropriation of the lament genre in the life and worship of Tanzanian Christians to take place we need to realize the following colonial indoctrination: In trying to do away with the hard language in the Bible, the colonial-Christian mission overlooked lament texts from the Bible.

I have indicated that the Lutheran Church in Tanzania places the Bible at the core of its teachings. The question, then, is, how do they deal with parts of the Bible which contain hard languages such as lament and imprecatory elements? First, most of the Scripture with hard language of lament and especially imprecations are not used in the church. In case the biblical text of lament is used because lessons in the lectionary are similar to other mainline church lectionaries elsewhere, strategic efforts are made by the church to eliminate the hard language through a shift in interpretation or emphasis. While most of the laments are prayers addressed to God for help, Christians in Tanzania associate these psalms with the confession of sins, thus interpreting lament psalms in the light of penitential psalms. This shift in interpretation distorts the focus of the laments; it not only undermines, or covers, the lament but also brings divergence in the theology of these psalms. In the prophetic literature, we encounter the question of the hiddenness of God because of sin. Since Israel had sinned against God, God withdrew from people; and this withdrawal causes calamities to both the individuals and the community as a whole. But the Psalms do not often make this claim. In the laments, individuals do not bring the calamities on themselves. Rather, individuals come to God because they are oppressed by their enemies, by God, or sometimes by themselves. So the church has collapsed the contrast.

Another shift that occurs is when the lament elements in those psalms are read as expressions of Jesus' agony during the Passion Week. Westermann attests to this when he observes: "The element of suffering as such, and the language, in which it comes to expression, become of secondary importance" (Westermann 1994: 83).

Form-critical reading of the Psalms has contributed to the demise of the lament psalms as well. In learned circles, the form-critical approach to the psalms has emphasized the shift from lament to praise and hope, a shift which in one way is so sudden and in another is enforced or imposed upon the psalm. Some of the Psalms do not make this shift (e.g. Psalm 88, 89). In Psalms that seem to make such shift, one is left to wonder whether the shift involves emotional change or it is used to motivate God to act! In African traditional prayers we could call this bargain "language."[1] When the community laments mention God's past work, they do so strategically as a way of reminding God how things were, and how things should be for the present; they bring the contrast of human life and of God's activity. "The contrast of *how it was* and *how it is,* is calculated to get God to action, for he will find his present arrangement intolerable" (Brueggemann 1994: 69). The celebration of God's wonders remains a distant memory for the present (and in some psalms as a hopeful reality in a future that is not so distant).

What historical critics call "movement" is sometimes a form of bargain when seen in the light of some African traditional prayers. People's fate or loss is perceived as God's loss as in the Pare prayer for fertility: *You, god of the sky, if I get a male child, I will keep a porcupine until this child is old enough to bring it here to be killed and have together with it plenty of alcohol. If I do not get a child, you will only look at these waters (liquids)*. In another Pare prayer, if God does not give a child to a praying person, then that means God will not have anyone to sacrifice. A Giur prayer from Sudan reminds God that lack of children means discontinuity: no ancestral links and, more seriously, Jouk's name will be forgotten. So God (Jouk) has to act.

> **Leader**: Thou, Jouk [God], who art our Father and hast created all of us, Thou knowest this woman is ours, and we wish her to bear children–
> **Altogether:** Grant children to her!
> **Leader:** Should we die tomorrow, no children of ours will remain–
> **All:** Grant children to her!
> **Leader:** If she bears a son, his name will be the name of his grandfather; if she bears a daughter, her name will be the name of her grandmother.
> **All:** Grant children to her!
> **Leader:** Would it be displeasing to thee if many children surrounded us? Spirit of the Father, spirit of the grandfather, you who dwell now in the skies, are you displeased that we ask for children?
> **All:** Grant children to her!
> **Leader:** Should we die without those who guard the family? Your name and ours shall be forgotten upon the earth.
> **All:** Grant us this night good dreams, that we will die leaving many children behind us.

In the communal lament, the reference to God's great deeds in history is not a statement of praise or even movement to praise; history is used to show the contrast between the past and the present, and in this way to motivate God to act. Prayers of lament are offered to God because the situation at the moment is different from what they know from history (see Psalms 44, 74).

A form-critical approach treats all Psalms in the same category, e.g. invocation, lament/complaint, petitions, praise/movement to praise trust etc. This kind of reading influences not only our reading

and making shifts in interpretation but also affects our pastoral ministry. We run away from the reality of pain and talk about trust, praise,
hope etc. As a result, pastors do not listen to the painful stories;
rather they would tend to say quickly, "in all things give thanks and
praise to God, for such is God's will in your life."

Ultimately, this tendency has implications on the practical life of
the people. People opt to live and put on a "churchly" face. When
there is fear, anxiety, pain and loss, these are covered and supple-
mented with talk of hope, trust, a thanksgiving attitude, and praise.
This is the way it worked during the missionary days, and it is the way
it works now. But deep inside, this teaching intensified the contrary.

> Mission was understood as urgent scramble to abandon the world and
> prepare for the inevitable confrontation. Psychologically, mission stressed
> the idea of individual responsibility, which heightened the sense of fear,
> isolation and insecurity. It sought to meet this individual crisis by offering
> security, assurance, and the safety of a redeemed and supportive fellow-
> ship. The individual disposition of fear and anxiety was turned into an
> attitude of faith and trust, and the reliance of inner resources in what
> would otherwise be a menacing world. Instead of being confronted to
> the world and thus exposed to its ways, Christians looked forward to the
> reign of God as the final security (Sanneh 1988: 12).

The pattern of the digression and avoidance of "hard or difficult"
texts in the church combined with the exegetical methodology that
is still in use in the academic arena have had a very negative effect
on the practical lives of both clergies and parishioners. The disadvantage originates from the fact that, when pastors do their pastoral
visitations to the afflicted, they tend to help the sufferers hide their
pain and complaint. The pastors do not give people sufficient time
to grieve and express their agony in words. They are encouraged to
trust, hope, thank and praise. There is this quick shift to gratefulness
to God even in the midst of pain.

One pastor from South Africa, Vivian Msomi (Feb 1999), once
recounted this "counselling" procedure to a woman who lost her
child. He said: "When the pastor visits the bereaved woman he encourages her to calm down and thank God." This is what the pastor
will say: "Daughter of so and so … do not cry and grieve a lot. Be
grateful for God needs flowers to decorate heaven, and he has chosen your child to decorate his abode. Children are God's flowers to

decorate his home." Anyone can join Msomi to wonder why God would choose a child to decorate heaven? If God chose this child to decorate God's home, what about the mother of the child? She too needed that child to decorate her life with the joy and the happiness of motherhood.

The shift in emphasis occurs also when these psalms are put in a different context in the lectionary. In our church calendar, Psalm 80 was used as the first reading at the second and third Sundays in Advent from 1995–1998. What does the community lament do in the Advent season where the emphasis is on the coming king? This psalm was placed in the Advent season simply because of verse 17: "But let your hand be upon the man of your right hand, the son of man whom you have found (made strong) for yourself." The context and the content of the psalm are subsumed in this single verse, which diverts from the rest of the psalm in both translations and context. The lament is never an issue here for our church calendar; the emphasis is on "this man" who is at the right hand, alluding to Psalm 2 and its messianic implications for the Christian community.

Lament Psalms as Endangered Texts

The Tanzanian Church has overlooked and failed to integrate two of her religious heritages in prayer and worship. It is my conviction that the devaluation of the lament psalms stems basically from the lack of proper interpretation of these texts. From the time of its inception to the present, Tanzanian Christianity has inherited not only a "lament-less Church," but also a pre-understanding of lament psalms from the Christians of the West who were their missionaries. The lament or complaint prayer was thought to be incompatible with the proper behaviour towards God; consequently it was "thought inappropriate to lament before God" (Westermann 1994: 81). Piety or a pious attitude towards God was and is still only associated with the praise or thanksgiving prayers. Such an attitude has severed the lament psalms from prayer in Christian piety, in worship and their function in Christian ministry. The lament psalms have become some of the endangered texts in the Tanzanian Church.

Subsequently, there is another paradox. Christians in Tanzania, as others in the world, live in a reality of pain and suffering. When faced by critical situations such as severe drought, famine, death, traumatic diseases or incidences, people tend to seek concrete ways and places for intervention and refuge. In pre-Christian Africa and even today in many societies where traditional beliefs hold, people lament to deities for intervention and answers to their particular problems. Painful emotions are expressed in utterances, prayers and actions. In times of calamity or distress, Africans offer lament and petition prayers that are often accompanied by concrete rituals, aiming at lessening and eradicating the pain in the community or in the life of individuals.

The stripping of the lament psalms in the liturgical setting of the church, at times of terror, fear, pain and loss, becomes an inadequate means to deal with those issues. Since these problems are pertinent, the African experience becomes a way to remedy or lessen the pain, even when it means doing such things in secret. This is happening because the important side of human emotional experience has been overlooked in the church's teaching and practice. Oduyoye comments: "The individual African in the process of being saved was told that witches do not exist, though the community continued to believe in the reality of evil that witchcraft represents" (Oduyoye 1986: 41). Consequently, the faith becomes so superficial; people move from one church to another, as well as from one faith to another for relief and cure.

Pre-fabricated Christianity could not reach the deeper needs of the people, nor could it give answers and directions to the pressing questions about God and life. God is protected from the people in the ELCT; there are no means to reach this protected God through complaints. African Christians live in a dilemma of faith praxis. Since God of the Christian faith is aloof and protected, they voice their complaints to the ancestors, spirits, chiefs, cultic functionaries, and other mediums who seem to be operative in day-to-day living.

In African spirituality, pain or suffering was never taken for granted or covered under the guise of spirituality. Many manifestations of suffering were thought to be life-threatening. Troubles were always brought to God for two particular reasons. First, for Africans, every aspect of life is tied to the spiritual realm. Existential issues were treated lightly over against the spiritual ones; in fact, the two were regarded as inseparable. There is no distinction between the sacred and the secular in African thought pattern. Everything that happens to human beings is always spiritual and has to deal with the spiritual world. Difficulties and troubles of daily life are associated or linked to evil or enemy, and the way out of this dilemma is to bring it to a higher power in the spiritual world. This worldview of Africans fits with that of the early Israelite society, as Dennis Sylva comments:

> The composers of the Psalms brought the difficulties which they encountered and the anguish which they experienced into the light cast by their religious traditions. They found in these correlations of tradition and experience the means to live trustingly and confidently rather than giving in to anxiety and despair (Sylva 1993: 9).

Secondly, in the same vein, every life-threatening experience was dealt with seriously because, for both Africans and ancient Jews, there was less emphasis on eschatology. Life was to be fully lived right here on earth. For this reason life and wholeness has to be experienced when one is living. There was no way of spiritualizing the problems and putting them far away to another realm of life. There was no "opium theology." Instead, people turned to God because God is a life-giver. This understanding empowered them to turn to God/s in crisis so that life could be restored, ensured and protected.

In the African lament is a relationship that is demonstrated in the process. Both the people and God/s participate in dealing with the situation. This participation is fostered and made possible because of the relationship that exists between the people and god/s and, most evidently, because of the past involvement of the god/s in the lives of the people. In these interactions, the deity has proven powerful in such a way that human beings can count on them for help. There are times when people have to comply with the wishes of the god/s even in crisis. However, these wishes are prescribed before and are thus known to the people. They are not wishes or requests that come to them as surprises.

For Tanzanian Christians this fact has been neglected. When one is faced with deep difficulty, the answer or the oracle they get from the church is that there is hope some day; in a distant future, all will be well! The church has failed to find the language that speaks to the people. The lament psalms provide us with that language which is healing in many ways, but the church has failed to provide a ritual and a place where people can concretize and name their problems in an honest, positive, healing and freeing manner. Because of this failure and negligence on the part of the church, many Christians join with non-Christians in conducting rituals that deal with community or individual afflictions. When this happens, Christians are blamed and sometimes excommunicated/alienated from the rest of the believing community. When Christians participate in such functions, they are labelled as "syncretistic." But Christianity has not given them alternatives.

The Western Christian Church not only devalued the biblical laments in its theology, faith, prayer and worship, but it also dismantled the power of African laments by regarding them as pagan and animistic, as they did to other aspects of African culture. African Christians inherited a "lamentless" church. But this church has the Bible in which are numerous treasures of lament psalms. What does the church do with this part of the Bible? The African Church, like its forbearers, uses psalms of praise and thanksgiving in her prayers and worship; in doing so, it has thrown aside a major part of the Psalter. This fact confronts African Christians with identity crises.

As Africans, lamenting is part of who we are, even when the church has removed that from worship. It has not, however, taken it from the people. The church still operates in the midst of people who lament, speak, and concretize their pain as part of life that forms human reality. Thus, removing lament from the church sphere brings another identity crisis. Do we have to throw away our cultural identity or spirituality in order to become Christians, especially when those aspects of culture do not contradict the message of the Gospel? Do we have to adopt another culture that presents itself as civilized in order to be Christian? As Christians, are we faithful to the Bible?

This is the gap which exists between the church and the lament psalms. By neglecting the lament psalms, the Tanzanian Church is at odds not only with the Bible that the Church uses as the norm for faith but also with her own cultural heritage. The Church has become an alien in search of faith and identity. The Bible is used in a manipulative way, in such a way that it suits our inherited culture. Brueggemann rightly remarks:

> We are expected and required to speak the language of safe orientation
> and equilibrium, either we find it so or to pretend we find it. For the
> normal, conventional functioning of public life, the raw edges of disori-
> entation and reorientation must be denied or suppressed for the purpose
> of public equilibrium. As a result, our speech is dull and mundane. Our
> passion has been stilled and without imagination. And mostly, the Holy
> One is not addressed, not because we dare not but because God is far
> away and hardly seems important (Brueggemann 1982: 19).

While Brueggemann speaks from the Western experience, his words
fit the Tanzanian context as well. African Christianity tends to adopt
the experience that contradicts who we are while betraying our
piety in which there is more god-talk than in the Western culture. In
Africa, life has to be lived as it is experienced, rather than pretend
that life runs smoothly. Although the Bible may not specifically address all of our problems or answer all of our questions, it will help us
draw near to God who loves and cares for us through it all.

If this tendency does not change, the true meaning of prayer will
be lost in the ELCT and other churches whose view of the lament
psalms, teachings and theology are similar to ELCT. As Christians, the
biblical traditions and worship materials that are derived from biblical texts and worship resources from the past guide our modes of
prayer and worship. The psalms themselves function as prayers, and
they can be used as prayers for all since almost every human experience is expressed in these psalms. The biblical lament corrects our
understanding of prayer as only praise and thanksgiving.

There are times in human life when the language of praise and
thanksgiving does not match personal or community need. In times
of deep troubles and disaster, one cannot burst into praise or thanksgiving; for in doing so we are neither honest to ourselves nor to God,
but covering our pain and underestimating our need. Both lament
and praise are offered to "a known, named identifiable **'You'** …
Prayer is a direct address to, and conversation and communion with,
an agent known from a shared, treasured past" (Brueggemann 1995:
34; bold in original). In both modes of prayers, God is acknowledged
as doing wonders in relation to the people. But there is a contrast
as well: in the praise the transforming wonders are experienced as
both a past and present reality. What is more distinct in praise is
that "the wonders of this **'You'** are marked by covenantal loyalty

and costly companionship" (Brueggemann 1995: 50). In the lament psalms, however, this relationship of God's deeds to the people sounds like something distant. God did wonders in the past, but for the time being God's actions are not seen and God's presence not experienced.

Embracing Lament Tradition and African Worldview

An effective reading, therefore, requires a release from this attitude as well as an "incarnation" into African culture and worldview. John S. Pobee delineates the elements of African culture, experience and history that make for African-ness. "First, *homo Africanus homo religiosus radicaliter* and, thus, had a religious and spiritual epistemology and ontology" (Pobee 1996: 166). The "incarnation" here means embodiment of one's own cultural heritage, when one embraces his/her own culture and realizes that God became incarnate in a culture too. A person has to know the elements of their religion such as prayers, rituals, and methods and ways of expressing those. This knowledge is not just the mental capacity to perceive things, but more dynamic interaction, participation and identification. In other words, a reflective knowledge enhances reflective religion.

Effective appropriation of the lament psalms in the life of the church implies effective hermeneutical principle(s) applied by the reading community. Although culture and context play a major role in interpreting the Scriptures, there are timeless issues that affect humanity in their finitude and frailty. As David Pleins puts it:

> We can immerse ourselves at the beginning of the tradition to wrestle with the sociopolitical contexts and questions of the text. We can locate ourselves at another stage of the tradition and meditate on these texts as documents imparting spiritual instructions. Or we can place ourselves in yet another stage of tradition to be moved by the Psalms to sing songs of tragedy and trust, lament and praise. However, no matter what our port of entry, the issues of suffering, social justice and worship continually confront us in our engagement of the texts. The questions are critical to our continued appropriation of the psalms as living documents in church and synagogue today (Pleins 1993: 5).

Psalms of lament are not simply living documents that can be twisted as befit the interpreter or the reader. They are living voices, voices of real people who lived in real adverse political and social situations.

The place of Lament in history of salvation

Cry for help is the core of the OT salvation history. In Exodus 3:7-8 God comes down to save the enslaved Israelites because "God has seen their misery, God has heard their cry, and God knows their works of affliction" (my translation). This is where it all started.

Psalm 13, for example, presents us with the theology of God who comes down and hears our groaning just as God did to the Israelites in Egypt. The language of "how long will you forget" is tied to God's remembrance of the covenant which is indicated clearly in the Psalmist's appeal to steadfast love as a covenantal concept of faithful relationship established by God to Israel. In this way, Psalm 13 brings both the psalmist's situation and God to the Exodus event, to that larger and decisive event in history. This history of relationship is reclaimed through dialogue between God and the sufferer. In this historical deed, Yahweh took initiatives to deliver the suffering nation and to give them a future with hope.

Psalm 102 describes a close relationship between the petitioner and God. This relationship is grounded in the understanding of the incomparable character of God who sides with the oppressed, raises the lowly and delivers them from those who are too strong for the oppressed. This conviction is rooted deep in Israel's memory. Like Psalm 13 the covenant relationship between Yahweh and the petitioner is particularized. In the Exodus-covenant memory and in the prophetic traditions, Yahweh aligns with the poor and the needy and intervenes powerfully on their behalf. "This covenant reality helps to explain the element of boldness that is so characteristic of these psalms (see, e.g., Pss. 44:23; 88:13-14). Because of the nature of the covenant, we have the right to complain to this God and ask for a hearing" (Craghan 1985: 116). Often the petitioner(s) invokes God by recalling God's deeds to Israel in the past. This is more prevalent in the community Psalms but also in the individual Psalms (e.g. Ps. 28:8-9; 44:1-3; 74:12-17; 80; 89:32-33).

The relationship of God in creation, redemption and sanctification is explained in a variety of ways which are concomitant with people's realities at given times and places. When Israelites lament, they make use of the language and a pattern of religion of which they are a part. Westermann makes the following observation:

> The Old Testament cannot pin God down to a single soteriology; it can only speak of God's saving acts within a whole series of events, and that necessarily involves some kind of verbal exchange between God and man [sic]. This latter includes both the cry of man [sic] in distress and the response of praise which the saved make to God (Westermann 1981: 259).

God's redemption activity began as an event between God and humanity. God heard and saw the cries and affliction of God's people Israel. Thus, "the lament is an inevitable part of what happens between God and man [sic]" (Westermann 1981: 261).

The lament psalms provide us as a community of believers, who suffer and grieve today, with the canonical and covenantal contexts in which to express our grief and give lament legitimacy, form, and healing direction. In discussing the role of the lament in the community of faith, Andre Resner, Jr. comments:

> When we are enveloped in the biblical lament (either through reading, study, or worship) and when we are in the context of today's covenant community of faith, we have, as it were, a bracket of perspective surrounding us in and through which God works. We are not left alone but we are swept up, rocked, and called back to live now. We are given a context and words for our weeping. And in that context of asking the great questions of our lives and wailing with what seems like our life's last breath, we come to realize that the one who rocks us and beckons us back from giving up is the Present God, who himself laments with us (Resner 1990: 142).

If this happens, human existence is made meaningful and livable even during distressful times. When we cannot find words to speak to God, lament psalms provide us with words and in this way voice our deepest fears, angers, doubts and desires. Psalms of lament do not only give words to suffering people, but they also give form to the painful experiences of life. "The prayers of lament in the Psalter give a form to the worst experience of life which follows the movement innate to human suffering and yet places it in the presence of the one who alone can be a decisive word to those who suffer" (Brueggemann 1977: 263). What the suffering person needs is not only right words to say to God and to the community, but also the need to hear a comforting word from the Maker and Restorer of all life. The speech of the sufferer and God's speech form the healing process in which communication takes place. A life of faith is not a life of denial but acceptance of a reality. It is a life that sees the breadth, length, depth and heights of human life in relation to God and in relation to society in which they are a part. It is also a life that is willing to be nurtured by the rich traditions of Scripture and its own tradition. It is a life that recognizes its heritage, and a life that embraces the fullness of its theological heritage, which, in turn, is embraced by the tradition.

The laments pervade the whole of the OT, from the patriarchal narratives, Exodus event, historical books, prophetic literature, the Psalms and Job. They are important in understanding the human situation because they address existential issues. A human being in the psalms is not idealized or spiritualized. He is portrayed as a finite being that fears suffering, pain, loneliness, abandonment, and most of all death. A human being is a being with limitations of transitoriness and failure as Psalm 13:3 makes very clear. The mortal psalmist is set over against God who is forever and everlasting. The perils created by these limitations are part and parcel of human existence and one cannot escape them, except that we can bring them to God for redress so that God can change one's plight. The lament takes humanity and its situation seriously. The lament is concerned with the removal of those perils and this is why there is, in many cases, movement towards praise as an anticipation of that transformation.

Lament psalms are songs of life addressing mortality and life transience (see e.g. Psalm 39). They are songs of defiance/resistance over suffering and/or death that touches the core of human life. The main part of lament/complaint reveals this reality, in which the petitioner addresses his/her pain to God in a raw language that challenges God to act. The Psalms exhibit a sense of a real power of spoken word from a human point of view – the power to concretize, give force, meaning and effectiveness to what would otherwise remain nebulous realities of life and inner longings. Psalms give possibilities and the prowess to search our own hearts that might have been closed to the realities of life. They challenge and extricate our euphemistic speech, reorienting our words to concur with those realities. Our Christian faith has created euphoria, a sense of wellbeing that, on one hand, narrows and deflects our understanding of life as a straight, one-dimensional adventure. But, on the other hand, these concrete life-threatening re- alities give permanent numbness to pain and suffering that people face from day to day. Christian faith, by its teachings, has made harsh realities temporal, deluding its believers to masochism, in hope of that otherworldly and permanent life. Christians live in *quasi de facto* cir- cumstances. As a result, faith and worship becomes less authentic and lethargic.

Lament addresses God and community to hear hurts and pains, similar to the way that, for instance, Bob Marley addressed the issues of injustice and oppression through songs of liberation (com- pare Psalm 35).

Concluding Remarks

The cracking of complacency is a wonderful thing, but it is only the beginning. An immense effort lies ahead of us, to engage in removing this hard crust of habit and custom and to allow effective interpreta- tions of biblical texts as a major concern in our faith. When we wrestle and engage with "hard psalms" we maintain our concern for truth and justice, honesty and fidelity to our own lives. More concretely, we are more fully engaged with the complex circumstances of career, family building, the interpretation of our faith, and our compassion toward the suffering, the afflicted and the oppressed.

It is the task of the church to engage seriously in exposing people to the cultural treasures that are hidden by our Christianization pro- cess. People need the cultural context of which they belong; they need the church, which is the authority to value the culture of the people. It can be done by working fervently to introduce cultural elements that enable the church to communicate better in their cul- tural locations. The church has to dig out these hidden treasures and place it in front of the people to see and appreciate the richness and closeness of their world to that of the Bible.

Inculturation does not need to be done in theological schools alone. It has to start from the grassroots. Instead of concentrat- ing on the traditional melodies in our church choirs, it would be appropriate to make use of important phrases and images used in traditional songs to express our pleas to God in the form of songs. We can harmonize these traditional creations with the biblical texts of the same nature, and finally make a new creation in the light of the Christian faith. In the lament psalms, both the theology and the mode of expression draw out of us a response to suffering and injustice. This can only happen when we have truly engaged ourselves with the context of the text. The attempt to avoid this serious and daring encounter results in the denial of our own reality as well as the reality that encompasses our societies and our communities. "Wrestling with these questions we, as individuals and as community, come face-to-face with Israel's God of justice in a world touched by both eros and dust" (Pleins 1993: 1). Pleins also reads the Psalms with political eyes, taking into account liberation theology, a theology that speaks against the oppressive institutions in this world, and that tries to bring the voice of the oppressed to the world of religion as well. But he also affirms that when "we read these texts with both canon and context in mind, we are confronted by language textured by human experience before God" (Pleins 1993: 5).

For Pleins, issues of suffering and social justice are the main agenda of the Psalms, and these issues can be brought forward regardless of the methodological approach one uses. He comments:

> We can immerse ourselves at the beginnings of the tradition to wrestle with the sociopolitical context and questions of the text. We can locate ourselves at another stage of the tradition and meditate on these texts as documents imparting spiritual instruction. Or we can place ourselves in yet another stage of tradition to be moved by the psalms to sing songs of tragedy and trust, lament and praise. However, no matter what our port of entry, the issues of suffering, social justice and worship continually confront us in our engagement of the texts. These questions are critical to our continued appropriation of the psalms as living documents in church and synagogue today (Pleins 1993: 5).

Of course this approach has already placed the issues of social justice and suffering at the centre, so that the agenda is already known and the psalms have to comply with this agenda. In other words, Pleins is looking at these psalms with the eyes of a liberation theologian, and he intends to find the ways these psalms grapple with the contemporary issues of oppression and liberation (Pleins 1993: 5).

His observation might not be applied to all the psalms, but reading the psalms by looking at their context might yield diverse issues that transcend our limited agendas. In fact, human issues and concerns are more diverse and complex than those brought out when we apply specific cultural and religious oriented modes of interpretations.

Reading the psalms by taking into account its varied contexts throws light on various aspects of God's character, as liberator, mother and redeemer. When we realize these various attributes we will be equipped to identify our sufferings and oppression with the lament psalms.

The continent of Africa is ravaged by HIV, wars, poverty, cultural injustices, and so on. Which songs shall we sing? What are songs of life? Can laments be songs of life?

Works Cited

Abogunrin, S. O. (1986). "Biblical Research in Africa: The Task Ahead." *African Journal of Biblical Studies* 1: 7–24.

Brueggemann, Walter (1977). "The Formfullness of Grief." *Interpretation* 31: 263–75.

Brueggemann, Walter (1982). *Praying the Psalms*. Winona: Saint Mary's.

Brueggemann, Walter (1994). *The Message of the Psalms*. Minneapolis: Augsburg.

Brueggemann, Walter (1995). *The Psalms and the Life of Faith*, ed. Patrick Miller. Minneapolis: Fortress.

Craghan, John F. (1985). *The Psalms: Prayers of Ups, Downs and In-Betweens of Life: A Literary-Experiential Approach*. Wilmington: Michael Glazier.

Hagena, Otto. (1949). *Schatten des Todes-Light of Leben*. Bethel bei Bielefeld: verlangschandlung der Anstalt, 3rd edn. Bethel.

Holladay, William (1993). *The Psalms through Three Thousand Years: Prayerbook of a Cloud of Witnesses*. Minneapolis: Fortress.

Oduyoye, Mercy Amba (1986). *Hearing and Knowing: Theological Reflections on Christianity in Africa*. Maryknoll, NY: Orbis.

Pleins, J. David (1993). *The Psalms: Songs of Tragedy, Hope, and Justice*. Maryknoll, NY: Orbis.

Pobee, John S. (1996). "Bible Study in Africa: A Passover of Language." *Semeia* 73: 161–79.

Resner, Andre (1990). "Lament: Faith's Response to Loss." *Restoration Quarterly* 32.3: 129–42.

Sanneh, Lamin (1988). *Translating the Message: The Missionary Impact on the Culture*. Maryknoll, NY: Orbis.

Sylva, Dennis (1993). *Psalms and Transformation of Stress: Poetic-Communal Interpretation and the Family*. Louvain: Peeters.

Westermann, Claus (1981). *Praise and Lament in the Psalms*. Atlanta: John Knox.

Westermann, Claus (1994). *Lamentations: Issues and Interpretation*. Minneapolis: Fortress.

13 Retelling Tamar's Story (2 Sam. 13:1-22) in Postcolonial Terms

Joseph Mathew

Introduction

"Biography is the footprint of history walked in the life of an individual," says V. Padma in a recent issue of *Bhashabhoshini* ("Nurturer of Language"), a Malayalam monthly publication (Padma 2004). Despite the limits of biographies and the biases of biographers, biographies are nonetheless windows to history. This echoes Phyllis Trible's claim that "stories are style and substance of life" (Trible 1984: 1). She coined "texts of terror" in retelling the stories of abused women, and how it becomes a significant hermeneutical exercise of "remembering the past the present embodies" (Trible 1984: 3).[1] Texts such as 2 Sam. 13:1-22 are often neglected and marginalized, and are found in few lectionaries on account of the disgusting story they present. Such texts are seldom read or preached publicly. However, as Mark Gray observes, "this story is dealing with the depiction of the process whereby Tamar's humanity is obliterated" (Gray 1998: 39). Therefore the attempt of the present enquiry is to revisit the story of Tamar addressing the issue of displacement that it poses, taking into consideration insights from postcolonial theory.

Postcolonial studies have emerged as a meeting point and battleground for a variety of disciplines and theories (Gandhi 1999: 2). Postcolonial theory inevitably commits itself to a complex project of historical and psychological "recovery" (Gray 1998: 39). Musa W. Dube contends that "Given that imperialism has been a recurring phenomenon in the history of the world, post-colonial applicability to various other classical texts in human history is legitimate" (Dube 1997: 15). What postcolonialism and feminist movements have in common is their resistance to any form of oppression – be it patriarchy or colonialism (for that matter, both patriarchy and colonialism function on similar ideologies). Both of these principles enrich and complement each other in their function.

Unless we know what colonialism implies, it is difficult to understand what postcolonialism means.[2] It is too simplistic to assume that colonialism was confined only to European nations. There were other forms of colonialism before and after the European expansion and withdrawal. There is internal colonialism within countries which were once under colonial rule, where indigenous people, especially women, and their histories and cultures have been annexed and annihilated by local "elites." Thus in this study "colonialism" is used to refer to the tendency to dominate, aggression, impulse of conquering, authoritarianism and imperial arrogance. This could appear in the form of cultural, intellectual, economic and political totalitarianism.

"Postcolonial" signifies a reactive resistance discourse of the colonized who critically interrogate dominant knowledge systems in order to recover the past from Western slander and misinformation of the colonial period. "Postcolonialism" as criticism, more than being a science, undertakes a social and political commitment, "as life-enhancing and constitutively opposed to every form of tyranny, domination and abuse" (Said 1991: 29). It is in this sense that postcolonialism is understood in this study.

Placing 2 Samuel 13:1-22

Samuel is a transitional figure with whose birth-report the book starts. Later he assumes the role of the kingmaker commissioned by YHWH. Since 1 and 2 Samuel deal with the stories of the origin of monarchy and of the first two kings of Israel, it is an "Empire Narrative." We have more detailed reports about David than about any other king. Such accounts are essentially contained in two great literary complexes: 1 Sam. 1 – 2 Sam. 5 records "the History of the Rise of David to the Throne"; and 2 Sam. 9 – 1 Kgs 2 comprises the "Succession Narrative." In the first instance, the record presents a prelude to David's reign which in essence is his conflict with Saul; and the second account addresses the question of succession which reflects the struggles for power (Rendtorff 1985: 29-31). The story of Tamar appears in the "Succession Narrative" of which 2 Sam. 13–14 serve as a prologue to the rebellion of Absalom.

As generally seen in the Old Testament, this case indicates the image and role of women during this period as reflecting the patriarchal ideology that governed the social system. This system gave a subservient, and dependant status to women. Phyllis Bird comments, "discrimination against women was inherent in the socio-religious organization of Israel" (Bird 1974: 50). The virgin daughter or bride are depicted with erotic metaphors in the Bible. A young woman who is ripe for love is called a "virgin," "young woman," "maiden" or "bride" in the conventions of ancient Near East poetry. A woman's sexuality was guarded by her father before marriage (Deut. 22:13-21, 28-29) and by her husband after marriage. Woman was considered as property along with other possessions of the male.

Displacement as Colonial Disaster

Displacement is a disastrous consequence of colonization, which is to be understood within the wider question of diaspora. Robin Cohen has explained that the term diaspora primarily meant "migration and colonization" among Greeks in the Archaic period (800–600 BCE) and was used to describe the colonization of Asia Minor and the Mediterranean region. The dominant features of displacement, and war that dispersion caused, according to Robin Cohen, were seen as "an expansion through plunder, military conquest, colonization and migration" (cited in Sugirtharajah 2002: 180). Thus displacement figures as a crucial issue in postcolonial criticism. It refers to the displacement of cultures (Spivak 1990: 26) under the guise of development. It is the imposed alienation upon the native within the "home." It is the marginalization and an altered representation of social geography in the colonies with specific strategies of rule (Stoler 2000: 797). Along with the notions of hardship and suffering, the term displacement, attested to the notion of diaspora, stands for the epitomized meaning of "victimhood" with the metaphorical meaning of being thrown away from the inherent location.

Tamar's Story as a Story of "Displacement"

Tamar was a displaced woman abused by the male powers that were in a struggle for exclusive power. Identifying Tamar as a displaced woman raises questions about the colonial conspiracy of the patriarchal powers and the intensity of her victimization. A discussion on certain dimensions of displacement such as displacement by the law, colonial instrumentality of language, false imaging, metaphor of travelling and finally the use of physical violence will further clarify the situation. This enables us to see Tamar as a victim of displacement who suffered estrangement and marginality on account of the sexual assault she was dragged into.

Law: The Primary Colonizer

The first tool of displacement in the society in which Tamar lived was the law itself. The politics of writing the law under male-dominated rule favoured men to safeguard its agenda while it marginalized the women. Law was the primary source in reconstructing the ideals and practices of Israel. The Israel law was characterized by severity in sexual transgressions. Law presupposed full membership of the society to man. One can infer from the Old Testament that the status of women in Israel before the Law was constructed within the masculine formulated direct address (e.g., Exod. 20:17) or in literary subordination to a male subject (e.g., Exod. 21:3; Jer. 44:25).

This disparity is evident in the law concerning virginity, which has to do with taboos and impositions on "young woman," "bride" or "virgin." The law presents well-defined stipulations on the virginity of woman where the sexual perversion of an unmarried man is surprisingly ignored. So, as a woman, Tamar was already displaced in the society by the law. The psychological pressure on Tamar by the law makes her life continue in constant guilt and shame and in total frustration after the instance of violence. The irony is that, as Eryl W. Davis says, "it is not the rapist, Amnon, who feels shame, but his half-sister Tamar" (Davis 2003: 76). The taboo of virginity as a pre-requisite for marriage leaves no room for Tamar to have recognizable existence, because her life is now torn apart – as she symbolically does by tearing her garment (2 Sam. 13:19) – between rejection and the urge to survive.

Language as a Colonial Instrument

"One of the main features of imperial oppression is control over language" (Brydon 2000: 52). Language can be manipulated to gain the goals of dominance. To this end, the language of the peripheries is shaped and dictated by an oppressive discourse of power. Further, in colonial strategies, language becomes the medium through which a hierarchical structure of power is perpetuated and the conceptions of "truth," "order" and "reality" become established (Brydon 2000: 52). This is to say that the manipulative operation of language by the colonizer to hegemonize the colonized has been a feature of colonialism.

The story of Tamar reveals such a manipulation of language. All that Amnon and his corollaries speak is perverted and feigned fact presented through equivocation. Amnon uses language as an instrument for plotting secrecy. His pretence of sickness and the desire expressed in his words when he says that "Tamar will come and bake food for me" as well as "come and make some special bread in my sight, so that I might eat from her" (2 Sam. 13:6) is a scheme-full twist. This became the weapon of seduction for Amnon on Tamar.

False Imaging

The colonizer imposes false image upon the colonized. Often the colonized are perceived by the colonizers as helpless, evil, weak, vulnerable, inarticulate, backward, savage, pagan and so on. This imposing or false imaging is strategically employed to validate the domination of the colonizer on the victims. Such a contrast is evident in the characterization of Tamar by Amnon and Jonadab, with the sanctioning of the narrator, and the self-image portrayed by Tamar through her words and responses.

However, against this weapon of false imaging, what is revealed of Tamar in her words in verses 12 and 13 invites serious attention.

She is prudent, wise and morally strong, and she evokes introspection even to the victimizer. Tamar resists the overpowering tide of Amnon's lust. She calls the act of Amnon as a "wanton folly" (*nebelah* v. 12), done only by "wanton fools" (*nebalim*) in Israel. Gerald O. West presents a categorical explanation marvelling the wit and wisdom with which Tamar reasoned (West 2004): First, she says a clear "No" (13:12), which should be enough. Second, she reminds him that he is her "brother" (13:12). Third, by using the word "forcing" she expresses her unwillingness to be his sexual partner (13:12). Fourth, she reminds him of the cultural heritage, "for such thing is not done in Israel" (13:12). Fifth, she declares his intention to be evil (13:12). Sixth, she calls attention to the consequences thereby to consider her plight (13:12). Seventh, she turns to the question of consequence on him saying what will happen to him (13:13). Eighth, she offers a way out by suggesting that he can marry her (13:13). Still Amnon fell prey to his unbridled passion. But the image of Tamar is highly elevated as a woman of wisdom proving wrong the false imaging of the victimizer.

Metaphor of Travelling

Travelling is another metaphor in the colonial narratives. This metaphor works in two ways. First the metropolitan travellers who are neither ignorant nor dependent on the natives, entering a "foreign" land with their authority claimed from their advantage of race, religion, technology and knowledge. Second, the subjugated travel of the colonized to the lands of their masters as powerless strangers – such as in exile – slaves, servants or refugees (Brydon 2000: 52).

Tamar travelled as a refugee from the house of her father to the house of her brother Absalom in Hebron who had already been imaged as rebellious to the King in terms of the politics of succession. Mark Gray traces the progression of this process (Gray 1998: 39):

> Tamar, at the behest of her father, goes [or travels] from the safety of home to the danger of [Amnon's room] where she is robbed of her humanity and discarded to a state of wandering homelessness until, a shell of her former self, finds some shelter [in Absalom's house].

This movement was a displacement from the palace to asylum; from princesshood to refugeehood, making Tamar a dependant waiting for society's acceptance and favour.

Physical Violence: The Last Resort

The use of physical power and violence such as military operation was a colonial strategy of conquering.

Refusing to heed the plea of Tamar by coming to terms with the wise reasoning she presents, Amnon moves to his last resort of violence: physical assault on Tamar. The text obviously refers to the exertion of physical power. "He [Amnon] was stronger than she; thus he 'forced' (RSV) her and laid her" (13:14b). Amnon "grabbed (*hzq*) hold of her" (13:11) and "he was stronger (*hzq*)" and "he *raped* (*'nh*) her." It is further recorded that Amnon ordered "Lie (*skb*) with me" (13:11) and finally "he laid her." In between, the plea of Tamar is heard as "Do not violate (*'nh*) me" (13:12) (Trible 1984: 46).

The verb *'nh* depicts sexual violation. Traditionally rendered "humbled" or in some readings "violated" or "forced her to sleep/lie with him," many translators now see strong evidence for the use of the word "rape." The verbs *'nh* and *skb* denote rape in the context of v. 14 because of the inclusion of Amnon's use of his superior strength (Gravett 2004: 298). Tikva Frymer-Kensky observes that

> the key term, [*'nh*] does not mean rape… In the story of Amnon and Tamar, specially where Amnon raped Tamar, narrator says specifically he overpowered her, abused her and lay with her… Both the use of the verb "over power" and the word order are significant. In Amnon's case, where the text tells us specifically that the rape was by force, [*'nh*] comes before the word "lay with" (cited in Gravett 2004: 298).

Thus by resorting to physical violence Amnon pushes her displacement to more or less an irrecoverable point.

Hermeneutical Challenge of the Story of Tamar

Reading the story of Tamar as an instance of displacement poses significant challenges in approaching biblical texts. The act of engaging with texts such as 2 Samuel 13:1-22 gives us the space to listen to the voices otherwise unheard, and to confront issues that are often swept under the carpet. Norman K. Gottwald opens the discussion on "biblical scholarship in public discourse" and says that biblical scholars are not just to exegete the texts; but are to take a deliberate hermeneutical option engaging with life challenges seeking how far the biblical text would inform the present-day culture, especially in the context of gender roles and other "public issues" (Gottwald 2003: 559). The dimensions of race, gender, third world realities, caste – all these perspectives need to be addressed with due commitment. However, one should not be ignorant of the reality that the Bible speaks with many voices, as the biblical scholars decide to "go public."

The question of displacement of women and the challenge of recovering the space is a poignant issue. Spivak suggests that for the "retrieval of lost origin or reclaiming one's history" "the subaltern women can speak only by embracing the self-erasure" (cited in Dube 2002: 106). The woman should come to "represent" herself. As Andrea Dworkin rightly points out, "all struggle for dignity and self-determination is rooted in the struggle for actual control of one's own body, especially control over physical access to one's own body" (cited in Exum 1993: 171). The real challenge for a woman in male-dominated social structures is the struggle to retrieve her dignity and to actualize the right to be in her own space, not in male-constructed spaces.

The church and the theological community, in particular, must actualize the challenge given by Jesus who made a conscious effort in public to recognize the space of women through his ministry (e.g. women with flow of blood in Mark 5:25-34; Canaanite woman in Matthew 15:21-28; and Mary Magdalene whom he regarded as a worthy partner in his mission) by deliberately "violating" the patriarchal imposition that displaces and marginalizes women.

Concluding Remarks

The text is silent on what happened to Tamar eventually. This is another example of textual violence (or rape) on women in the Bible.

The narrator uses the story of Tamar as a plot that invigorates the scene of the struggle for succession and ignores it when the purpose is served. Tamar is again "used" here not as a person but as a political object. J. Cheryl Exum refers to this as "literary rape" but it should not be compared with actual rape (Exum 1993: 171). This kind of textual violence calls into critique the reports in the media and damage it does to the identity of the victim who is in double disgrace both by the actual event of violence and then by its reports in the public arena.

The story throws light on several issues such as incest, sexual violence, discrimination by law, marginalization of women, insecurity of women in families and so on. Tamar, the protagonist of the story, comes out both as a vulnerable victim of patriarchy and a critic of the wickedness to which the text witnesses. To recap the prophetic voice of the biblical text, which often lies enmeshed in the ideology of the time, is the challenge as we confront realities of displacement. This recovery needs to be done with a commitment to liberative praxis, to ensure the space that each deserves in society.

Works Cited

Bird, Phyllis (1974). "Images of Women in the Old Testament." In *Religion and Sexism: Images of Woman in the Jewish and Christian Tradition*, ed. Rosemary R. Ruether, 41–88. New York: Simon and Schuster.

Brydon, Diane (ed.). (2000). *Postcolonialism: Critical Concepts and Cultural Studies*, vol. 1. London and New York: Routledge.

Davis, Eryl W. (2003). *The Dissenting Reader*. Aldershot: Ashgate.

Dube, Musa W. (1997). "Toward a Post-Colonial Feminist Interpretation of the Bible." *Semeia* 78: 11–26.

Dube, Musa W. (2002). "Postcoloniality, Feminist Spaces and Religion." In *Postcolonialism, Feminism and Religious Discourse*, ed. Laura E. Donaldson and Kwok Pui-lan, 100–120. London: Routledge.

Exum, J. Cheryl (1993). *Fragmented Women: Feminist (Sub)versions of Biblical Narratives*. Pennsylvania: Trinity International.

Gandhi, Leela (1999). *Postcolonial Theory: A Critical Introduction*. Delhi: Oxford University Press.

Gottwald, Norman K. (2003). "Biblical Scholarship in Public Discourse." *Biblical Interpretation* 11.3/4: 555–65.

Gravett, Sandie (2004). "Reading 'Rape' in the Hebrew Bible: A Consideration of Language." *Journal for the Study of the Old Testament* 28.3: 279–99.

Gray, Mark (1998). "Amnon: A Chip off the Old Block? Rhetorical Strategy in 2 Samuel 13: 7-15. The Rape of Tamar and Humiliation of the Poor." *Journal of the Study of the Old Testament* 77: 39–54.

Padma, V. (2004). "Theendal" [untouchability]. *Bhashaposhini*, Book 27 Vol. 9 (February): 30.

Rendtorff, Rolf (1985). *The Old Testament: An Introduction*. London: SCM.

Said, Edward (1991). *The World, the Text and the Critic*. London: Vintage.

Spivak, Gayatri C. (1990). *The Postcolonial Critic: Interviews, Strategies, Dialogues*, ed. Sarah Harasym. New York: Routledge.

Stoler, Ann Laura (2000). "Colonial Studies and the History of Sexuality." In *Postcolonialism: Critical Concepts in Literary and Cultural Studies*, ed. Diane Brydon, 797–812. London and New York: Routledge.

Sugirtharajah, R. S. (2002). *Postcolonial Criticism and Biblical Interpretation*. Oxford: Oxford University Press.

Trible, Phyllis (1984). *Texts of Terror*. Philadelphia: Fortress.

West, Gerald O. (2004). "1 and 2 Samuel." In *Global Bible Commentary*, ed. Daniel Patte et al., 92–104. Nashville: Abingdon.

14 What is in a Name? Abishag the Shunammite as *sokenet* in 1 Kings 1:1-4

Mercedes L. García Bachmann

Introduction

The book of Kings opens with a simple story. David has become old and cold: his life is evidently fading and he cannot keep himself warm any more. So his servants decide to bring a young woman who would attend to him. Abishag from Shunem is the chosen one. She accompanies him constantly, even "laying in his bosom," but no sexual relations are involved. She seems to be present as Bathsheba and Nathan manage to get David to appoint Solomon as his successor. Much later, after Adonijah had lost his chance to be appointed king, he requests through Bathsheba that Abishag be given to him as a wife. This turns on Solomon's rage, so that he orders Adonijah's execution for his pretence to the throne (1 Kgs 2:17-22).

Abishag is not mentioned again. She is never given direct speech or even a hint of her feelings or thoughts. She is clearly not a character, but an agent in the plot (Berlin 1982: 74–76). The plot is much wider than Abishag's story. It is well known that scholars do not agree on many important issues, such as whether we are dealing with the "succession narrative," the "court history" or some other plot (not to mention its tendency for or against Solomon, especially its beginning). These are not essential for our goal; yet they must be kept in mind because in that whole picture Abishag is not only a non-character; she is *one* among several agents. Since the "succession narrative" is not my main concern here and it would take too much space to deal with it, I will select certain elements from the whole story; elements that pertain to the argument I am making here.

In this chapter I want to explore the ways a text uses names in order to speak of a woman who happens not to be an important character in the story, but rather an agent for its development. Particularly, I am concerned with how women are systemically denied our rights to proper names. Playing with terms, I think of "proper names" in the grammatical sense of "Abishag," "Shunem" and so on, but also in what is due a person, what would be proper – at least from my own perspective – for a person to be called.

At first glance, this interest may look too minute. Nevertheless, language greatly influences ideologies (how people see and order the world into a system more or less coherent). Thus effort should be given to unmasking languages that belittle people (or events of great import). Furthermore, if language is used to belittle a person and hide her real import there is the challenge to look behind it, testing whether in the scant information we have about her, we may get a broader political picture of palace and kinship as presented in the last events of King David's life.

The Broader Context of the Story

The story of Abishag cannot be fully grasped without understanding the broader story of King David, his family, and his way of doing politics, i.e., of dealing with his "kingdom."[1] There are enough commentaries dealing with these books' composition, unity, date, and other vexing issues. Thus, I will not deal with those here. Whenever it is unavoidable to take a stand, I follow Fokkelman's literary analysis.

The broader frame of 1 Kings 1–2 has several peculiarities. On the one hand, as several scholars have noted, the way David is portrayed in these two chapters strongly contrasts with how he is portrayed in the previous book: from active to passive, from assertive to doubtful, from powerful to powerless, and so on (Fokkelman 1981: 345–46; Walsh 1996: 5; Gunn 1982). On the other hand, while it is the beginning of the book of Kings, it recounts the end of David's life and, whether that is this story's main concern or not, it has a clear bearing on who will reign after David: Will it be Adonijah, the first-born, or will it be Solomon (see Fokkelman 1981: 353–58, 365, 367)? And how will this happen?

The (Known) Story of Abishag

There are three texts in 1 Kings 1–2 which mention this young woman. The way she is presented and the events her presence unleashes are different in each of these episodes. In none of them is she given a voice.

Abishag is appointed personal assistant to David (1 Kings 1:1-4)

The first and most important text for our purposes is 1 Kgs 1:1-4, the beginning of the book of Kings. The main character of the story is King David, even though he hardly speaks. His servants make an assessment about him that sets the plot in motion. He is unable to keep himself warm any more. His last recorded decisions are made not from his throne, but from his bed-chamber. Yet they are still authoritative, as one learns in the following chapters. It is in this political *crux* that Abishag is brought in.

1 Kgs 1:1-4 recounts why she was chosen and brought to King David's chamber. The story is straightforward and the Masoretic text presents no textual problems:

> In those days, King David had become old and they covered him with clothes, but he could not get warm. And his servants told him: "Let a young 'girl' be sought for my Lord the king, and she would stand in the presence of the king and be his personal assistant. Let she lie in your bosom and may the king my Lord get warm." They sought a pleasant/pretty "girl" within the borders of all Israel and they found Abishag the Shunammite. And they brought her to the king. The "girl" was very pleasant/pretty and she was the king's stewardess. And she attended/ministered to him. And (but?) the king did not know her (sexually).[2]

In this story, actions are performed by a group of "servants" ('abadim) of the king, whose number and names are unknown to the reader. David's situation, assessed by the narrator in v. 1, no doubt represents what his servants had also realized by themselves and perhaps commented upon. Blankets proved not to be enough, so they come to the king with the proposal of looking for a young body that would attend to him and keep him warm by sharing his same bed. That young body to keep him warm is, of course, that of a young woman, of marriageable age. I will return to this text below.

David appoints Solomon as King (1 Kgs 1:15-53)

The next time Abishag is mentioned, she is in the king's chamber. First Bathsheba and, shortly after her, Nathan, appear to speak to David and force him to appoint his successor. Abishag is mentioned by the narrator, who records her presence when Bathsheba enters to talk to her husband:

> And Bathsheba went unto the king into the chamber. The king was very old; and Abishag the Shunammite was ministering to the king (1:15).

There is not much here to be known about her, except that she is there, present, where the queen is not: Batsheba notices her when she enters the king's chamber (the text is silent about Abishag staying or leaving the room). Yet her presence need not be seen as a sign of a higher status than Abishag. To the contrary. Servants of different kinds are needed as part of the scenario, so to speak; precisely because they are disposable or, at least, interchangeable. This is not to celebrate how lower-class people are treated; on the contrary, it is a sad observation of how different writers construe their scenes, and it applies to men and to women as well. This has to do with the ambivalence inherent in the concept of slavery or chattel, in which a person is a sort of mobile object owned by someone.

Abishag as an excuse for the last succession fight (2 Kgs 2:13-25[26-35])

The last mention of Abishag does not even have her physically present. The event is one that unleashes Solomon's "cleaning-up" of his last enemies: his brother Adonijah, and his supporters Abiathar and Joab.

This last episode is useful in exemplifying or clarifying how people may become an excuse for actions within state politics, which would not be otherwise acceptable. Adonijah first approaches Bathsheba and asks her to intercede on his behalf unto his brother and king, Solomon. He requests that Abishag be given to him as a wife:

> And he (Adonijah) said: "Please speak with Solomon the king – for he will not deny (anything) to you – that he give me Abishag the Shunammite as wife" (2:17).

This request is taken by Solomon as a claim to his throne. Thus, he has his brother and two of his close supporters executed on the assumption of treason to the king appointed by David and already governing. Whether this request of Adonijah carried by Bathsheba on his behalf was indeed an indirect claim to the – by then lost to Adonijah – throne of Israel, or whether this was the excuse Solomon needed to dispose of his last enemies, has long been a matter of discussion among scholars. At any rate, Abishag is a pawn in a game between contending parties – one more woman disputed by males who, in the end, do not care about her, only about what she might represent in their power games. And as such, Abishag is also in danger of being raped – of having to give her body for sex to a man without her own consent, which is rape.

Abishag's lot after these events is not recorded. In all probability, she remained in the palace, since nothing is said here about her being taken as part of this plot by Adonijah and punished accordingly. She might have become one more concubine in Solomon's harem, or might have been given in marriage to someone Solomon wanted to reward. We do not know.

With this last mention, this woman vanishes from the Bible. Which makes sense, due to her status of "support personnel" (in terms of her occupation), of na'ara ("dependent," in social or legal terms), and of agent (narratively). Yet there remain several intriguing facts about her; or, to be more precise, about the way she is presented and described, especially in the first two texts reviewed here. To these we turn next.

A "One-of-her-Kind" Woman

In this chapter I am not dealing with the historicity or not of Abishag or any of the other people mentioned in this story, including Nathan, Joab, Solomon, and David himself. As anyone conversant with current scholarship knows too well, there is a deep disagreement on these issues. I can imagine a core of truth in it, especially in what has to do with how "Solomon," and not his elderly brother, became king because of a political move, almost a *coup d'etat*, that needed some explanation in order to gain acceptance. Were there a core of historical verity in Solomon, Nathan, Bathsheba, Abishag and the others, we would still be left with a literary depiction of them and not with a historical essay.

Therefore, what I am asking here is not "Who was Abishag?," but "How is Abishag depicted in this story?" The main source for answering this question is the first of the texts mentioned, because the remaining two texts do not add new data.

How is Abishag depicted? The information about her can be organized into four categories: (a) usefulness for the purpose of the search; (b) reason for her being chosen over other candidates; (c) her social condition; and (d) personal information. These categories overlap, but it might be useful simply to organize the information; an organization that a verse-by-verse reading would not allow.

Usefulness for Purpose of Search

The first and most important of all data is that Abishag is somebody brought in to the palace in order to perform a duty or task, to provide a service, related to keeping David comfortable and warm. This is the reason for her being brought in: she is a servant to the king. This intention is confirmed by the assessments that she was his stewardess or personal assistant (*sokenet*), and that "she ministered to him" (1:4, and also 1:15, when the reader sees through Bathsheba's sight: "And Bathsheba went unto the king into the chamber. The king was very old; and Abishag the Shunammite was ministering to the king").

Not only is her task enunciated by the words used, but also by the structure, as Fokkelman shows in his analysis of the servants' proposal to find someone:

a   ...Young girl for my lord, the king
b   and she will stand in front of the king
x   and she will be a *sōkenet* to him
b   and she will lie in his bossom
a   and make warm my lord, the king[3]

Fokkelman understands the three components of this chiasmus, a-a', b-b' and x as related to each other in the sense that they all would explain the centre, the "axis upon which the plan rotates"; which is to say, Abishag's task – and person, because both go together in this story – and would not be different elements:

> A paradoxical use of words reflects the particular nature and equivocality of Abishag's position, for her service "stand in-front-of/the king" consists of "lying/in the bosom/of you." Serving as *sokenet*, here linked to *škb*, is repeated in v.4b where *sokenet* = *šrt*. This reiteration with variation proves once again that lying with David is the essence of her duties (Fokkelman 1981: 348).

What kind of social position would a *sokenet* have had? Would she have been highly regarded? These are very difficult questions to answer, starting from the difficulty of telling how a culture, far in time and geography, would have assessed its members. What would "highly regarded" mean? Would diverse factors balance each other, so that being Israelite but indentured would be equal, for instance, to being foreigner but free? Which aspects would bear more weight? Morals (especially honesty and sexual propriety)? Gender? Ethnicity? Closeness to the sacred? Power? Age? Beauty? Ability to conceive? An "advantageous" marriage?

What is striking here in 1 Kgs 1:1-4 is the use of two particular terms to describe her service, *skn* and *šrt*. A second reason for considering it of interest lies in that in Isa. 22:15, a *soken* has a name, is a well-known person, and his social status is clearer than Abishag's. Thirdly, it is of interest because scholars who have studied that text have analysed the term's cognates – analysis which in turn can be used here. And, finally, it shows how similar terms are not assessed in the same way when they apply to men or to women (including their translation into modern languages or their explanation in commentaries).

(a) *sokenet*. The other text of interest in the Hebrew Bible is Isa. 22:15, for several reasons. First, being the only corresponding masculine term, it allows for close comparison. While most dictionaries parse it as a participle Qal form *skn* I, "be of use" and thus "waitress," "attendant," E. Lipinski traces these two terms to northwest Semitic origins (Sumerian *s/šakina*, Ugaritic *sà-ki-ni*, Akkadian *šaknu*, and others), changing the *qātil* form into Hebrew *qōtēl*. Thus, he translates *sōkēn* as "intendant" and *sōkenet* as ""intendante" or "gouvernante" (Lipinski 1973: 195–96; Heltzer 1987: 87). In my view, his proposal

explains the fact that there are no other terms in the Hebrew Bible
which share this meaning (three meanings usually proposed are
"be of use or service," "incur danger" and "be poor") – dictionaries
notwithstanding.

In Isa. 22:15, Shebna, the king's *soken*, is confronted by the
prophet. He is criticized for having erected his own tomb in a high
rocky place, unduly exalting himself. Besides his being described as
"that steward," *hassoken hazze*, he is also "the one who is over the
house," *'ašēr 'āl habbayit*, thus "overseer," "majordomo" or "minister." The expression is almost exclusive of higher servants of royal
houses, such as Obadiah (1 Kgs 18:3) or Eliakim (2 Kgs 18:18; Isa.
36:3).[4] Scholars agree that Shebna's office was one of high status or,
at least, high responsibilities.

Given Shebna's high office, how does that fit with him being also
a *soken*? Are both epithets contrary to each other, in the sense that
being a *soken* he would be less than a high officer? Or are both terms
of high rank, so that he is being accused of never having enough
power or honour? Any answer to these questions would influence
our further comparison with Abishag.

The biblical texts alone do not give us much help in solving this
puzzle. Studies of cognate terms show that there were both male
and female officers holding this title.[5] From the neo-Assyrian material
recovered at Fort Shalmaneser and Nimrud, M. Heltzer concludes
that,

a) The neo-Assyrian *šakintu* of the Sargonid period was connected with a certain royal palace located in different places.
b) She was a woman of a high administrative position and had
   her male and female administrative staff.
c) The *šakintu* could possess considerable property and freely
   participate in legal transactions.
d) We know that the *šakintu* could have a daughter. But nothing
   is till now known about her husband.
e) The fact that the *šakintu* had at her disposal a *rēšû*, "eunuch"
   can be interpreted also that she was connected with the
   supervision of the royal harem (Heltzer 1987: 89).

A person's status is a composition of several factors which largely
depend on his or her society; and since we do not have access to

information on those factors, it would be highly risky to affirm that a neo-Assyrian or Nuzian *šakintu* had a high status in society. What *can* be affirmed is that they had responsibility over other personnel and, thus, a certain amount of power and privilege; power and privilege that – were we able to measure them – would have been relative always subject to their master's or mistress's whims. Yet, power and privilege are important components of any person's status, even thought there could be others, such as ancestry, freedom or land, which could have been even more important.

Caution is advisable in an area where so much is unknown as that of labour in antiquity. Yet it is also important to assess critically what lies before our eyes and wonder to what extent there is a bias here, whereby the status conferred to the same term is not of equal value when applied to a man and to a woman – status conferred both by the biblical text itself and by ancient and modern scholarship. According to the text, when Abishag is destined to lie on the king's bosom and try to keep him warm, her counterparts in the ancient Near East and Shebna enjoyed a higher status, set "over the house" of their kings or queens. Examples from ancient and modern scholarship are abundant, starting from translations of these two terms (e.g., "let her cherish [the king]" KJV; "be his attendant" NRSV; "y lo atienda" *Biblia de Jerusalén* with regard to Abishag; but "this treasurer" KJV; "this steward" NRSV; "mayordomo" *Biblia de Jerusalén* for Shebna") and going through most commentaries.

(b) *šrt*. With regard to the second term applied to Abishag, *šrt*, it is an imperfect (*wattesaretehu*, 3rd fem. sing. Piel with 3rd p. masc. sing. suffix) in 1:4 and as participle (*mešaret*, Pi. fem. sing) in 1:15. There are several masc. participles (and a few imperfects), which refer to the Levites' service in the temple (e.g., Ezek. 43:19; 1 Chron. 6:17), to Israelites serving the king as mighty warriors (1 Chron. 27:1. 28:1, etc.); to attendants at Ahasuerus' court (Est. 1:10); to Joshua as servant of Moses (Num. 11:28, Jos. 1:1) and to other servants. The majority of instances are plural and do not indicate the servants' numbers, rank, or names. One can infer that at least some of them were Israelites and did not belong to the lowest social strata. This is especially obvious in the stories of apprentices who afterwards inherit their masters' place (Elisha, Joshua) or in the lists of Aaron's descendants, ministers of YHWH's sanctuary. In other stories, they were bound to their masters, at least for some time.

Among these, two stories deserve special attention for comparison with Abishag. One is 2 Sam. 13, the story of Amnon's rape of his sister Tamar. A personal assistant or servant, a *mešaret*, appears in his room when Amnon wants to throw Tamar from it, after having raped her (2 Sam. 13:17-18). This is the one text in which an assistant is in a task closely similar to that of Abishag in that the servant is to carry out the orders and wishes of his or her master, and that the location for such services is the master's bedroom.

Playing with the same elements in yet another way, the story of Joseph in Potiphar's house also combines service, slavery, a bedroom, and the danger of being raped as part of what the master or mistress expects from a bound servant. Of Joseph, it is said that he had been sold as a slave, that his mistress wanted to have sex with him, that he served his master (*šrt*), and also that he was made overseer of his household (*wayšaret 'oto wayyapqidehu al beto wekol-yeš-lo natan beyado*, Gen. 39:4). It is apparent that he started with a low social status (a foreign slave). But he is also the main actor of the story, an Israelite (and not just any, but the favorite), male, and is made overseer of his master's properties. These facts make a huge difference between him and Abishag!

And there is also a difference between him and the anonymous servant of Amnon (2 Samuel 13), of whom it is *not* said whether he was an Israelite or that he would hold responsibility as overseer, and who, furthermore, did not have to face the danger of being raped by his master (he did not have a mistress).

Finally, two other pertinent texts appear in the book of Isaiah. Here there is an announcement that tables will be turned and those who now mourn will laugh and vice versa. In this song of promise to Zion, the flocks are said to become her servants (*šrt*) and be acceptable at YHWH's altar (Isa. 60:7). Three verses later, the poem announces that those who have been servants until now will witness, in a reversal of lack, how the kings of the nations will serve (*šrt*) them (Isa. 60:10). This type of reversal-of-fate announcement is quite common in the prophetic literature and thus easy to overlook. Yet, by its very nature, it shows that being a servant was on the other tip of the scale from being king.

At least for those sharing the social ideology of "Isaiah," a servant (*mešaret, mešarat*), would be on the lower social ladder; and a woman, even more so. And while it is clear that Isaiah 60 is not 1 Kings 1, they also share a broad common understanding of society, in which one of the pairs of a binary is higher than the other, to wit, male–female, Israelite–foreigner, queen–concubine, free–indentured, master–slave, king–subject, active–passive, and so on.[6]

To sum up this section, the intriguing fact about Abishag's job as described in 1 Kgs 1:1-4 lies in the two terms used: "be of service, stewardess" (*skn*) and "ministering, attending to" (*šrt*). These are not combined in any biblical text and neither is used of another woman. Both terms are ambiguous with regard to the type of work expected and, especially, with the status of both the job and the persons involved. There are clear instances in which *skn* refers to someone (generally a man) with responsibilities in court or palace over other people; *šrt*, on the other hand, alludes to different realms and status, from the cultic to logistics.

The ambiguity found in what pertains to Abishag, then ("lying in the king's bosom to keep him warm" – a rather uncommon job description!), cannot be dispelled by other texts. The only sure affirmation is that it could have been seen as menial service (a kind of maid or waitress, like Amnon's servant) or it could have been seen as a promotion (a kind of minister, like the overseer Shebna of Isa. 22:15). Why would the redactor choose these two verbs, I am unable to say. Perhaps it has to do with the fact that the much more common verb *'abad* does not appear, to the best of my knowledge, pursed in feminine forms – nor is there a female noun from that root either.[7] This lack of description is typical of most workers in the Bible, whose tasks are taken for granted and not described. In fact, most servants of any type appearing in a given story seem to be there more for the sake of a proper scenario, at most accompanying their masters, rather than doing any work.

This analysis leaves us with the painful awareness that there is much we do not know about labour in the ancient Near East, to say nothing of gender division of labour. This leads any scholar to have to construe some answers in the hope that further scholarship, including new evidence, might one day confirm or correct those informed guesses.

Reason/s for Being Chosen

Second, we may infer from the fact that a search was conducted within the whole territory of Israel that she had special characteristics that made her the chosen one from among many. What special characteristics or charms she had are not made explicit – except for her great fairness, repeated twice: "they looked for a pleasant *na'ara*" (v. 3) and "the *na'ara* was very pleasant" (v. 4). It is to be noted that being *yapa* (pleasant, beautiful, fair)[8] is not an explicit requirement when the proposal is first made to King David, but perhaps it was presupposed. What was mentioned then was the search for a youngster (*na'ara*), who would be in his presence, attend to his needs, and make him warm by lying in his bosom. Thus we are left with the choice between thinking that this was a beauty contest and she won it; or that, among many beautiful or at least pleasant women, she was chosen because of other (unstated?) reasons.

Another expression also points to the importance of this contest. The text states that they looked for a pleasant youngster *bekol gebul yisrael*, literally, within the whole border of Israel, thus indicating a national search. This expression appears in other texts as well, often indicating the need for an urgent or dangerous, nationwide, measure. Within the DtrH are especially notable Judg. 19:29 (where the "wronged" Levite sent her concubine's body to every tribe), 1 Sam. 11:3, 7 (Saul appears as the only saviour from King Nahash), and 1 Sam. 27:1 (David decides to flee to Philistine territory to dissuade Saul from continuing to persecute him).[9]

Such an expression, then, is used purposefully to indicate that Abishag's coming into the palace was not just any common event; or, said differently, that it *did* make a difference whether it was her and not any other youngster. The reader is still unable to see why it was her and not any other, apart from what the text states, but that is not the point here. The reader is invited to accept the fact that, even if only for bed service, a thorough search was conducted and the best one (for whatever reasons) chosen (or was she Bathsheba's *sokenet*?).

The text is not abounding in reasons decisive for selecting Abishag and not any other young woman within the kingdom. Explicitly stated are her condition of *na'ara* (translated as "girl" in order to emphasize her lack of autonomy or "coming of age") and her beauty or fairness. The fact that the search was nationwide implies that she was above any other contestant. Above in what aspect the reader is not told, except for her beauty.

Legal Social Status

Two aspects of hers mentioned in these few verses are her condition of *na'ara* and *betula*. What was a *na'ara betula*? Neither of these nouns translates easily, as there are no equivalent Western categories. Furthermore, they do not form a fixed pair; in fact, in our own text, *na'ara* appears alone (v. 4) and also modified by an adjective (v. 3). To the best of my knowledge, *na'ara* is a term indicating the socio-legal condition of a woman who is not under the male authority of her father or husband. I have chosen to translate it using the term "girl" to indicate that depending condition which is the core of the Hebrew terms *na'ar* and *na'ara*. On the other hand, I have used quotation marks because these terms do not automatically indicate male or female teenagers (though Abishag probably was one), but people who nevertheless remained legally under a "father" and thus, somehow, always "minors."[10]

The second term, *betula*, is usually associated with physical virginity, although this does not hold for every instance where this word appears in the Hebrew Bible. A translation more related to a social category between puberty and, perhaps, becoming a mother, seems better to me. It is true that law and custom commanded that women did not have sexual intercourse before marriage. Yet, as is well known, in every age and every culture trying to impose such a custom, there have been occasional (and sometimes notable!) exceptions. *Betula* does not indicate, in the first place, physical virginity, but a woman being of marriageable age who, presumably, would *also* "have not (sexually) known a man," as the Hebrew biblical expression so often states.

Since, as it was seen in the previous section, Abishag did get elected after a considerable search process, I assume she was both of marriageable age and also a virgin.

I have named this category "socio-legal" for lack of a better term and for lack of more precise information on legal issues pertaining to social groups. What is meant by this term is that *na'ara* and *betula* are two different social categories, which could coincide in a person or not: that of lack of protection from one's own family, and that of being a woman who has yet to prove that she can procreate. Besides, there might have been specific legal implications for these and other groups of people – implications we are hardly aware of, besides, for example, those in Deut. 21:10-14 and 22:13-30.[11] As far as the biblical text allows us to know, Abishag never left these two categories. The remaining text in which Abishag is mentioned, 1 Kgs 2:17, 21, 22, only adds to this information the fact that she could be asked by a prince as a wife:

> And [Adonijah] said [to Bathsheba]: "Talk to Solomon the king, for he will not deny you (anything), that he would give me Abishag the Shunammite to be (my) wife" (or as a wife) (v. 17).

Since there are many aspects of law and customs that remain unknown, I will not draw any further consequences from this text, except the recognition that she was asked and not forced; and that the expression used is the one used for marriage ("take or give as wife/woman," *le'iššā*), while the vocabulary related to "concubinage" (*pilegeš*, which might be some kind of second-class marriage) is never mentioned in relation to her.[12]

Personal Information

Finally, we learn very little about her own personal characteristics: her first name, Abishag, and her provenance, Shunem. "The Shunemmite," her gentilic, always accompanies her name. Logic would indicate that a *na'ara*'s identification would not be accompanied by her father's name, since her very situation is that of being outside his control but also his protection. On the other hand, there are several examples of women who became wives or concubines of kings, who maintained their former identity – at least in the narrator's view: Rizpa, the daughter of Aiah, Saul's concubine, and Bathsheba, the wife of Uriah the Hittite are two cases in point.

Patricia Franklin claims that the only way a man could be Israelite was through possession of patrimonial land. Thus a resident alien (Hbr. *ger*) could never become part of Israel; the only possibility for him and his family was to be identified by a gentilic. Since Abishag was not married, she must have been the descendant of a resident alien (Franklin 1990: 21).

But why Shunnem? What is important about this place? Granted, one could argue that this is a remnant of a historical fact, which the narrator wanted to keep. It is hard to believe this is all there is about this fact. There must have been other facts that contributed to keeping record of her Shunammite origins: Are there traditions related to this place? Why a Shunammite and not a "Judith," a woman from Judah, where David was strongest? Does it have any political implications that she was from Shunem?

To the first question, whether there are elements related to this place that might help make sense of this story and bring Abishag out of the shadows, the answer seems to be "No." Shunem is mentioned in Jos. 19:18 as one of the borders of the land allotted to Issachar, together with – among other towns – Jezreel, Bet-shemesh, and the Jordan River. It was a rich, yet dangerous territory, very close to the Philistine territory. And the Jezreel valley was the corridor to any invading army going North or South.

The next mention of Shunem occurs in 1 Sam. 28:4. Saul is fighting the Philistines and David as his opponent. Here, Shunem has become the Philistine camp, while the Israelites are encamped at Gilboa. Saul is unsure of how this battle will turn, as YHWH does not answer him. So he disguises himself and seeks Samuel's spirit through a medium at Endor. In terms of Shunem or the Philistine-Israelite war, nothing happens. The next event (1 Sam. 29:1) has the Philistines encamping in Aphek and the Israelites in Jezreel, still in the same region of Issachar. The last mention of this city and of a "Shunammite" is an anonymous, yet great woman, who built an upper chamber in her home for Elisha, the man of God, and who, in exchange, became a mother (2 Kgs 4:8-37). Literarily speaking, this distinguished lady comes many chapters later, during the times of Elisha, when the united kingdom was long gone.

In short, Shunem is only mentioned (aside from the three references to Abishag) as pertaining to Issachar when the land was allotted (Jos. 19:18), as endangered by the Philistines in Saul's times (1 Sam. 28:4) and as hospitable towards Elisha through one of its richest women in later times (2 Kgs 4:8). There is, then, no strong tradition related to Shunem, which might have been made on purpose – at least, none that I can detect here.

If a tradition related to Shunem is not the reason for the redactor(s) to have kept her gentilic, there must be another reason. Considering the – acknowledged weak/ambiguous – evidence of a *sokenet* (in this case, Abishag) as a high-officer in court, the reason why she is always remembered as "Abishag the Shunammite" may be that she was such a well-known person that it would have been impossible to change her gentilic without altering her identity too much. I pose an example from another important person. It is hard to imagine Uriah the Hittite by any other name. He would not be "Uriah the Hittite," the one faithful to death to David, the one married to Bathsheba... Given the fact that non-Israelites lack identification by patronymic, the only way of making sure that someone as important as Uriah be remembered is by constant use of his name-plus-gentilic.

This is one reason, I believe, why Shunem was not taken from Abishag's identification. The whole search process and her role as *sokenet* – even with all the ambiguity inherent in her being an officer, a woman, and not having become David's concubine or wife – indicate, as already stated, someone with responsibilities and, thus, with a certain status. Her constant identification as "Abishag, the Shunammite" is yet another signal of her (relatively) high status as officer of King David's court.

Whether she was responsible for David's harem, as Heltzer proposes upon comparison with her neo-Assyrian "sisters," or whether she belonged to that harem even though David had been impotent, it is hard to know. As so often when one tries to get into women's lives – especially poor or everyday women – we do not have enough information to be able to make a decision. Considering what this text tells us about her and the use of these particular expressions, my inclination is to consider that she had a position of high responsibility in the social organization of the palace, thus probably not belonging to the royal harem.

Looking at the Story from the Political Arena

Yet the choice of Abishag is not an innocent nor a private matter. She is not the village's nurse who is called to take care of "a nobody," any feeble old man or woman who cannot keep her/himself warm. The way the narrator explains her selection indicates her importance over other candidates. Besides, the one to be cared for is not any man, but King David. A king who is evidently fading and whose power and ability to keep control over regal matters may be doubted, but he is still able to ensure "long life" for one of his sons and his supporters, as events in 1 Kings 1–2 show.

In this scenario, Abishag's presence may just be part of the king's commodities, part of the scenographic setting, but nevertheless, an agent in the narrative. Even if mute, an agent. Her presence in the king's chamber when Abishag comes to ensure Solomon's succession to the throne is clearly indicated, with no apparent function: "And Bathsheba went unto the king into the chamber. The king was very old; and Abishag the Shunammite was ministering to the king." Most commentaries suppose this contrast functions to stir Bathsheba's jealousy and perhaps, as a foil to her, once a beautiful, young and desired woman. Yet, this is not, in my view, the purpose of this information. Far more serious matters are at stake here. And to consider that two women facing each other only have in mind the king's bed is to underrate them and to foster patriarchal bias. There are, for sure, two women competing here, but these are not Bathsheba and Abishag. These are Bathsheba and Haggith, knowing all too well that their own future and perhaps even their own lives depend on their son's positions in court (Fokkelman 1981: 352). What a fate! To have been the king's wife, to have given him son(s), to have spent the whole life in a harem and finally to have to fight for one's own life through the sons' succession claims to that throne!

Since Abishag is not a mother (*betula*), and thus not "eligible" for succession, Abishag is not an opponent to Bathsheba – unless her position in court gives her such a power as to be important by herself and not because of a son. The information the narrator provides twice (vs. 1-4, 15), then, regarding their relationship (service on the part of Abishag, no sex) aims at something else. On the one hand, the fact that she did not become a concubine or wife makes her eligible for marriage and thus provides an element for the plot to be developed later in chapter 2. (Whether the fight between Adonijah and Solomon over her is just an excuse for claims to the throne does not matter here.)

Yet this is not a decisive issue, as there are, in David's story itself, other events in which concubines are raped for the sake of making a political statement (e.g., Rizpah).

Growing up in a continent and a time filled with political upheaval, military dictatorships and economic instability, my reading cannot help but ask about the political aspects of this story and the narrator's way of telling it. And, in this reading, I intuit that this woman who never speaks – but sees and hears too much – is there for a purpose. The fact that there is much in this story that cannot be proved makes assertions look risky; yet I dare to make this one in the hope that, in this dialogue that is scholarship, someone else will take it up and confirm or refute it with other arguments that escape me.

Depending on translation, from the narrative in 1 Kgs 1:1-4 it is possible to interpret that the contest was made in order to check David's potency:

> [1]In those days, King David had become old and they covered him with clothes, but he could not get warm. [2]And his servants told him: "Let a young 'girl' be sought for my Lord the king ... Let she lie in your bosom and may the king my Lord get warm." [3]They sought a pretty "girl" ... [4] The "girl" was very pleasant/pretty and she was the king's stewardess. And she attended/ministered to him. But/And (we) the king did not know her (sexually). [5]But/and (we) Adonijah, the son of Haggith exalted himself, saying: "I will be king."

The Hebrew particle *we* can have several meanings, from conjunctive to adversative. It is possible to translate the *we* of v. 4b as "but" (the king did not know her) and the *we* of v. 5 as consecutive: "Then Adonijah...," thus assuming continuity between that piece of information on David's impotence, and Adonijah's decision to claim the throne or, at least, to prepare himself to succeed his father (Bar-Efrat 1997: 49-50; Walsh 1996: 5; DeVries 1985: 12–13).

Sexual potency equalled to political power. This is not new and it is not over either. The question that remains unclear is this: Whose decision was it to search for a woman to see whether David would still be able to keep power? Who were "his servants" (v. 2, *'abadayw*) who made the proposal of searching for a *na'ara* and carried it along with David's compliance? Answers to this question would shed light on the political overtones of this decision. Conversely, knowing the political overtones of such a decision would make it possible to

perceive the intention behind such a proposal: to counter or to enhance Solomon's cause? To counter or to enhance Adonijah's cause?
This is yet one more ambiguity in this master tale. As ambiguous are
Abishag's family, social status both before entering the king's service
and at court, and marital status.

One thing, however, is clear to me, namely, that Abishag had to
be part, willingly or unknowingly, of this plot. Her selection among
the choicest young women of the whole country, Israel and Judah,
had to have considered her reliability to live and work in a place
where much was "cooked," i.e., her ability to be loyal to those
who chose her and set her in that post. Now, the story ends up
with Solomon getting rid of his last enemies, Abiathar the priest, his
brother Adonijah the prince, and Joab the chief commander of the
army. Given the importance of these three men, especially in comparison to Abishag; given the fact that they did not face all the same
fate (Abiathar was banished from Jerusalem, the other two were executed); and since Abishag was the reason or excuse for their punishment, it is clear that Abishag was not perceived by Solomon or
his party as a danger or even as involved in Adonijah's "revolt." Her
innocence would be stronger if she was all along an ally to Solomon's
party. Then, Abishag's presence at the king's chamber as Bathsheba
entered the room would not be a signal of any peril or discomfort,
but a kind of hidden ally, watching the king's health deterioration or
amelioration, hearing and seeing any political moves, and reporting
to her "bosses." All matters considered, this hypothesis is quite plau-
sible. Yet there are no elements in the story or more broadly in the
Bible that would link her or Shunem to Zadok, Benajiah, Bathsheba,
Nathan or Solomon himself. Thus it remains a hypothesis.

What is in a Name?

In this study, I have attempted to call attention to the possibility that
this hardly known young woman at King David's court would have
enjoyed a higher status than usually recognized. The narrator presents her in a very ambiguous way, so that one can choose to make
her into a bedfellow, an attendant, a "could-have-been-concubine,"
or a vizier in charge of the king's harem, for instance.

No doubt, the cultural, social and literary distance between us and the text is partly responsible for such a range of opinions. When a term is not well attested, the context is helpful in trying to determine its best possible translation. Thus, many opt for a term in the line of "personal attendant" or "bedfellow." The text itself is also partly responsible, as it uses a term that otherwise implies a high court position, does not explain what would have been a *soken/et's* tasks, and relates her presence to keeping the king warm. Thus, after much consideration, our translation opts for "stewardess" because it is a term that does not immediately imply sexual or bed services.

Unfortunately, this dilemma is not the only one in the Bible. Using a term with different values when ascribed to men or to women is one of the strategies of patriarchal power.[13] At least in this part of the world in which I live, it is not the same to be a public man or a public woman, a male or a female assistant, and so on. A "public man" is well known in the media, whether from politics, the arts or some other area, while a "public woman" is a prostitute or a woman too easily available for sex. Finally, a *soken* was a high officer and a *sokenet* was a bedfellow!

Another strategy often used by patriarchy for keeping power is that of disguising its own sins by euphemisms or just dismissal of their effects on women and on other weaker parties. Examples of this strategy are also, unfortunately, plenty. For instance, the Empire's speeches about "developing countries" which will never develop under the present system, or collateral effects of war for massive destruction of civilians, villages, and so on.

In her analysis of narratives in which slaves or concubines are used for sex without their consent, which means they are raped, Scholz concludes that

> in all of these stories, men regard women as objects to be violated sexually. The focus on the men and their behavior exposes the destructive consequences of androcentrism. Women, especially as slaves and concubines, are acted upon by men who view them as symbols of male power. Whether raped or not, the women are quickly forgotten, as the long history of androcentric interpretations demonstrates abundantly. Yet when we identify these texts as rape stories the fate of the women is exposed for what it is: a fate that either destroys women's lives or co-opts women into androcentrism. The tales do not offer optimistic answers,

but, to their credit, they make visible some of the dynamics that shape many women and men's lives even today (Scholz 2004: 31–32).

Abishag's story is but one of those tales that, "to their credit, ... make visible some of the dynamics that shape many women and men's lives even today." That her story differs from others' in that Adonijah could not have his wish fulfilled or in that there was a petition of marriage makes a certain difference in how the *men* involved are presented. No difference as to Abishag's room for negotiation, feelings, or anything that would require her voice.

Rape was and is bad enough that unmasking it and its (often unrecognized, diminished or ignored) consequences in a sacred text would already merit a study. Androcentrism, as any particular vision that would not dialogue with other visions, is just unable to be sensitive to certain issues and interests that run against its own interests. Scholz brought Abishag as one of several female slaves and concubines, who are raped (or almost raped in the case of Abishag) in a political game in which they are only pawns.

From a different perspective and with due caution to calling Abishag a concubine, our study wants to contribute to the same purpose of raising a voice against any form of injustice and violence against the weakest members of society, including its largest group, women – especially when such violence is sanctified by the book that millions of people consider Sacred Scriptures/Word of God.

The way to do that has been by calling attention to an androcentric perspective that makes of an officer in court, the king's bedfellow. An androcentric perspective that, by so degrading her post, also prevents later generations from knowing better how life was for society at large and women in particular.

Works Cited

Bar-Efrat, Shimon (1997). *Narrative Art in the Bible*. JSOTSup, 70. Sheffield: Sheffield Academic Press.

Berlin, Adele (1982). "Characterization in Biblical Narrative: David's Wives." *Journal for the Study of the Old Testament* 23: 69–85.

DeVries, Simon J. (1985). *1 Kings*. Word Biblical Commentary. Waco: Word.

Fokkelman, J. P. (1981). *Narrative Art and Poetry in the Books of Samuel: A Full Interpretation Based on Stylistic and Structural Analyses, I: King David (II Sam. 9-20 & I Kings 1-2)*. Assen, The Netherlands: Van Gorcum.

Franklin, Patricia N. (1990). "The Stranger within their Gates: How the Israelite Portrayed the Non-Israelite in Biblical Literature." Unpublished PhD dissertation, Duke University.

Heltzer, M. (1987). "The Neo-Assyrian *Šakintu* and the Biblical *Sōkenet* (I Reg. 1,4)." In *La Femme dans le Proche-Orient Antique. XXXIIIe. Rencontre Assyriologique Internationale*, ed. Jean-Marie Durand, 87–90. Paris: Editions Recherche sur les Civilisations.

Henshaw, R. (1967). "The Office of *Šaknu* in Neo-Assyrian Times. Part I." *JAOS* 87: 517–25.

Henshaw, R. (1968). "The Office of *Šaknu* in Neo-Assyrian Times. Part II." *JAOS* 88: 461–83.

Leeb, Carolyn. (2000). *Away from the Father's House: The Social Location of na'ar and na'arah in Ancient Israel*. Sheffield: Sheffield Academic Press.

Lipinski, E. (1973). "*skn* et *sgn* dans le Sémitique Occidental du Nord." *Ugarit Forschungen* 5: 191–207.

Scholz, Susanne. (2004). "Gender, Class, and Androcentric Compliance in the Rapes of Enslaved Women in the Hebrew Bible." *Lectio difficilior* 1. http://www.lectio.unibe.ch

Walsh, Jerome T. (1996). *1 Kings* (Berit Olam). Collegeville: Michael Glazier/ Liturgical.

15 Return, Medium of En-dor

Jione Havea

Out Again

As you exit this site, or turn back if you wish, I bid you farewell with
the story of a woman character whose assistance King Saul seeks,
even though her craft was outlawed. This is the story of the Medium
of En-dor, whom Saul asks to recall prophet Samuel from the dead
in order that the torn king might receive counsel from him. This is
the last time Saul seeks anyone (Gunn 1980: 108). The woman was
banned; the king was redundant; the prophet was dead. Three *out-
of-place* (for different reasons) characters appear in this story but
they did not really "meet" because Samuel did not affirm Saul or acknowledge the Medium of En-dor. You might wish to first consult the
biblical narrator's version in 1 Sam. 28:3-25, for this chapter is an
out-of-place telling of a night encounter of characters under disguise,
in fear, robed, angry, weak, caring and faring-well.

My telling is unapologetically biased on behalf of the proscribed
Medium of En-dor, while at the same time mindful of the riddle
(*mashal*) that the story of Saul may have answered for Israel:

> The story of Saul, and indeed the character himself, is – or may be re-
> sponsibly read as – the long and subtle answer to the question: When
> the exile community prepares to return to Judea from Babylon, once it
> is possible to do so (after 539 or so), shall the people return under the
> leadership of kings or not? In retrospect we can see that the answer is
> pretty clear: without kings… [T]he answer, made clear in and by the story
> of Saul as he embodies the monarchic experience of Israel, shouts "no
> more kings!" (Green 2003: xvi).

In other words, I respect the biblical narrator's point of view (see
Yamasaki 2007: 1–9). But this chapter is accountable to Mieke Bal's
call for *countercoherence*, which is about critically examining texts
for their *coherences* of kingship, nation-building and empire, which

are thoroughly androcentric, in order to account for patterns of governance and subjects at their undersides (Bal 1988: 16–21). Instead of focusing on the story of Israel and its kingship, I favour *out-of-place* characters. This creates a dilemma because there are several *out-of-place* characters in 1 Sam. 28 and they oblige me in different ways. My response and answerability (see Green 2003: xviii–xx; cf. Gunn 1980: 11) to these characters are not the same, for I lean in the direction of the Medium of En-dor and of Saul, ahead of Samuel. This is not an easy move for me to make because Samuel represents the ancestors and I have been conditioned to respect the ancestors.

The motivation for this move is simple: the Medium, who is banned (by Saul) for her craft and overlooked (by Samuel) because of her gender, is a figure for people who are banned because of their crafts and subjectivities. I have in mind here not only the menial workers and labourers, who do not hold "real jobs" and are damned by birth and lack of privileges, but also the many people who are persecuted, rejected and shamed because of who they are, what they do and how they think. They might be physically and mentally disabled persons, social critics and protestors, political activists and reformers, religious and community workers, radical and organic intellectuals, and so forth. It is in solidarity with them that I bid you farewell with the story of the Medium of En-dor.

Banned Medium

"Medium of En-dor" is not the proper name for the woman character in 1 Sam. 28. She too is nameless (like the wife of Potiphar, the wife of Jephthah, and their daughter, and many other women biblical characters) and readers over the years have called her by several names, such as "Witch of Endor," "Woman who consults familiar spirits," "Ventriloquist," "Woman who masters over ghosts," "Necromancer," and more recently, "Belly-Myther" (see Greer and Mitchell 2007: xi–xviii). I have decided to use the vaguer tag "Medium of En-dor" – even though it does not express the compound biblical Hebrew (which has to do with "mastery" and "ghost") and Greek (which has to do with "belly" and "myth") words (see Greer and Mitchell 2007: xi–xviii) – because "medium" underscores her subjectivity. She was banned but she is the *medium*, the opening, the threshold, who can enable the penetration of worlds, and of sides, over and through frustration, passions and physical weaknesses.

The servants of Saul introduce the Medium of En-dor into the story (1 Sam. 28:7) and she enters as an outcast, for Saul had previously, after the death of Samuel, expelled the mediums and the wizards from the land (1 Sam. 28:3b). She enters the story as a member of a banned group, and the narrator is not clear if Samuel was among their numbers. Was Samuel a friend or a protector of the mediums, or may have been a medium himself? Did Saul finally get the chance to cast the mediums out since Samuel has died? Is this a craft for women only (cf. Jobling 1998: 186)? Or did Saul cast mediums out in order to remove any chances of calling Samuel back? Samuel was not always friendly to Saul (see, e.g., 1 Sam. 15), and now that he was dead, it makes sense to get rid of mediums so that, so to speak, Samuel will not be resurrected so Saul may live in peace.

The Medium of En-dor enters the story because YHWH would not answer Saul through dreams, Urim or prophets (1 Sam. 28:6). She comes as one who could make things happen, through whom Saul could inquire of YHWH and Samuel. She was special because she had the ability to mediate, to affect; she was a woman with power. Was she so powerful that her name is not revealed? Before she enters the story, the narrator establishes her subjectivity, as a medium, and pricks the interest of readers by leaving her nameless. On the one hand, namelessness suggests that the narrator does not really care about the subject. A nameless character is not a full subject. On the other hand, nameless is seductive, for it draws the attention of readers and listeners to the subject in question. Who is this nameless woman? This is a question that the narrator does not answer, and thereby frees the character from the control of readers and listeners.

The Medium of En-dor enters the story as an observer of regulations. When the disguised Saul asks her to bring up one particular spirit, she replies, "You know what Saul has done, how he has banned [the use of] ghosts and familiar spirits in the land. So why are you laying a trap for me, to get me killed?" (1 Sam. 28:9b; NJPS). But she is willing to bend the rules, as one would expect from a medium. She enables the return of Samuel, as an old man wrapped in a robe (1 Sam. 28:14). She disturbs the rest of a dead character so that he would return in response to the request by the person who outlawed her craft. She also enables the "return," the turning back, of the rule against mediums and wizards in Israel, hence her entry to the story marks the "return" of medium-hood to the memory of Israel. The story of this nameless character is filled with returns. She is the medium of returns.

I don't know how old she was, or if she had a family, but she is a person of substance (see 1 Sam. 28:24). Her gender may have been the reason why Samuel disregarded her to address Saul directly. Saul needed her to bring Samuel up (1 Sam. 28:11-14), but Samuel ignored her completely (in 1 Sam. 28:15). This kind of treatment usually happens to mediums. They are often, easily and quickly, overlooked. They are at once necessary and unnecessary, as are *out-of-place* subjects, without whom it would not be possible to identify who is "in."

Unheard King

The Philistines had gathered to fight against Israel, and Saul did not know that David was serving as bodyguard, or deceivingly pretends to be one (so Gunn 1980: 107), for Achish, king of Philistia (1 Sam. 28:1-2). Y HWH did not respond to Saul during this anxious time, and consequently Saul's heart trembled greatly (1 Sam. 28:5). Nothing could be more frustrating for a distressed person than to be ignored and disregarded, especially when it is one's master that does so. In not responding to Saul Y HWH treats him as if he is "voiceless." In this story, as far as Y HWH is concerned, a voiceless king seeks the help of a banned nameless woman. Could Saul have done more wrongly?

In seeking out the Medium of En-dor, Saul acts against his own decree:

> Both Saul's egregious violation of his basic charge to mind the Y HWH-Israel bond and his more pedestrian ineffectual leadership are demonstrated as he violates his own law and makes evident that others have done so as well, including his own men, who seemed well informed about the woman (Green 2003: 107).

Saul appears too desperate to worry about how he breaks his own words. He did not come to the Medium in order to seek her advice about what to do, but for her to provide the link to another character, Samuel, who used to be his link to YHWH. Saul did not come for her agency but for her craft, her service. In this regard, Saul was not fully enlightened. She appears to be his last chance, and she did not turn him away. She is the one character who listens to Saul, who takes him seriously.

The Medium "listened" to Saul even before he approached her. This is one way of understanding her initial response, "*Surely* you know what Saul has done..." (1 Sam. 28:9; NRSV, emphasis added). She expects everyone to know, and honour, the leadership and words of Saul. Yet she was willing to transgress the words of Saul on behalf of, she thought, another man who seem troubled and desperate. That man turns out, later, to be Saul himself. The Medium gives Saul his voice, both for and against himself. She returns his voice, and his decision, to him, unless she was being sarcastic, as Jobling suggests (Jobling 1998: 188).

The Medium did to Saul here what Hannah did to Eli in 1 Sam. 1:26-28, when she brought her weaned child to the temple. Hannah reminded Eli that she is not a stranger: "I am the woman who was standing here in your presence, praying to the LORD." She was referring to an earlier occasion when Eli was sitting beside the doorpost of the temple when she came to *ask* YHWH for a son. Eli thought that she was drunk, and after Hannah corrected him, he gave her his blessing: "Go in peace. May the God of Israel grant you what you have *asked* of him" (1 Sam. 1:17, emphasis added). Hannah returned Eli's words to him when she brought the child she had asked in order to *lend* him to YHWH. The Hebrew language is playful here, for the words translated as "ask" and "lend" are from the same root (*š'l*; see below). The son that Hannah asked and lent is Samuel, thus the stories of the Medium and of Hannah, which frame 1 Samuel, link (so Jobling 1998: 185).

The Medium's ability to bring back a dead man, to make a dead man walk and talk, accentuates her place in the story. It is not clear if she did use her power or Samuel simply appeared (Miscall 1986: 168), but the narrative feels like a birth story, if I were to listen with native ears. There was an appearance, a shrieking scream, and a recognition of "a divine being coming up from the earth" (1 Sam. 28:13). Could a being be more divine than when it is born? Earth, as mother, and as home of the ancestors, gives birth to a son whose name was Samuel, who was Hannah's son, and the Medium served the midwifery role. The Medium enabled the re-birth of Samuel, and the return of Hannah, to the story of Saul.

The disguising king came to the Medium, and she met what he asked, and more. Much has been said about Saul's dis-guise. Whom did he try to deceive? From whom did he disguise himself? Whether from Israel, the Philistines, the Medium, or from himself, Saul indeed "adopts the guise of a 'not king,' the very role to which God has been persuading him" (Green 2003: 107). In this regard, the Medium exposes, and thus returns, Saul to himself: "You are Saul!" (1 Sam. 28:12). The Medium hears Saul into himself, once again.

The Medium practised a craft associated with foreigners, and her location at En-dor, which is at the border of Israel and Philistia, suggests that she may have been "a Philistine, or of mixed blood" (Jobling 1998: 186). "She is a member of a class of religious practitioners who must be expelled from official Israel. Indeed, her place is not merely outside of Israel, but outside of acceptable human character as the Bible can otherwise conceive it" (Jobling 1998: 304). She is *out of place* in person, in practice, and in location. But she is the one that gave Saul a hearing, embracing him in his own *out of place*.

Angry Prophet

Early church fathers brought a different set of questions to this story. Did the Medium actually resurrect Samuel, or did she only bring up his soul (but not his body)? Did she have anything at all to do with the appearance of Samuel? Justin Martyr and Origen believed that Samuel's soul did indeed come up, but were ambiguous whether she brought him up in body also (in Greer and Mitchell 2007: 1–5, 32–61). The more troubling question for the church fathers relates to the place from where the Medium called Samuel. Did she, as a woman who has power over spirits, call him back from "hell" (compare 1 Sam. 28:13b)? Eustathius, who refutes Origen by insisting on the resurrection of the body, argues that the soul of Samuel was indeed in hell until the Medium called him back (in Greer and Mitchell 2007: 62–157). Theological positions and doctrinal biases of course influenced the views of these Christian leaders, with the story of Jesus lurking in the background. Whatever they say about Samuel in 1 Sam. 28 impact, and is impacted by, their understanding of the story of Jesus. If Samuel the prophet was in hell, then Jesus could have been there too; if Samuel was not resurrected in body also, then the resurrection of Jesus had to be different; and there is the issue of a woman having power over the soul and/or body of a dead prophet. How did the raising of Samuel relate to the resurrection of Jesus?

The biblical narrator seems, on the other hand, convinced that the Medium succeeded in bringing Samuel back as a "divine being" (*'elohîm*) wrapped in a robe, who came up out of the earth (1 Sam. 28:13-14). Whether the divine being is only spirit is not clear (cf. Frymer-Kensky 2002: 312), but Saul bowed and paid his respects to the raised and wrapped being as Samuel himself (1 Sam. 28:14). I honour Saul's discernment, for he reminds me of the protestor in Garibay's *Jacob Wrestling with G*d* (on cover). What matters to me is that Samuel did appear, and I take that to mean that the Medium has delivered what Saul asked of her.

Saul went to all this trouble so that Samuel may tell him what to do (1 Sam. 28:15). He was hoping that Samuel would not turn away from him, as G*d did. But instead of telling Saul what to do, Samuel announces his fate: YHWH has become Saul's enemy and has torn the kingdom from Saul and given it to David, and "tomorrow you and your sons will be with me" and Israel will be given into the hands of the Philistines (1 Sam. 28:16-19). Saul already knew that the kingdom was torn from him, but this is the first time for him "to learn that YHWH has been backing David and that Saul's opponent in this matter has been God" (Green 2003: 110). He did not know that he has lived his whole life at cross-purposes with G*d (Green 2003: 122).

Samuel's anger was obvious. "Samuel does not do the one thing that Saul asks of him: he does not tell Saul what to do. This omission echoes in the words he does say: Saul's fate is sealed and there is nothing he can do" (Frymer-Kensky 2002: 313). Samuel did not care for Saul, who did not want to be king in the first place (see 1 Sam. 9–10), and he disrespects the Medium. When Samuel appeared, he addressed Saul directly (1 Sam. 28:15) as if the Medium was not present. These behaviours give me the impression that the figure whom the Medium raised was none other than Samuel himself.

Samuel was raised, but there is no record of him leaving again. The narrator seems to have forgotten to get rid of him after he had dumped his heartbreaking speech against Saul. As the narrative continues with the effect of Samuel's words on Saul (1 Sam. 28:20-21), I want to believe that the Medium zapped Samuel again, making him disappear, out of respect for the safety of Saul. Whatever she did towards making Samuel appear worked, and I imagine that she could have made Samuel disappear, return to being dead, again, as easily as she made him rise.

The return of Samuel from the dead was supposed to help Saul, whom the Medium recognized, ironically, when she saw Samuel: "Then the woman recognized Samuel, and she shrieked loudly, and said to Saul, 'Why have you deceived me? You are Saul!'" (1 Sam. 28:12; NJPS). Samuel's appearance revealed who Saul was, as if the recognition of Saul depends on the presence of Samuel. In this light, the devastation that Samuel's words caused for Saul is tremendous. To be rejected is already bad; to be rejected by the one upon whom one's recognition depends is disgraceful. The return of Samuel seals the fate of King Saul: he will fall in the hands of the enemy and his son will not inherit the throne of Israel. The message of *coherence* is clear: the house of Saul will fall together with Israel, and the house of David will take over.

At his birth, Samuel appeared in response to a prayer in which Hannah *asked* YHWH for a son. The root of the Hebrew verb for "to ask" is *š'l*, which is also the root for the name of Saul, *ša'ul*. The characters of Samuel and Saul thus intersect early in 1 Samuel, at least at the literary level. There is an interesting interplay in the stories of Hannah and of the Medium. When Hannah presents her son to Eli, she declares "He [Samuel] is *ša'ul*" (1 Sam. 1:28), which prefigures what the Medium says when she sees Samuel. She turns to expose Saul, "You are *ša'ul*" (2 Sam. 28:12) (so Green 2003: 108). Samuel and Saul are linked, from the prayer of Hannah up to the exclamation of the Medium. In this regard, Samuel has been displacing Saul throughout his life, at his birth and at his return, his second coming. Samuel is the reason why Saul is both king and at once *out of place*.

The way Samuel phrases his words against Saul are haunting: "tomorrow you and your sons shall be with me" (1 Sam. 28:19). *Immediately*, Saul falls on the ground, filled with fear "because of the words of Samuel" (1 Sam. 28:20). This is not the first time Saul has heard that YHWH has torn the kingdom from him or that Samuel no longer supports him (see 1 Sam. 15:28-29). But this is the first time that Saul is presented with the possibility that he will be with Samuel again, at death. Given the troubles Samuel brought upon Saul during his life, what peace will Saul receive at death if he ends up alongside Samuel? Is this the reason why Saul *immediately* became weak? In other words, Saul lost his strength not so much because it finally sunk into his mind that YHWH has turned away from him but because he found out that he will never escape Samuel. Death will not part them. In this regard, he would have greatly regretted seeking Samuel out in the first place.

In contrast to the enablement that the Medium of En-dor presented for the distressed Saul, the return of Samuel was a dead-end for Saul. Samuel did not deliver the guidance for which he was brought back; he was more an irritation than a resolution. On the night before Saul died, Samuel did not have a comforting word to say to God's anointed (cf. 1 Sam. 15:35). In this reading, which sympathizes with Saul (see also Gunn 1980), the angry Samuel is *out of place*.

Farewell, Strangers no Longer

Samuel's "death sentence" (Miscall 1986: 170) sucks the energy out of Saul. He had been fasting (1 Sam. 28:20b), maybe because of depression or for some religious reason (Frymer-Kensky 2002: 313), and his strength left him when it became clear that death is imminent. The time is set for the next day. Assuming that the Medium heard Samuel deliver the death sentence, what she did next is sacramental. She insists on serving Saul a meal, to break his fast, and this ends up being his last meal before he returns to his army and before his death. The Medium serves the last meal for Saul's servants as well, and they return into the night as "dead men walking."

The Medium emphasizes the act of listening (*šm'*): "Your hand-maid listened [*šm'*] to you; I took my life in my hands and heeded [*šm'*] the request you made of me. So now you listen [*šm'*] to me: Let me set before you a bit of food [*pat lehem*]. Eat, and then you will have the strength to go on your way" (1 Sam. 28:21bf., NJPS; cf. Miscall 1986: 171). Having listened to Saul, she now demands Saul to listen to her. But he refuses. Then his servants step in and together with the Medium they make Saul listen (*šm'*) to them (1 Sam. 28:23). I would have liked Saul more if he had listened to the Medium the first time, accepting her demand, her voice, her sub-jectivity, but what else should I expect from a king. Notwithstanding, they got him off the ground and onto the bed. The intervention of the servants reminds me of the servants of Naaman, who talked their master into submitting to the direction of the prophet Elisha (2 Kgs 5:13) to go and bathe seven times in the Jordan. The servants play significant roles in both stories.

The Medium's persistence brings to mind Jacob's perseverance, for he would not let his antagonist go unless he received a blessing from him (Gen. 32:26). But in what sense would Saul's acceptance of food from the Medium be a blessing for her? This would surely be a blessing for Saul. Gunn suggests that in eating Saul accepts life, even though what life offers him next is death (Gunn 1980: 109). His death and the death of his sons is the *gift* that awaits the next day. It is thus appropriate that Saul receives his last meal at a place named "En-dor" (*'ên dôr*), a Hebrew construct that can mean, "there is no generation." It is at En-dor that Saul learns that his line will end, that he has no generation from the next day on. In this regard, the bless-ing for the Medium is the opportunity to offer hospitality to a cursed man. Frymer-Kensky sees in the Medium

> the very model of Israelite hospitality. Like Abraham, she offers a *pat lehem*, a "round" of bread (Gen. 18:5), but then provides meat, giving her guest what might be her only fatted calf. Like Abraham, she *hurries* (Gen. 18:6) to prepare the meal, and as with Abraham, the details of bread baking are recorded to show that the bread is prepared absolutely fresh and new for the visitors (though in Genesis, Abraham can tell Sarah

to prepare the bread, Gen. 18:6). Her meal marks a fitting end to Saul's kingship (Frymer-Kensky 2002: 314).

Hospitality is not cheap, but it can be fulfilling for the host. The extent of the hospitality is indicative of the will and wealth of the host. The Medium is not a pushover, and she has means and strength. She prepares an extensive meal, serves her guests, and they leave the same night (1 Sam. 28:25). This is extraordinary, and she stands out as the authoritative character in this story. The Medium strengthened Saul

> to do what he must face, perhaps finally to make some decision for himself. No alibi, no pretending: no one can tell him what he needs to do; were any to do so, there is no guarantee the advice would be right when the moment came. So wisdom's strength is the best gift the king can be given. Having eaten wisdom's meal, Saul and his servants melt away into the night (Green 2003: 112).

"Her ability to communicate with spirits does not make her evil. Her craft is outlawed because it is an uncontrollable and ungovernable access to divine knowledge. But it is effective, and it can be benevolent" (Frymer-Kensky 2002: 314). The Medium is not evil but hospitable, generous and powerful. She serves ministerial (Jobling 1998: 189) and prophetic (Frymer-Kensky 2002: 314) roles, even as an *out-of-place* character. At the end of the story, with Samuel ceasing to speak and Saul and his men departing into the night, the Medium remains the last person standing. Samuel returned to the ancestors, and Saul and his servants will soon join them, farewelled by the Medium of En-dor.

As a native of Oceania, I find the task of giving farewell to be more significant than, while it at the same time depends upon, the offer of hospitality. This is because farewell involves departure and return, and the interruption of links and relationships, made more difficult when the departing are doomed to imminent death. It makes good sense therefore that the Medium insists that Saul receives her hospitality, for that would make the farewell possible. This is her blessing.

As the one who is sought, in order that she might return a dead man (to life, then to death again), and who hosts and farewells the departed and the departing, the Medium of En-dor at once *is* and *is not* out of place. To what extent, then, is it fair to talk of her as if she is *out of place* only?

Works Cited

Bal, Mieke (1988). *Death and Dissymmetry: The Politics of Coherence in the Book of Judges*. Chicago: University of Chicago Press.
Frymer-Kensky, Tikva (2002). *Reading the Women of the Bible*. New York: Schocken.
Green, Barbara (2003). *King Saul's Asking*. Collegeville: Liturgical.
Greer, Rowan A., and Margaret M. Mitchell (2007). *The "Belly-Myther" of Endor: Interpretations of I Kingdom 28 in the Early Church*. Atlanta: SBL.
Gunn, David M. (1980). *The Fate of King Saul: An Interpretation of a Biblical Story*. Sheffield: JSOT.
Jobling, David (1998). *1 Samuel*. Collegeville: Liturgical.
Miscall, Peter D. (1986). *1 Samuel: A Literary Reading*. Bloomington: Indiana University Press.
Yamasaki, Gary (2007). *Watching a Biblical Narrative: Point of View in Biblical Exegesis*. New York: T&T Clark.

Notes

Foreword

1. This term refers to the mass migration of Caribbean people to the UK, between 1968 and 1965. In that period, approximately 500,000 people travelled from the then British colonies to the so-called "Mother Country" of Britain. For further details see Mike Phillips and Trevor Phillips, *Windrush: The Irresistible Rise of Multi-racial Britain* (London: HarperCollins, 1999).

2. I address aspects of the ambivalence to England, the country of my birth, in Anthony G. Reddie, "Black Theology in Britain," *Expository Times* 120, no. 1 (October 2008): 16–23.

Chapter 3

1. An earlier version of this chapter appeared under the title "Gott und die globale Marktwirtschaft" in *Oikos Europa zwischen Oikonomia und Oikumene: Globale Marktwirtschaft, EU-Erweiterung und christliche Verantwortung*, ed. Dietmar W. Winkler and Wilfried Nausner (Innsbruck/Vienna: Tyrolia Verlag, 2004), 73–85. For a more detailed account see Rieger 2009.

2. One of the most surprising things about the economic growth of the 1990s was that only the elites benefited from it. The wages of CEOs, for instance, increased at incredible rates. Even though some still contend that many people have never been as well off as now, even in the so-called "first world" more and more people, including significant parts of the middle class, are worse off than before (cf. Wolman and Colamosca 1997).

3. "I do not mean to employ theological reflection as an argument for or against any form of political economy. My aim is more modest. The point of Incarnation is to respect the world as it is, to acknowledge its limits, to recognize its weaknesses, irrationalities, and evil forces, and to disbelieve any promises that the world is now or ever will be transformed into the City of God" (Novak 1982: 341). The third part of the book, from which this quotation is taken, is titled "A Theology of Economics." Novak's titles speak for themselves. See also Novak 1990.

4. Good and evil, favourite categories of former President George W. Bush, are manifestations of this focus on otherworldly matters. People are

either good or evil, depending on how they are connected to this other world. Moral distinctions are not needed to identify good and evil. Even the killing of others in times of war is therefore not necessarily evil or good: it all depends on the right kinds of connections to the right kind of other world. Likewise, "supporting the troops" in situations like the war in Iraq means to support ideas like freedom rather than people; loss of life or the increasing numbers of those who are severely injured without immediate loss of life are not of central concern to most supporters of the war.

5. An important exception to this rule is "Covenanting for Justice in the Economy and the Earth," a statement developed by the World Alliance of Reformed Church at its meeting in Accra, Ghana, July 30–August 13, 2004. The Confession of Faith developed in this document centres on the question of God. What is not recognized in this statement, however, is that those who support free-market economics also assume God's presence and believe that this economic system will ultimately improve the living conditions of the poor.

6. Carsten Herz 2003a and 2003b.

7. *Dallas Morning News*, September 5, 2001. In 1999 the relation was 419:1 and in the late 1980s it was 70:1.

8. Luther reminds us furthermore that "money and possessions," "knowledge, intelligence, power, popularity, friendship, and honor" can also take the place of God.

9. Smith prefers talking about the nature of things rather than talking about God, although the outcome is the same. In book I, chapter II of *Wealth of Nations*, he argues that human nature is the reason for the division of labour. He finds "propensity in human nature … to truck, barter, and exchange one thing for another." In addition, he argues that while animals are independent, human beings need each other. Franz J. Hinkelammert identifies the early roots of this approach which says that the laws of the market have been placed in nature by God, in the developments between the sixteenth and the eighteenth century (Hinkelammert 1991: 68).

10. The basic problem of modernity in terms of religion can now be seen in a new perspective. The problem is not secularization but a kind of religiosity which promotes the worship of idols. Jung Mo Sung (1994: 207) identifies the core of this religiosity in the promise to achieve the impossible, namely an equilibrium in which all needs and desires are completely satisfied.

11. Both perspectives, where images of God come from and where they lead us, are important and must no longer be separated. In this regard, we need each of the two opposing classical approaches, the approach of Max Weber, who has shown how theology influences economic developments, and the approach of Karl Marx, who has shown how theology is shaped by economic interests.

12. In the European situation, where other religious images are scarce, the images promoted by the market have little competition. In the US, where religious images abound, the situation is not necessarily much different if the economic images manage to assimilate those other images – this is often the case where theology fails to search for explicit alternatives.

13. This is expressed in the famous statement of Smith, *Wealth of Nations*, book I, chapter II: "It is not from the benevolence of the butcher, the brewer, or the baker that we expect our dinner, but from their regard to their own interest. We address ourselves, not to their humanity but to their self-love, and never talk to them of our own necessities but of their advantages." Nelson reports about different contemporary interpretations of self-interest in the tensions among economists between the followers of Samuelson and the so-called "Chicago School" (Nelson 2001: 120).

14. In the US, most retirement plans are based on faith in progress and the growth of the market; the Bush administration continues to lobby hard to introduce changes in social security that would make it completely dependent on market performance.

15. There were one million homeless children in the US in 1999; this is the highest since the depression in the 1930s. *Dallas Morning News* (July 1, 1999), 4A. It is interesting to note that the phenomenon of child homelessness does not exist in most countries in Europe, due to different regulations and a stronger social security net.

16. The fact that theology may be shaped by economics has received little attention. It is explored in Rieger 2002 and 2009. Theology needs to learn from the study of economics; the study of economics can enable theology to take into account its own formation by the now all-pervasive forces of the economy and to develop a more self-critical perspective.

17. The approach of natural theology attempts, in short, to understand God in terms of what is identified as natural laws and conditions.

18. Economist Friedrich Hayek, for instance, believes that economic hierarchy and disparity is beneficial for progress, since all progress is introduced by those on top and from there trickles down to the masses (see Hayek 1960: 42, 45). But even if Hayek were correct, is this trickle-down process sufficient to raise the masses out of their misery?

19. Karl Barth is the most famous representative of a theology which emphasizes God as Other and rigorously rejects natural theology.

20. It is often overlooked that Barth himself saw God not only as the "wholly Other" but as the other who locates himself alongside the oppressed and against the oppressors (see Rieger 2001: 52, 211). In this context, transcendence does not first of all refer to what is otherworldly. Rather, transcendence means a break with certain kinds of immanence in favour of other kinds of immanence. The Roman Catholic theologian Jung Mo Sung, arguing from a different perspective, arrives at a similar

insight. Sung notes that the cry of those who suffer because of the market is transcendent because it breaks through the totality of the oppression and transcends the boundaries of the system (Sung 1991: 92). At the same time, Jung observes, those who do not hear the cry are unable to grasp the work of God in the world. In an earlier book, Jung argued that the critique of economics is what truly distinguishes different forms of Latin American theology of liberation (Sung 1994).

21. Here is another place where the approaches of Weber and Marx need to be connected. Images of God cannot be transformed in a vacuum but in relation to concrete material conditions, as Marx has rightly seen. Nevertheless, images of God that have been transformed in this way can also have important implications for social dynamics. Such implications were studied by Weber.

22. The preferential option for the poor gains fresh importance in a postmodern world where concern about the poor is either seen as special interest or gets lost in pluralistic perspectives.

Chapter 4

1. This is a problem that, e.g., black theology raises insistently against "melting-pot" theories.

2. Haraway wrote this more than a decade before the Iraq War.

3. Philip Hefner, "Onco Mouse as Creation: Art Portrays the Ironic Unity of Science, Technology, and Religion," the first of his three spring lectures on the Created Co-Creator on March 1, 2004 at the Hillel Center at the University of Pennsylvania sponsored by the Metanexus Institute on Religion and Science.

4. Alves' doctoral dissertation barely passed at Princeton, presumably because of some hybridity. It was published in 1968 as *A Theology of Human Hope*, a title given by the editor who did not find the author's original title, "A Theology of Liberation," marketable. It was published in Portuguese more than a decade later, with a new introduction saying that he hesitated publishing it again for it was too bookish and pedantic.

Chapter 5

1. For some years now I have preferred to think in categories of the cross cultural rather than the multicultural. The reason is partly theological. The cross-cultural focus can turn attention to the resurgence of interest in a

theology of the cross which has roots deep in the Christian tradition as well as key insights for a theology today seeking to distance itself from more triumphant Christologies. It also lends itself to a more energetic, active hermeneutic of crossing over and engagement. The term multicultural has been widely used in Australia in more political and sociological ways. It has its origins in the departures from immigration policies which had largely been based on "whiteness" and theories of "blood" (see Tavan 2005). Its current usage (which is widespread) has become more diluted in meaning than it once was. The growing international ambivalence to the term "multiculturalism" is reflected in recent texts such as Baber 2008.

Chapter 6

1. Mimesis is a cyclical interpretative process because it is inserted into the passage of cosmological time. As time passes, our circumstances give rise to new experiences and new opportunities for reflection. We can redescribe our past experiences, bringing to light unrealized connections between agents, actors, circumstances, motives or objects, by drawing connections between the events retold and events that have occurred since, or by bringing to light untold details of past events. Of course, narrative need not have a happy ending. The concern of narrative is coherence and structure, not the creation of a particular kind of experience. Nevertheless, the possibility of re-describing the past offers us the possibility of re-imagining and reconstructing a future inspired by hope. It is this potentially inexhaustible process that is the fuel for philosophy and literature.

2. Stuart Hall defines cultural identity in terms of "one, shared culture, a sort of collective 'one true self,' hiding inside the many other, more superficial or artificially imposed 'selves' which people with a shared history and ancestry hold in common" (Hall 2000: 22).

Chapter 7

1. Mary Daly talks about "Verbicide" as "killing of the living, transformative energy of words" in her proposal to change from God the Father, Being, to God the Verb, Be-ing (see Daly 1985: xvii).

2. When the where-are-you-from question is asked to a Caucasian, it could be an innocent question. But when it is asked to an Asian by a Caucasian, for example, it carries a different political connotation.

3. Said contends, citing Theodore Adorno, that the "only home truly available now, though fragile and vulnerable, is in writing" (Said 1990: 365).

4. The title *Theology from the Womb of Asia* by C. S. Song is a good example of "naturalization" of Asia by adopting the metaphor, "womb", from feminine biology, as a ground of Asian theologizing.

Chapter 9

1. Several of my interviewees expressed to me their fear when travelling alone; others related incidents of gang violence perpetrated against them; Ratnam the solicitor related several cases of petty hate crimes against Sri Lankan refugee Tamils and of police negligence in dealing with them adequately.

2. We can discover the "generative words" of a community and so "read their world" by listening carefully and observing the words they use most often and with the strong intensity of feeling; those words will reveal their deepest longings, frustrations and aspirations (see Freire 1968: 75–118; cf. Freire 1968: 198; Freire and Macedo 1987).

3. The quality of village dogs has not improved a hair in the past two decades. Miserable, mangy refugees from the happy hunting grounds, they skulk around, apparently enduring a joyless, painful, half-starved existence; only showing signs of life when threatened by their own kind with the possibility of ending it. Only crows, cats and small rodents show them respect. Those that range the lanes and roads and slink about wherever humans gather, particularly at public functions where they vie with crows for crumbs and crusts, have neither personal appearance nor charm of personality to appeal to the viewer (Holmes 1980: 67–68).

4. The *nomos* of the universe is that principle that gives the multiplicity of elements their inner connection, their coherence and meaning for the whole. In a similar way, the *nomos* of a society is that ordering principle that turns the mere aggregation of individuals into a congregation of persons with a common purpose for life together. With *nomos*, the group of individuals becomes an organized society of persons; without *nomos*, a previously organized society turns into a group or a human mass, even as human horde; then society falls into what in Sri Lanka we call *mob rule*. In Greek thought the concept of *nomos* comes within a context of other equally important concepts, often complementary to each other. *Cosmos* is the ordered universe; *chaos* is the undifferentiated disorderly universe; *nomos* is the ordering principle of things; without *nomos*, *cosmos* falls back into *chaos*, and loses its essential meaning. *Nomos* is the outward expression of the *logos* or

inner nature of things or society. See entry "Physis and Nomos" in Edwards 1967; see also Winger 1992: chapter 2.

5. An example of that is the project of the UNESCO's World Federation for Mental Health to balance technological transformation of the modes of production in the developing societies with a healthy mental development of their components. The UNESCO prepared a manual under the title *Cultural Patterns and Technical Change* under the direction and editorship of the cultural anthropologist Margaret Mead. The insight underlying the entire project was that rapid technical development led to rapid social change, and that entire populations could not cope with such a change and consequently would fall under the condition that Durkheim and others would call "anomic state" (see Mead 1961).

6. Paul Tournier narrates numerous clinical cases of mental disturbances resulting from the pervading feeling of loneliness among his patients (see Tournier 1962). Both Eric Fromm and Paul Tournier agree that the sense of loneliness is universal and often leads to personal disintegration. Perhaps the difference between the solitude of Tamils living in London and the solitude of others living in their own culture is a question of degree and diffusion, not of kind. It would be safe to say that, in London, refugees in general, and Tamils in particular, suffer the melancholy of solitude at a higher degree than the rest of the population.

Chapter 11

1. By 1925, eleven of the eighteen Pentecostal churches planted in Australia were founded by women. Even by 1930, twenty of the thirty-seven churches (for which information is available) were initiated by women (see Chant 1999: 428).

2. Unlike the AoG in America, which began among the urban and the working classes, the movement in Australia (now called 'Australian Christian Churches') originated among middle-class and rural groups – but not academically educated. According to Barry Chant, "in Australia, its origins were among people of relatively comfortable socio-economic status" (Chant 1999: 38).

3. While it is not the place of this essay to debate the authorship or historical origins of the text of Isaiah, it is sufficient to say that most scholars would agree that the intended audience of the prophetic declaration is the Judean exiles if not also the historical location of the prophet themselves.

4. For example, Hoover in the 1930 *Australian Evangel* writes, "Healing is an evidence of faith, and where there is no faith there is no healing."

Though the prayer may be instantaneous or delayed in its actualization, the programme of God for healing is unchanged.

5. Bridges-Johns also notes that "Healing and deliverance from the demonic powers of this age are fused with the biblical witness and the age to come in which all will be healed and restored. Thus, Pentecostals live in the tension of the already but not yet consummated kingdom" (Bridges-Johns 1996: 46).

Chapter 12

1. The prayer for fertility among the Pares of Tanzania goes like this: Gods, I am poor (lit. "I have a poverty of a child"); if you give me a child, I will have a child who will be behind (following) me; I will bring here a bull and plenty of alcohol (dengelua, a local brew) so that people can come, and drink and sing joyful songs. If you do not give me a child, I will not do or offer you any ritual offering since I too have no one to sacrifice for me.

Chapter 13

1. Recollecting such stories involves critique of culture and faith in the light of misogyny, feminism as a prophetic movement, examining the status quo, pronouncing the judgement and calling for repentance. The first step is to document the case against women. Second is to discern the critique of patriarchy within the Bible. Third is to incorporate the two. It is a process of searching for remnants in unlikely places, noting that the Bible mirrors life in holiness and horror similar to the way art reflects life in varied forms.

2. I use the terms "imperialism" and "colonialism" interchangeably. When "imperialism" refers to the "empire" and its rule over a distant territory, "colonialism" implies settlement and the consequent controlling and "civilizing" of the indigenous people (Sugirtharajah 2002: 24–25).

Chapter 14

1. In speaking of the monarchy, I do not enter the discussion of its historical validity; the narrator, however, intends to have us believe that such was the story.

2. Translations of biblical text are mine unless otherwise stated. I have tried to stay as close to the Hebrew as possible, to the disadvantage of "good" English (and kept transliterations simple; my apologies to "good" scholarship). Quotation marks for the term "girl" are explained below.

3. Adapted from Fokkelman 1981: 347. For the sake of simplicity, I have used Fokkelman's chiasmus but adapted his transliterated Hebrew original into English, except for the words "Young girl" and *"sōkenet,"* which I have left as in the original.

4. The exception is Joseph, set over his master Potiphar's house (Gen. 39:4), an important household but not the king's.

5. There are some extra-biblical witnesses, but they are hard to assess in what they say about our text. On the one hand, the cognate terms point to high officers in court; on the other hand, the term's origins are obscure. Apart from these difficulties, there is the additional difficulty in dating the Dtr History, which thus hinders any comparison based on dates. See Heltzer 1987: 89. According to Heltzer (1987: 89), "the *šakintu* does not appear in Old- and Middle Assyrian texts, and in Neo-Assyrian the term appears only in the Sargonide period. Therefore it is not impossible that the office of the *šakintu* came to Assyria from the West, but the word by itself is not of West-Semitic origin." See also Henshaw 1967: 517–25 and 1968: 461–83; Lipinski 1973: 191–207.

6. Obviously, trying to prove anyone's intention is to beg for trouble, especially when so many centuries and cultural differences interfere between the biblical narrator and us. Yet I believe Isaiah's view of king-slave was also in the Deuteronomist's mind when he called Abishag a servant. "The Deuteronomist" is, of course, an abstraction, a convention to speak of those (men) responsible for the compilation of what we today call the Dtr History.

7. There are a few texts that might be exceptions to this statement. Ezek. 36:9 has a *Nifal* 3 fem. sg., but its subject is not a woman but the land being tilled. There are also some uses of the masc. pl., e.g. Exod. 1:13, which presumably included women.

8. One is tempted to translate *yapa* as pretty or beautiful on the basis of her condition of being a young and desirable woman, sleeping with the king and being coveted by Adonijah if not by Solomon also. Yet the adjective is applied also to men (Saul, David) and to animals. Thus, perhaps, "pleasant" or "nice" would suit best a less gender-tainted translation of this term.

9. Outside the DtrH, 1 Chron. 21:12 is of interest, because here it refers to a choice between three forms of punishment from Y$_{HWH}$ because of David's sin: to wit, three years' famine; three months' persecution or three days' destruction by Y$_{HWH}$'s angel over the whole country.

10. Carolyn Leeb (2000) has demonstrated that what all instances of these two terms have in common is the condition of lack of protection from

a senior male, a *paterfamilias*. Such lack may be permanent (e.g., Gehazi, Elishah's servant or Ziba, Mephiboshet's servant) or momentary (e.g., Ruth as a widow before she marries Boaz). There are several other examples, but these have been chosen precisely because they indicate people who were not youngsters any more.

11. The redaction/compilation of these laws is later, but they probably reflect earlier practices and, in this sense, they may be considered here.

12. It is to be noted, on the other hand, that this is an argument from the negative: it only states what it is *not* said of her. For the expression *le'iššā* (for/to wife) is used also of Hagar (Gen. 16:3), Bilhah and Zilpah (Gen. 30:4, 9), and three slave women given by their mistresses to bear children for their husbands; here there was no asking the women involved and their status remained secondary to their mistresses. Also the law on captive women (Deut. 21:11) speaks of them as "wives" (*le'iššā*). So the use of the expression "as wife" for these women tells us not to put too much weight on it as a sign of prestige over against that of concubine (*pilegeš*), for instance.

13. Other, rather common, examples are those of calling names related to one's enemy's mother; of using language related to female sexuality to speak of a totally different reality, such as idolatry.

Index of Names

Index of Subjects

Index of Biblical Characters

Lightning Source UK Ltd.
Milton Keynes UK
09 April 2011

170654UK00001B/1/P